# BRITISH LABOUR STRUGGLES:
# CONTEMPORARY PAMPHLETS 1727-1850

# THE TEN HOURS MOVEMENT

## IN

## 1831 AND 1832

*Six Pamphlets and One Broadside*
1831-1832

## Arno Press

A New York Times Company/New York 1972

Reprint Edition 1972 by Arno Press Inc.

Reprinted from copies in the Kress Library
Graduate School of Business Administration,
Harvard University

BRITISH LABOUR STRUGGLES:  CONTEMPORARY PAMPHLETS 1727-1850
ISBN for complete set:  0-405-04410-0

See last pages for complete listing.

Manufactured in the United States of America

Library of Congress Cataloging in Publication Data
Main entry under title:

The Ten hours movement in 1831 and 1832.

        (British labour struggles:
contemporary pamphlets 1727-1850)
    CONTENTS: An enquiry into the state of the manu-
facturing population, by W. R. Greg [first published
1831].--A memoir of Robert Blincoe, by J. Brown [first
published 1832].--A letter to Sir John Cam Hobhouse
[first published 1832].  [etc.]
    1.  Hours of labor--Great Britain.  2.  Factory
system--Great Britain.  I.  Series.
HD5166.T45        331.2'572        72-2548
ISBN 0-405-04439-9

# Contents

AN

# ENQUIRY

INTO THE STATE OF THE

## MANUFACTURING POPULATION,

AND THE

### CAUSES AND CURES

OF THE

### EVILS THEREIN EXISTING.

## LONDON:

JAMES RIDGWAY, 169, PICCADILLY.

M.DCCC.XXXI.

TILLING, PRINTER, CHELSEA.

AN

# E N Q U I R Y,

*&c.*

---

In an article published some time since in the Edinburgh Review,[*] written, it is supposed, by Mr.
M'Culloch, it is stated, that the number of individuals employed in the different branches of the cotton
trade, amounted to about 1,100,000.   This number
cannot now, we think, be far short of 1,500,000,
and we may, therefore, compute those who directly,
or indirectly, derive their subsistence from this great
staple manufacture, at about 4,000,000.   According
to the British Census of 1821, exactly one third of
the population of Great Britain is employed in agricultural occupations, and two thirds in handicraft, or
manufactures of some kind.   Monsieur Dupin gives
the same calculation ;[†] and though we have not the
data requisite to enable us to come to any minutely
accurate conclusions, we shall be safe in assuming

[*] No. XCI. p. 22.
[†] Dupin—Forces Productives et Commerciales de la France.

B

that at least 8 or 10,000,000 of our present population are employed in, or subsist by, manufactures.

Such being the case, it is wonderful how little curiosity has been excited respecting the moral and physical condition of so large a portion of our fellow countrymen, and how lamentable and pernicious an ignorance prevails on these subjects in almost every part of the kingdom. The effects of manufactures on the health and morals of those engaged in them, are scarcely known or thought of, even amongst those who live in the very heart of the districts where they abound, and have never, we believe, been publicly noticed, except by Mr. Southey, for the purposes of poetical declamation; by Mr. M‘Culloch, for the sake of corroborating his economical and commercial doctrines; or by some Member of Parliament, whose philanthropy has not been equalled by his knowledge of the fact, or his discernment of the cause.

We think it is high time that the attention of the public should be directed to this momentous question, that they should be informed, not merely of the advantages attendant on manufactures, which we fully allow, but also of the evils which accompany these advantages, but which are not inseparable from them; in order that they may be able to investigate the cause, and to suggest the remedy. It is with this view that we have commenced the following Enquiry, which we earnestly trust may be productive of good, believing, as we do, that the benefits resulting from the establishment and extension of manufactures, are intrinsic and essential, and that the vice and misery attendant upon them, are, for the most part, accidental, and removable by zealous and well-directed efforts. As individuals, we are friendly to manufactures, and extensively engaged in them. We shall not, therefore, be suspected of a wilful exaggeration of the evils we lament. We shall not conclude, like Mr. Southey, that the houses of the manufacturing poor must be the abodes of wretchedness and immorality, because, instead of being surrounded by gardens, and embowered by creepers, they are built " naked, and in a row."* Nor shall we, like a celebrated political economist of the day, infer, that, because the proportion of deaths is not much greater in Lancashire than in Westmoreland, manufactures must, therefore, be favourable to health.† We shall assume nothing—infer nothing—exaggerate nothing—extenuate nothing,—but simply state the nature and amount of the evil, lament its existence, and suggest its cures.

Domestic manufactures are almost extinct. The population which was formerly scattered throughout the country, is now congregated into large towns, and is impressed with a distinct character. In the following observations, we have principally in view the cotton manufacture, in the form in which it exists in the towns of Manchester, Bolton, Blackburn, Bury, Rochdale, Stockport, Stayley Bridge, &c.

We come to consider, in the first place, the state

---

* Colloquies on the Progress and Prospects of Society.

† Edinburgh Review, No. XCI. p. 34.

of *health* of those engaged in manufacturing occupations.

The advocates for the salutary influence of these employments, are fond of referring to tables of Mortality, arguing that, if the proportion of deaths to the population be not greater in manufacturing districts than in others, their alleged unhealthiness is disproved. Let us examine, first the fact, and then the argument.

The proportion of deaths to the population in Lancashire is 1 in 55,* which is greater than in any other county of England, except these four, Warwick, (52,) Surrey, (52,) Kent, (50,) and Middlesex, (47,) and considerably greater than the average of England, which is 1 in 58. The annexed Table will shew the case clearly.

* British Census, 1821.

| Manufacturing. | Deaths to Population. | Agricultural. | Deaths to Population. | Wales. | Deaths to Population. | Towns. | Deaths to Population. |
|---|---|---|---|---|---|---|---|
| Middlesex | 47 | Sussex | 72 | Anglesey | 83 | Paris (Houses) | 51 |
| Chester | 55 | Monmouth | 70 | Brecon | 67 | Paris (with Hospitals) | 32 |
| Lancashire | 55 | Gloucester | 64 | Cardigan | 70 | London | 40 |
| Yorkshire | 60 | Suffolk | 67 | Pembroke | 83 | Manchester | 45 |
| Stafford | 56 | Wilts | 66 | Carnarvon | 69 | Birmingham | 40 |
| Warwickshire | 52 | Hereford | 63 | Glamorgan | 69 | Leeds | 45 |
|  |  |  |  |  |  | Glasgow | 47 |
|  |  |  |  |  |  | Northampton | 51 |
| Average | 53 |  | 67 |  | 73 |  | 44 |

See *Berard*, Discours sur les Ameliorations progressives de la Santé publique.—*Villermé*, Memoirs on Comparative Mortality of Rich and Poor.—*Dr. Hawkin's* Medical Statistics.—British Census for 1821.

It would appear, from this Table, that manufacturing counties are far worse than others in their average rate, which may, however, in a great measure, arise from the number of towns they contain. We have not, indeed, from want of room, given all the counties of England,—and we have even selected those which most strikingly exemplify the fact,—but our Table may easily be verified by a reference to the proper sources.

As far, therefore, as tables of longevity and mortality can be relied on, they rather tend to prove that manufactures are *unfavourable* to health. But we do not think, that in a discussion of this kind they are entitled to much consideration, for this simple reason, (among many others,) that a great number of deaths is compatible with a great degree of general health; and that one district in which the deaths are numerous, may be more healthy than another where they are less frequent, if the prevalent diseases are of an *acute* kind in the first instance, and of a *chronic* nature in the second. To exemplify this :

By far the larger proportion of the diseases to which agriculturists are subject, are either cases of rheumatism or of acute inflammation. Inflammatory fevers, the constant effects of exposure to the inclemencies of the weather, are frequently and rapidly fatal, especially where the patient is in circumstances which preclude him from that degree of warmth, comfort, and unremitting attention, which in such cases are indispensable. Acute inflammation, so frequent in country districts, which chiefly attacks those of robust and plethoric health, if not speedily suppressed by prompt and vigorous measures, is most generally fatal. Cases of this kind require immediate medical aid, which, in the country, is seldom to be procured without considerable delay, and often does not arrive till all assistance is unavailing. These considerations make it obvious, that deaths may be frequent and sudden in agricultural districts, while by far the greater proportion of the living are in the full enjoyment of health and strength.

In manufacturing towns the case is widely different. Few, if any, die from want of medical assistance. They are supplied with every aid which skill or charity can bestow. But the diseases which prevail, are of a nature, which, without suddenly destroying life, or even shortening it materially, deprive it of health and enjoyment, and render existence itself little else than a chronic malady. The disease which we find by far the most frequent, among those engaged in manufactures, is a species of *Gastritis*, or chronic inflammation of the membranes of the stomach, or a morbid irritability of that organ which has been termed *Gastralgia*.\* This fact has been stated to us by several medical gentlemen, and is fully confirmed by a reference to the records of dispensaries.†

But without dwelling longer on these distinctions,

---

\* See a valuable Paper, by Dr. Kay, in the second Number of the " North of England Medical and Surgical Journal."

† We may here observe, also, that epilepsy appears to be more frequent among the manufacturing labourers than in other classes; and that varicose enlargements of the veins, and ulcers

(though of extreme importance,) we will boldly appeal for the confirmation of our views on the *present* un-wholesomeness of large manufactories,* to any one who has been long and intimately acquainted with the interior of these establishments ; who has seen children enter them at ten or twelve years of age, with the beaming eye, and the rosy cheek, and the elastic step of youth ; and who has seen them gradually lose the gaiety and light-heartedness of early existence, and the colour and complexion of health, and the vivacity of intellect, and the insensibility to care, which are the natural characteristics of that tender age, under the withering influence of laborious confinement, ill oxygenated air, and a meagre and unwholesome diet. We have witnessed all this repeatedly, and we have found it impossible to resist the obvious conclusion—a conclusion which we think cannot be gainsaid by any man of experience and observation.

We will now proceed to develope the causes which produce this unhealthiness among those employed in large manufactories, and the peculiar class of diseases which prevail among them, viz. general lassitude and debility, dyspepsia, and gastralgia.

of the lower extremities, are common among them, in consequence of their being obliged to stand so large a portion of the day. In cases of accidents, their wounds heal slowly; and all their diseases, whether medical or surgical, are characterized by a deficiency of energy in the system.

* Malthus, I. p. 415.

I. First, among these noxious causes, to which we shall give a somewhat detailed consideration, is the *diet* of the people. This is for the most part unwholesome and inadequate. The severity of their labour, and the confined atmosphere in which they work, demand an ample supply of solid and nourishing food. We should prescribe as the diet, likely to keep men in health under similar circumstances, a sufficiency of animal food, wheaten bread, and malt liquor, and as little liquid of other kinds as possible. These we should consider indispensable. Now let us see what their aliment actually consists of. Potatoes, butter, sometimes pastry, sometimes bread, often oatcake, and *occasionally*, *though rarely*, a small sprinkling of bacon or other meat, constitute their dinner six days out of the seven. For breakfast and supper they take sometimes fruit-pies, sometimes coffee, (or what they call such,) but far more generally tea,* diluted till it is little else than warm water, and the materials of which never came from China,† but are the production of one of those innumerable frauds which are practised upon those of the poor, who are desirous to imitate the rich. Under any circumstances, we should deprecate the too liberal use of weak tea, as extremely debilitating to the stomach ;‡

* Tea is often taken as their mid-day meal.

† See Sir Henry Parnell's remarks on the adulteration of tea, in his admirable work on Financial Reform. p. 41.

‡ Cabanis. Rapports du Physique et du moral de l'homme. II. p. 92.

but the practice is fatal to the constitution of all hard-working men. At first, they make use of tea as a stimulant to relieve the internal languor and depression, which always accompanies an unhealthy and ill-regulated digestion ; it affords a temporary relief at the expense of a subsequent re-action, which in its turn calls for another and stronger stimulus ; and it is generally the case, that those among the work-people who have been long habituated to the use of tea as a frequent meal, are at length reduced to mix a large proportion of spirits in every cup they take. This pernicious practice prevails to an inconceivable extent among our manufacturing population, at every age, and in both sexes.*

Nor is it from any actual distress that they have recourse to this unsatisfactory and noxious diet, but from bad management, and bad habits. Milk is cheaper than tea, and would afford them double the nourishment at half the price; but on all these points they are sadly ignorant, and their domestic arrangements are, for the most part, totally devoid of economy. A vast proportion of them have very good wages, amply sufficient to supply them with a solid and substantial food, were they well laid out, instead of being squandered in vain luxuries, or enervating excess. From the long hours of labour, and the warm and often close atmosphere in which they are confined, a very large proportion of our manu-

* This custom, we regret to say, is even more prevalent among females than the other sex.

facturing labourers feel the necessity of some artificial stimulus; and we regret to say, that many of them, especially those which receive the highest wages, are in the habit of spending a portion of their leisure, after working hours, more particularly on a Saturday evening, and during the Sunday, in besotting themselves with ale and beer; and, still oftener, with the more efficient stimulus of gin. It is customary for them in many of the towns to stop at the gin shops, and take a dram as they go to their work in the morning, and another as they return at night; and where, as is frequently the case, the houses of the work-people lie in a cluster round the factory, it is not uncommon for a wholesale vender of spirits to leave two gallons (the smallest quantity which can be sold without a licence) at one of the houses, which is distributed in small quantities to the others, and payment is made to the merchant through the original receiver. The quantity of gin drunk in this way is enormous; and it is painful to know, that children, and even girls, are initiated into this fatal practice at a very tender age.* This is a picture which it is impossible to contemplate without

* It is useless to dwell for an instant on the lamentable effects which must, and do result from this general use of spirituous liquors. We may, however, mention, (from Dr. Willan's Reports on the Diseases in London,) " that considerably more than one-eighth of all the deaths in the metropolis above twenty years of age, happen prematurely, from excess in drinking ardent spirits."

See also Cabanis Rapports, &c. vol. ii. p. 83, 84.

sentiments of sorrow and regret, that such a state of things should exist within reach of a remedy, and yet that remedy not be applied; for, as we shall endeavour to show in the subsequent pages, all these evils may be greatly mitigated, if not altogether removed. But this is not all. Ardent spirits are not the only stimulus which this class of people indulge in. Many of them take large quantities of opium in one form or another; sometimes in pills, sometimes as laudanum, sometimes in what they call an *anodyne* draft, which is a narcotic of the same kind. They find this a cheaper stimulus than gin, and many of them prefer it.* It has been in vogue among them for many years when wages were low, and the use of it is now continued when there is no longer this excuse.

II. As a second cause of the unhealthiness of manufacturing towns, we place the *severe and unremitting labour*. Cotton factories (which are the best in this particular) begin to work at half-past five, or six in the morning, and cease at half-past seven, or eight at night. An interval of half an hour, or forty minutes, is allowed for breakfast, an hour for dinner, and generally half an hour for tea, leaving about twelve hours a day clear labour. The work of *spinners* and *stretchers* is among the most laborious that exist, and is exceeded, perhaps, by that of mowing alone; and few mowers, we believe,

* Confessions of an Opium Eater, P. i.

think of continuing their labour for twelve hours without intermission. Add to this, that these men never rest for an instant during the hours of working, except while their *mules* are *doffing*, in which process they also assist; and it must be obvious to every one, that it is next to impossible for any human being, however hardy or robust, to sustain this exertion, for any length of time, without permanently injuring his constitution. A collier never works above eight, and a farm labourer seldom above ten hours a day; and it is, therefore, wholly out of all just proportion, that a spinner should labour for twelve hours regularly, and frequently for more.

The labour of the other classes of hands employed in factories, as *carders*, *rovers*, *piecers*, and *weavers*, consists not so much in their actual manual exertion, which is very moderate, as in the constant attention which they are required to keep up, and the intolerable fatigue of standing for so great a length of time. We know, that incessant walking, for twenty-four hours, was considered one of the most intolerable tortures to which witches, in former times, were subjected, for the purpose of compelling them to own their guilt; and that few of them could hold out for twelve;* and the fatigue of standing for twelve hours, without being permitted to lean or sit down, must be scarcely less extreme. Accordingly,

---

* Glanvil's Sadducismus Triumphatus.
Beaumont's History of Witchcraft.

some sink under it, and many more have their constitutions permanently weakened and undermined.

III. The third cause we shall assign, is perhaps
even more efficient than the last. The air in almost
all factories is more or less unwholesome.\* Many
of the rooms are obliged to be kept at a certain temperature, (say 65 degrees Fahrenheit,) for the purposes of manufacture, and from the speed of the
machinery, the general want of direct communica-
tion with the external atmosphere, and from artificial
heat, they often exceed this temperature. This, of
itself, is sufficient to enervate and destroy all energy
of frame. But in addition to mere heat, the rooms
are often ill-ventilated, the air is filled with the effluvia of oil, and with emanations from the uncleanly
persons of a large number of individuals; and from
the want of free ventilation, the air is very imperfectly oxygenated, and has occasionally a most over-
powering smell.† In a word, the hands employed

\* " The air which the children employed in manufactories
breathe, is, from the oil, &c., and other circumstances, very injurious: little attention is paid to their cleanliness; and the
frequent changes from a warm to a cold atmosphere, are pre-
disposing causes to sickness and debility, and particularly to
the epidemic fevers, so frequently to be met with in these factories."—*Dr. Aikin's Description of the Country round Manchester.*

† It is, however, important to mention, that cotton mills
are materially improved of late years in most of these particulars, and that in some mills they exist in a much less degree
than in others, which shows them *not* to be essential and inherent evils.

in these large manufactories, breathe foul air for twelve hours out of the twenty-four; and we know that few things have so specific and injurious an action on the digestive organs, as the inhalation of impure air; and this fact alone would be almost sufficient to account for the prevalence of stomachic complaints in districts where manufactories abound. *

The small particles of cotton and dust with which the air in most rooms of factories is impregnated, not unfrequently lay the foundation of distressing and fatal diseases. When inhaled, they are a source of great pulmonary irritation; which, if it continues long, induces a species of chronic bronchitis, which, not rarely, degenerates into tubercular consumption. Patissier † says, (speaking of cotton spinners,) "These workmen constantly inhale an atmosphere, loaded with *debris cotonneux très-tenus,* which excite the bronchi, provoke cough, and maintain a perpetual

* " Dans les ateliers clos, surtout dans ceux où l'air se renouvelle avec difficulté, les forces musculaires diminuent rapidement; la reproduction de la chaleur animale languit; et les hommes de la constitution la plus robuste contractent le temperament mobile et capricieux des femmes. Ajoutez que, si le nombre des ouvriers est un peu considerable, l'altération progressive de l'air agit d'une manière directe et pernicieuse, d'abord sur les poumons, dont le sang reçoit son caractère vital, et bientôt sur le cerveau lui-même. Ainsi donc, sans parler des emanations malfaisantes que les matières manufacturées, ou celles qu'on emploie dans leur preparation exhalent souvent, presque toutes les circonstances se réunissent pour rendre les ateliers également malsains au physique et au moral."— *Cabanis,* t. ii. p. 114.

† Sur les Maladies des Artizans, p. 245.

irritation in the lungs. They are often obliged to change their occupation, in order to avoid Phthisis." *

IV. The fourth cause of the ill-health which prevails among the manufacturing population, may be traced to the injurious influence which the weakened and vitiated constitution of the women has upon their children.† They are often employed in factories some years after their marriage, and during their pregnancy, and up to the very period of their confinement; which, all who have attended to the physiology of this subject know, must send their offspring into the world with a debilitated and unhealthy frame, which the circumstances of their infancy are ill-calculated to renovate; and hence, when these children begin to work themselves, they are prepared at once to succomb to the evil influences by which they are surrounded.

In consequence, also, of the mothers being em-

* For further particulars on this important subject, see a late Paper by Dr. Kay, in the North of England Medical and Surgical Journal, No. iii. p. 348.

† It is a curious circumstance, and one which amply merits attentive consideration, that the fecundity of females employed in manufactories seems to be considerably diminished, by their occupation and habits; for not only are their families generally smaller than those of agricultural labourers, but their children are born at more distant intervals. Thus the average interval which elapses between the birth of each child in the former case, is two years and one month, as we have found, upon minute enquiry; while in country districts, we believe, it seldom exceeds eighteen months. The causes of this fact we have at present no space to enter upon.

ployed from home, their children are entrusted, in a vast majority of cases, to the care of others, often of elderly females, who have no infant family of their own; and most of whom, having in their youth had their children nursed by others, have never formed those habits of attachment and assiduous attention to their offspring, which could alone afford a probability of a proper care of the children committed to their charge. These women often undertake the care of several infants at the same time; their habits are generally indolent and gossipping; the children are restless and irritable, from being deprived of a supply of their natural food; (as, when the mothers suckle them, they can only perform that duty in the intervals of labour); and the almost universal practice among them is to still the cries of the infant by administering opiates, which are sold for this purpose under several well-known and popular forms. The quantity of opium which, from habit, some children become capable of taking, is almost incredible, and the effects are correspondingly destructive. Even when the infants have a healthy appearance at birth, they almost, uniformly, become, in a few months, puny and sickly in their aspect, and a very large proportion fall victims to bronchitis, hydrocephalus, and other diseases, produced by want of care, and the pernicious habits we have detailed. We may mention also, that spirits, particularly gin, are frequently given when the infants appear to suffer from pain in the bowels, which, from injudicious diet; is very common among them.

We now come to the consideration of a still more interesting, and, if possible, still more important point—the state of the manufacturing population in respect to MORALS.  It is extremely difficult to come to any thing like satisfactory conclusions, in so involved and complicated a question.  Lists of convictions afford very uncertain data, unless where the *nature* of the crimes, as well as their number, is specified, which is not the case in any of the official returns for this country, which we have been able to procure ; and however accurately these were given, they would still be far from affording us the information we desire, which, in fact, can be procured only from the testimony of personal observers.  Official returns may enumerate the actual *crimes* committed, or at least discovered ; but what becomes of that mass of *vice*, that infinity of immoralities, which no law can recognize, and no magistrate can punish, and no census can record ; which escape the penetration of the statesman and the philosopher ; which are known only to the perpetrators of the guilt, and to those who are condemned to live habitually among them.  *Crime* may be classified and calculated ; *vice*, depravity, and secret licentiousness, are intangible ; they defy enquiry, and baffle calculation.

We shall endeavour, notwithstanding, to come to a few correct general facts, and we shall consider the state of the manufacturing districts,

1. With respect to crimes of violence and fraud.
2. With respect to licentiousness.

1. We find, as a matter of fact,* that wherever manufactures, and general civilization (to use the word in its common acceptation,) prevail, crimes of violence, crimes committed against the person, those which arise from the sudden impulse of an impetuous

*

| Countries. | Population. | Crimes against the Person. | Crimes against Property. | Personal Crimes to Population, one in | Property ditto to Population, one in | Year. |
|---|---|---|---|---|---|---|
| Netherlands | 6,676,000 | 231 | 935 | 28,904 | 7,140 | 1826 |
| England..... | 12,422,700 | 531 | 15,616 | 23,395 | 799 | .... |
| France ..... | 32,000,000 | 1,821 | 17,735 | 17,573 | 1,804 | .... |
| Spain...... | 13,732,000 | 3,610 | 2,313 | 3,804 | 5,937 | .... |

For the verification of this Table, and for further information, consult, Companion to Almanac, 1829, p. 89 and 98.—British Census.—Quetelet, Recherches Statisques sur les Pays Bas, p. 31, and Recherches sur les Population, &c. des Pays Bas, p. 53.— Foreign Quarterly Review, n. 9. p. 88; n. x. pp. 368—408; n. vii. p. 140, *et seq.*— Report of a Committee of the House of Commons in 1828.—Bulletin Universel, September, 1828.—Monsieur Charles Dupin, Forces Productives et Commerciales, &c.— Works of M. Ch. Lucas.—" Summary of a Statement of Criminal Offenders for the last Seven Years. Compiled at the Home Office, 1830."

passion, or a furious temper, are diminished in number; while theft, fraud, and all those crimes which are directed against property, and which arise from an habitual want of moral restraint, are considerably increased. We have examined this subject with the utmost care, we have made ample allowance for increase of population, and for every other contingent circumstance which could affect the correctness of the official returns, and the unavoidable conclusion which this investigation has forced upon us, is that crimes against property have regularly increased with the increase of commerce and manufactures, and the consequent concentration of the population into large towns. The above table shows this too plainly to be misunderstood. Spain, the most ignorant, degraded, and uncommercial of all countries pretending to civilization, is, in respect of crimes against property, *three times* less vicious than France, and *more than seven times* less vicious than England. This fact is a fearful one, and speaks volumes. England is more than twice as criminal as France in this department of offences. We also find a striking difference between the North and South of France. In the former, according to Mr. Charles Dupin,* the increase of manufactures and trade is attested by the mercenary nature of the crimes there committed, as compared with the southern districts of the same country, where offences against the person are substituted for offences against property, and are perpe-

* " Forces Productives et Commerciales de la France."

trated with a black and savage atrocity which almost baffles conception.* Spain ranks *Cannibalism* among her list of crimes,† but robbery is rare, and petty fraud still rarer. Ireland again, especially the South, where manufactures have not penetrated, exhibits much violence and bloodshed, but comparatively little of dishonesty or larceny; while our own country, whose civilization we are so apt to vaunt, *far* exceeds all others in the career of mercenary crime; and has increased for many years back, and is still rapidly increasing in this painful pre-eminence in guilt. ‡

* " Causes Criminelles Célèbres, &c." Paris, 1828.

† Bulletin Universel, September, 1828.—Foreign Quarterly Review, vol. x.

‡ It is but fair to mention, that, in all calculations of this kind, the state of the Police is an important consideration. This is, however, superior both in France, and the Netherlands, to that of our own country.

Let us finish this survey by a comparison of some of the manufacturing and agricultural districts of England.* For these we have no accurate returns of the *nature* of the crimes committed, though we have

1827.

| Manufacturing Counties. | Population. | Crime. | Crime to Population, one to | Agricultural Counties. | Population. | Crime. | Crime to Population, one to |
|---|---|---|---|---|---|---|---|
| Cheshire | 304,130 | 497 | 612 | Berkshire | 143,400 | 208 | 690 |
| Lancashire | 1,226,600 | 2,459 | 495 | Essex | 319,400 | 451 | 708 |
| Middlesex | 1,295,100 | 3,381 | 353 | Hertford | 144,300 | 205 | 704 |
| Northumberland | 220,500 | 96 | 2,300 | Kent | 468,900 | 632 | 742 |
| Nottingham | 206,300 | 298 | 695 | Hampshire | 314,000 | 341 | 920 |
| Stafford | 378,600 | 569 | 665 | Westmorland | 55,800 | 20 | 2,790 |
| Warwick | 310,500 | 602 | 515 | Wiltshire | 245,000 | 365 | 671 |
| York | 1,321,600 | 1,223 | 1,080 | Devonshire | 484,200 | 432 | 1,121 |
| Average | | | 840 | | | | 1,043 |

of the number of criminals, and these, as we anticipated, turn the balance decidedly against the manufacturing districts. We give an annexed calculation of the
crimes committed in 1827, in eight Counties, of each
class, selected at random, with the proportion they
bear to the population. The aggregate result shews,
that in the manufacturing districts, the criminals are
to the population, as 1 to 840; while in the agricultural, they are as 1 to 1043; and there can be little
doubt, that the difference consists chiefly in offences
against property.

It is proved then, beyond the possibility of a
doubt, that the increase and prevalence of manufactures has a tendency to diminish crimes of violence,
and to increase those of robbery and fraud. Is this a
moral gain? We are very doubtful if we can admit
it as such; but the discussion would be a dangerous
one, and we will leave it to the casuistry of our
readers.

It is to be remarked, in conclusion, and this is a
consideration which will depress the scale still more
against the manufacturing population, that the list of
convictions will afford a much fairer estimate of the
criminality of an agricultural than of a trading district, as the " greater crimes," (to use the common
expression,) which abound in the former, are all cog-
nizable by law, and from their nature can rarely
escape detection; while larceny and petty fraud are
often so difficult to discover, that we may safely
assume, that not one half of the offences of this
nature actually committed, appear in the official lists.

We hope we are not vilifying any portion of our countrymen. We have proceeded in our statement very cautiously, and have groped our way by the aid of known facts, official documents, careful calculations, and close personal observation. If we are mistaken in any point, our error should be forgiven, for we have spared no pains to understand the subject.

2. On the subject of the general licentiousness and illicit intercourse between the sexes, which prevails in manufacturing districts, we cannot, for obvious reasons, dwell as long, nor as minutely as the extreme importance of the subject would justify. In the few words we shall devote to this branch of our investigation, we shall be careful to keep within the limits of the most scrupulous accuracy, and to affirm nothing which we do not possess the materials for proving. First, then, we shall remark, that nothing but personal observation, or the testimony of eye-witnesses, can be relied on for satisfactory information. The returns of illegitimate children (in the few cases where they can be procured), are worse than useless, for it will be obvious, on a few moments consideration, that in such cases, they can afford us no possible criterion of the desired result. On this subject, some writers on political economy,* betray the same ignorance as in this assertion, of the extensive use of animal food among the manufacturing labourers. Both instances furnish an illustration of what appears to be a com-

* Edinburgh Review, XCI.

mon source of error with them, viz. a disposition to draw inferences from isolated facts, instead of resting their doctrines upon the basis of extensive and accurate observation. They conclude, that because the proportion of illegitimate births appears to be greater among the agricultural than the manufacturing population, the females of the former are the more immoral of the two. *We draw, without doubt or hesitation, exactly the opposite conclusion;* and every one intimately acquainted with the South of Lancashire will bear us out in this opinion. The deduction we draw is also materially confirmed by the practice, which it is painful to state, is far from uncommon among the abandoned females of these districts, of destroying prematutely the fruit and the evidence of their guilt.*

The fact, then, undoubtedly is, that the licentiousness which prevails among the dense population of manufacturing towns, is carried to a degree which it is appalling to contemplate, which baffles all statistical enquiries, and which can be learned only from the testimony of personal observers. And, in addition to overt acts of vice, there is a coarseness and grossness of feeling, and an habitual indecency of conversation, which we would fain hope and believe are not the prevailing characteristics of our country. The effect of this upon the minds of the young will readily be conceived; and is it likely that any instruc-

* Many facts have lately come to our knowledge, strongly corroborative of this statement, but they are such as we cannot relate here.

tion, or education, or Sunday schools, or sermons, can counteract the baneful influence, the insinuating virus, the putrefaction, the contagion of this moral depravity which reigns around them !

" Nil dictu visuque fœdum hæc limina tangat
" Intra quæ puer est."     *Juvenal.*

After all, what motive has either sex, in the class and situation to which we allude, for being virtuous and chaste ?   Where they are unshackled by religious principle, as is too generally the case, they have no delicate sentiments of morality and taste to restrain them from gratifying every passion : they have few or no pleasures beyond those which arise from sensual indulgence, and they have no motive for refraining from this indulgence ; it involves no loss of character, for their companions are as reckless as themselves ; it brings no risk of losing their employment, for their employers know, that it would be unsafe to enquire into these matters ; it is often a cause of no pecuniary loss, for in many cases the poor laws provide against this ; and all these circumstances considered, the licentiousness of the manufacturing population is a source of bitter lamentation to us, but of no astonishment whatever.

—————

Having now stated briefly, but we hope clearly, the state of health in the manufacturing districts, we shall proceed, still more shortly, to the second portion of our task, that of suggesting a few measures, which we believe would act either as palliatives or remedies of the evils we have enumerated.

That many of these evils may be, in a great measure, mitigated, even by individual exertion, is clear and certain. In several cases which we know, where the proprietors of factories have had the welfare of their people honestly at heart, much has been done towards an amelioration of their condition, both physical and moral; and it is important to mention, that *these houses are, without exception, among the most flourishing in the trade.* But in order to effect any thing like a complete reform in the manufacturing districts, a much more universal and systematic plan of exertion is required. It is no plaything we are about. Partial remedies will be of no avail. It is useless any longer to nibble at the evil,—it must be attacked in its strong holds,—it must be uprooted from its source. We call upon every one to assist us in this great and important object. As long as a man is suffered to remain upon the earth, we consider it as an intimation from Providence, that there is some duty for him to discharge, which it would be mean and criminal to decline; and we are sure that no cause can be more worthy, no duty more imperious, than that of labouring to promote the happiness and the virtue of four millions of our countrymen.

I. We hope we shall not greatly offend the prejudices, either of political economists, or practical tradesmen, when we state our firm conviction, that a reduetion in the hours of labour is *most important* to the health of the manufacturing population, and *absolutely necessary* to any general and material amelioration in their moral and intellectual condition. We are fully alive to the immense, and, at first sight, apparently insuperable objections to any measure of the kind. It will be urged, in opposition, that all legislative interference in commercial concerns is, *primâ facie*, objectionable, and involves the admission of a dangerous and impolitic principle. That legislative interference is in itself an evil, we deeply feel, and readily admit; but it is an evil, like many others, which necessity and policy may justify, and which humanity and justice may imperiously demand. Legislative interference is objectionable only where it is injudicious, or uncalled for. It will also be objected, and with more sound reason, that a reduction of the hours of labour would cause a corresponding reduction in the quantity produced, and, consequently, in the wages of the workmen; and would also diminish our power of competing with other manufacturing nations in foreign markets, and thus, by permanently injuring our trade, would be productive of greater evils to the labouring classes than those we are endeavouring to remove. This objection, though very reasonable, we think is considerably overstated. That " a reduction of the hours of labour would cause a *corresponding* reduction in the quantity produced," we entirely deny. What *would* be the actual loss consequent upon a reduction of the hours, it is impossible to state with any cer-

tainty, but it is probable, that if factories were to work
ten hours instead of twelve, the loss in the quantity
produced would not be one sixth, but only about
one twelfth, and in Mule Spinning, perhaps, scarcely
even so much. We *know* that in some cases, when the
mills only worked four days in the week, they have
often produced five days' quantity, and the men earned
five days' wages. That this would be the case to a
considerable extent, every one must be aware; as all
men will be able to work much harder for ten hours
than they can for twelve. The objection above mentioned, therefore, we consider to be much overstated;
and we are convinced that the *loss* incurred would
only amount to a *part* of the reduction. And we
think that *all* loss to the masters might be prevented,
and the necessity of a *real* reduction of wages ob-
viated, were all duties on raw materials, and those
taxes which greatly raise the price of provisions,
abolished by the legislature. It is principally the
shackles and drawbacks to which the Cotton Manufacture is subjected, which renders it so difficult,
and, as some think, so impracticable, to adopt a
measure without which all extensive and general Plans
for improving and regenerating our manufacturing
poor, must approach the limits of impossibility.

At present (in the cotton trade, at least, which is
already restricted by law) the hours of work generally
extend from half past five or six in the morning till
half past seven or eight at night, with about two hours
intermission, making in all about twelve hours of

clear labour. This we would reduce to *ten* hours,* (if such a measure should be rendered practicable and safe by a removal of all taxes on manufactures and provisions); and we again express our conviction, after regarding the subject in every possible point of view, that till this measure is adopted, all plans and exertions for ameliorating the moral and domestic condition of the manufacturing labourer, can only obtain a very partial and temporary sphere of operation. We say this with confidence, because in every project of the kind which we have been enabled to form, in every attempt for this purpose which our personal acquaintance and habitual intercourse with the people could suggest, we have been met and defeated by the long hours (absorbing in fact the whole of the efficient day) which the operative is compelled to remain at his employment. When he returns home at night, the sensorial power is worn out with intense fatigue; he has no energy left to exert in any useful object, or any domestic duty; he is fit only for sleep or sensual indulgence, the only alternations of employment which his leisure knows; he has no moral elasticity to enable him to resist the seductions of appetite or sloth;

* It must not be supposed, that we are supporters or well-wishers of the Bill, lately introduced by Mr. Hobhouse. We disapprove of it in every point of view. Many of its details betray a sad want of acquaintance with the subject on which he undertakes to legislate; it will be utterly inefficient for the object it has in view, and will, if carried in its original form, be highly injurious to all parties, especially to those whom it is designed to benefit.

no heart for regulating his household, superintending his family concerns, or enforcing economy in his domestic arrangements; no power or capability of exertion to rise above his circumstances, or better his condition. He has no time to be wise, no leisure to be good, he is sunken, debilitated, depressed, emasculated, unnerved for effort, incapable of virtue, unfit for every thing but the regular, hopeless, desponding, degrading variety of laborious vegetation or shameless intemperance.* Relieve him in this particular, shorten his hours of labour, and he will find himself possessed of sufficient leisure to make it an object with him to employ that leisure well; he will not be so thoroughly enervated with his day's employment; he will not feel so imperious a necessity for stimulating liquors; he will examine more closely, and regulate more carefully his domestic arrangements; and what is more than all, he will become a soil which the religious philanthropist may have some chance of labouring with advantage. We do not say that a reduction in the hours of labour would do every thing; but we are sure that little can be done without it; it is indispensable as a preliminary measure; it will pave the

* Lest any should object to the boldness of this and other of our statements, we may state once for all, that we are throughout speaking of the manufacturing population *generally*. We by no means wish to deny the existence of many exceptions to the general character we give, especially in the case of those mills which are isolated, and in country situations, and whose proprietors attend to the comfort and welfare of their hands. There *are* such, and we are happy to be able to rank them among our friends.

way for the success of other plans, and render their execution comparatively easy.

II. This great plan once put in force, it will be in the highest degree desirable to introduce among the manufacturing labourers a better system of diet. This will contribute to strengthen their frames, and to preserve them against the necessarily noxious accompaniments of their occupation, as well as in a great measure to supersede the use of spirits, by preventing the occurrence of that craving of the stomach, and that general debility and lassitude, which so often, in the first instance, drive them to this fatal practice. The kind of food at present most in vogue among them, and which we have detailed in a former page, is expensive as well as innutritious; and the badness of their general diet arises far oftener from want of knowledge and of management, than from want of means. In fact, few families (those of hand-loom weavers excepted) who gain their living by manufacturing employments, can plead with any justice inability to supply themselves with solid and nutritious food; for their wages are in almost every case amply adequate to their support, were that portion which is now constantly spent upon luxuries, such as articles of finery, tea, opium, and spirits, devoted to provide the family with the necessaries and conveniences of life. It is absurd to say that those whose weekly wages amount to an annual income of £70., or £100., cannot afford themselves a sufficiency of wholesome food. But the fact is, that partly from thoughtlessness, partly from vanity, partly from habit, and partly from the love of selfish indulgence, but more than all from actual ignorance of domestic economy, their household affairs are carried on in the most unsystematic, slovenly, and expensive style, and display an almost incredible want of management, thriftiness, and care. We believe that a small pamphlet, pointing out the minute details of domestic economy, and showing where an advantage might be gained, and where a saving might be effected, if assiduously circulated among them, and aided perhaps by *vivâ-voce* lectures, would work a most materially beneficial change in their personal and family habits.

III. Among minor arrangements which seem to us essential for preserving the health and morals of the manufacturing population, we will just notice the following.—1. Great care should be taken to keep the rooms in factories as cool as is consistent with the nature of the operations carried on, and to insure free and constant ventilation.—2. More attention should be paid to the cleanliness of the hands, especially the children. *Weavers*, it is true, are and ought to be tolerably clean, nor is there any thing in their occupation to engender or excuse the contrary habits. The *Roving-tenters*, *Dressers*, and *Warpers*, generally, are, and always ought to be clean. But the *Piecers*, the *Scavengers*, the *Card Room*, and *Scutching Room* hands, neither are compelled to be clean and neat in their persons, nor are they ever so, nor is it possible they should be so. But a little attention to

D

this point on the part of the masters might ensure a general ablution every night, which is now only performed only at far more distant intervals.—3. The sexes should be kept separate, as far as this is practicable.—4. No mothers, whose children are too young to take care of themselves, should be allowed to work in factories, or indeed in any occupation which would preclude them from paying constant and vigilant attention to their offspring. The reasons for this suggestion obviously arise out of the facts we have stated in the first part of this enquiry relative to the conduct of mothers.—5. We would allow no children to work in factories till the age of twelve. At present, they are taken in at nine years of age, and indeed often before; for though this is the time fixed by law, yet the anxiety of parents to enable their children to support themselves, frequently induces them to violate the truth, and affirm their child to be older than it really is. At this early age, it is evident that neither mind nor body can have attained that firmness of texture and elasticity of constitution which are requisite to resist the noxious influences which both are called to encounter. Their education also is cut short almost as soon as it is begun, and they have few opportunities in after life of supplying this early deficiency. Add to this, that this is a most dangerous age to be thrown into close and constant intercourse with a set of companions, most of whom are only calculated to unteach what is good, and lead on to what is evil; and the importance of the regulation will be obvious to every one.

IV. Little advance can be made towards improving the morals of the manufacturing population, till a strict and scrupulous attention is paid by the masters to the character of those they employ. This is done in a few isolated cases, and with excellent effect; but these instances are very rare. The great body of master manufacturers pay no attention to the morals of their workmen, nor reprobate bad conduct, except as far as it interferes with their daily labour. A large number of their female hands are notoriously immoral characters, and a considerable portion of their men drunkards more or less confirmed. Were they, on the contrary, to refuse to employ any who could not produce certificates of their being persons of at least a *tolerably* correct behaviour, few measures would have a more immediate, more powerful, or more extensive agency of good. But when the men see that a moral character is in no way valued by their masters, they learn to value it still less than before; and as bad conduct, unless outrageously flagrant, little interferes with their worldly gains, they have no inducement sufficiently powerful to induce them to amend it. We conceive this point to be indispensable.

V. We must bestow upon the manufacturing population a judicious and effective education. We have placed this last, not because it is the least important, but because it must necessarily be subsequent to the other measures of amelioration. We admit the superior intelligence of the manufacturing labourers—

it is one of the great counterbalancing advantages of this system, the evils of which we are deprecating,— but it is still susceptible of great increase, and an improved modification. This subject, if it be not presumptuous to say so, has hitherto, we think, been viewed in erroneous lights. The system followed for the education of the *adults* of this class, at least, has been altogether faulty and inefficient. The efforts of its advocates have been ill-directed. " It has been the error of this age to substitute knowledge for wisdom, to educate the head, and to forget that there is a more important education necessary for the heart." Reading, writing, and arithmetic, are taught at the primary; and geometry, chemistry, and natural philosophy, at the secondary schools. This scarce deserves the name of education. The education which is efficient on the youthful mind is not that which he receives from a master on one day in the week, or for a few hours in the day,—but that which is derived from the example and fellowship of those with whom his days and nights are past in company,—from the contagion of the moral atmosphere with which he is surrounded, —from the combined influence of every thing which he hears and sees ; " for the constant dropping of daily circumstances on the character, wears in it deeper channels than the transient torrents of persuasion."* These "daily circumstances" are the mighty agencies, the incessant influences, which determine the stamp

* Dr. Gooch, on Puerp. Insanity.

and features of the future character,—these are the abundant sources of all that is excellent, and all that is detestable, in our moral nature; and it is to these that all our schemes for the reformation of mankind must be directed, if we wish them to succeed. It is a thankless, and a hopeless task, to palliate the *effects*, while the *cause* remains in undiminished vigour, and unchecked activity,—to suppress the symptoms, and spare the disease. If we desire to effect any material change in the character and habits of the people, we must apply such a system of education as will penetrate into the interior of their families, as will awaken their moral perceptions, strengthen and purify their moral principles, create a new sense, an unfelt desire, a novel want,— as will, in fact, affect the *character*, as well as modify the *conduct*.

The order in which we would arrange the subjects of such an education, is the following.

1. Domestic economy, on the importance of which we have already enlarged. We are of opinion, that information, on this head, would have a far more important *indirect* influence than that of a mere pecuniary saving. It would induce habits of sobriety, thriftiness, family care, and family affection, which at present exist only in a very feeble degree.

2. Instruction in their moral and religious duties. On this point we need not dwell. It is already liberally provided for.

3. Instruction in their political relations, and the duties arising therefrom. This division, which is

daily becoming more pressingly important, is of far too great moment to be hastily discussed in this place. It deserves, and will receive a separate consideration.

4. We would instruct the people in other branches of interesting knowledge, especially geography and history; intermingling such moral, and religious, and political lessons, as naturally grow out of the subject, and are calculated to come home to the popular mind.

And—5. Above all, we would labour to give them that delicacy and propriety of feeling, and civility of manner, which a friendly but respectful intercourse with the superior classes can alone bestow. We regard this as the most important branch of popular education. We know nothing which exercises such a powerful influence over the feelings and manners of the lower orders, as opportunities of associating with their superiors. " *Emollit mores, nec sinit esse feros.*" Wherever these opportunities have been afforded, the people seem to have risen many grades in the scale of society above their less favoured countrymen. In agricultural districts, this intercourse exists to a considerable extent, and might be greatly increased. In manufacturing towns, with a few rare exceptions, it has no existence. The masters and their men occupy two distinct spheres of living, to the mutual detriment of both. They are bound together by no ties beyond those of pecuniary service; and when these are broken, or suspended, that state of things ensues which has lately been alarming and inflaming the whole of the South of Lancashire, and spreading doubt and dismay throughout the kingdom. We entreat the attention of our readers to these considerations, as we feel convinced they are of the last importance. We shall recur to this part of the subject on a future occasion.

We have now laid before the public a concise, and, we hope, a correct view of the moral and physical condition of our manufacturing population,—of the lamentable evils under which they labour, and of the measures which seem to us, if adopted, likely to act as remedies or palliatives of these evils. We are not very sanguine as to the success of our statement, in arousing the philanthropic feeling, or stimulating the benevolent exertions of our more affluent and powerful countrymen. But though, from constitution and from principle, averse from feeling or acting as alarmists, we are certain— in as far as reasoning from the past and the present *can* make us certain of the future, that unless some cordial, faithful, vigorous, and united effort is made on the part of the influential classes, to stem that torrent of suffering and corruption, which is fast sweeping away the comfort and the morals of so large a portion of our poorer countrymen; and which, if not checked, will soon send them forth upon the world, desperate, reckless, ruined men—ruined both in their feelings and their fortunes ;—unless some such effort is made, and *that* speedily, there are silent but mighty instruments at work, like an evil that walketh in darkness, which, ere long, will undermine the system of social union, and burst asunder the silken bonds of amity, which unite men to their kind. But even in this day of anxiety and suspense, we will not, for the honour of our common country, suffer our minds to be borne away with these melancholy anticipations. We will believe and trust, that, notwithstanding despised sufferings, unheard complaints, unanswered entreaties, and neglected warnings, there is still a redeeming spirit in the feelings of the wealthy and the great, which will interfere, while interference may yet avail, and avert by a wise, a vigorous, and an enlarged philanthropy, the calamities which threaten the peace, the prosperity, and the virtue of the country.

Tilling, Printer, Chelsea.

A

# MEMOIR

OF

# ROBERT BLINCOE,

An Orphan Boy;

SENT FROM THE WORKHOUSE OF ST. PANCRAS, LONDON
AT SEVEN YEARS OF AGE,

TO ENDURE THE

# Horrors of a Cotton-Mill,

THROUGH HIS INFANCY AND YOUTH,

WITH A MINUTE DETAIL OF HIS SUFFERINGS,

BEING

THE FIRST MEMOIR OF THE KIND PUBLISHED.

## BY JOHN BROWN.

MANCHESTER:
PRINTED FOR AND PUBLISHED BY J. DOHERTY, 37, WITHY-GROVE.
1832.

# PUBLISHER'S PREFAC

THE various Acts Of Parliament, which have been passed, to regulate the treatment of children in the Cotton Spinning Manufactories, betoken the previous existence of some treatment, so glaringly wrong, as to force itself upon the attention of the legislature. This Cotton-slave-trade, like the Negro-slave-trade, did not lack its defenders, and it might have afforded a sort of sorry consolation to the Negro slaves of America, had they been informed, that their condition, in having agriculturally to raise the cotton, was not half so bad, as that of the white infant-slaves, who had to assist in the spinning of it, when brought to this country. The religion and the black humanity of Mr. Wilberforce seem to have been entirely of a foreign nature. Pardon is begged, if an error is about to be wrongfully imputed—but the Publisher has no knowledge, that Mr. Wilberforce's humane advocacy for slaves, was ever of that homely kind, as to embrace the region of the home-cotton-slave-trade. And yet, who shall read the Memoir of Robert Blincoe, and say, that the charity towards slaves should not have begun or ended at home?

THE Author of this Memoir is now dead; he fell, about two or three years ago, by his own hand. He united, with a strong feeling for the injuries and sufferings of others, a high sense of injury when it bore on himself, whether real or imaginary; and a despondency when his prospects were not good.—Hence his suicide.—Had he not possessed a fine fellow-feeling with the child of misfortune, he had never taken such pains to compile the

Memoir of Robert Blincoe, and to collect all the wrongs on paper, on which he could gain information, about the various sufferers under the cotton-mill systems. Notes to the Memoir of Robert Blincoe were intended by the author, in illustration of his strong personal assertions. The references were marked in the Memoir; but the Notes were not prepared, or if prepared, have not come to the Publisher's hand. But, on inquiring after Robert Blincoe, in Manchester, and mentioning the Memoir of him written by Mr. Brown, as being in the Publisher's possession, other papers, by the same Author, which had been left on a loan of money in Manchester, were obtained, and these papers seem to have formed the authorities, from which the Notes to the Memoirs would have been made. So that, though the Publisher does not presume to make notes for the Author, nor for himself, to this Memoir, he is prepared to confirm much of the statement here made, the personalities of Robert Blincoe excepted, should it be generally challenged.

Robert Blincoe, the subject of the Memoir, is now about 35 years of age, and resides at No. 19, Turner-street, Manchester, where he keeps a small grocer's shop. He is also engaged in manufacturing Sheet Wadding and Cotton Waste-Dealer. The Publisher having no knowledge of Robert Blincoe, but in common with every reader of this Memoir, can have no personal feelings towards him, other than those of pity for his past sufferings. But such a Memoir as this was much wanted, to hand down to posterity, what was the real character of the complaints about the treatment of children in our cotton mills, about which a legislation has taken place, and so much has been said. An amended treatment of children has been made, the apprenticing system having been abandoned by the masters of the mills; but the employment is in itself bad for children—first, as their health—and second, as to their manners and acquirements—the employment being in a bad atmosphere; and the education, from example, being bad; the time that should be devoted to a better education, being devoted to that which is bad. The employment of infant children in the cotton-mills furnishes a bad means to dissolute parents, to live in idleness and all sorts of vice, upon the produce of infant labour. There is much of this in Lancashire, which a little care and looking after, on the part of the masters of cotton-mills, might easily prevent. But what is to be done? Most of the extensive manufacturers profit by human misery and become callous toward it; both from habit and interest. If a remedy be desired, it must be sought by that part of the working people themselves, who are alive to their progressing degradation. It will never be sought fairly out, by those who have no interest in seeking it. And so long as the majority of the working people squanders its already scanty income in those pest-houses, those intoxicating nurseries, for vice, idleness and misery, the public drinking-houses, there is no hope for them of an amended condition.

# MEMOIR

OF

# Robert Blincoe,

## AN ORPHAN BOY.

## CHAP. I.

**B**Y the time the observant reader has got through the melancholy recital of the sufferings of Blincoe and his associates in cotton-mill bondage, he will probably incline to an opinion, that rather than rear destitute and deserted children, to be thus distorted by excessive toil, and famished and tortured as those have been, it were incomparably less cruel to put them at once to death—less cruel that they had never been born alive; and far more wise that they had never been conceived. In cases of unauthorized pregnancies, our laws are tender of unconscious life, perhaps to a faulty extreme; whilst our parochial institutions. as these pages will prove, after incurring considerable expence to PRESERVE the lives of those forlorn beings, sweep them off by shoals, under the sanction of other legal enactments, and consign them to a fate, far worse than sudden death.

Reared in the most profound ignorance and depravity, these unhappy beings are, from the hour of their birth, to the last of their existence, generally cut off from all that is decent in social life. Their preceptors are the veriest wretches in nature !— their influential examples all of the worst possible kind. The reports of the Cotton Bill Committees abundantly prove, that, by forcing those destitute poor to go into cotton-mills, they have, in very numerous instances. been consigned to a destiny worse than death without torture. Yet appalling as are many of the statements, which, through the reports of the Committees, have found their way before the public, similar acts of delinquencies, of a hue still darker—even repeated acts of murder, have escaped unnoticed. Much of the evidence brought forward by the friends of humanity, was neutralized or frittered away by timidity of their witnesses, or by the base subserviency of venally unprincipled professional men, who, influenced by rich capitalists, basely prostituted their talent and character as physicians, surgeons, and apothecaries, to deceive the government, to perplex and mislead public opinion, and avert the loud cry raised against the insatiate avarice and relentless cruelty of their greedy and unfeeling suborners.

It was in the spring of 1822, after having devoted a considerable time to the investigating of the effect of the manufacturing system, and factory establishments, on the health and morals of the manufacturing populace, that I first heard of the extraordinary sufferings of R. Blincoe. At the same time, I was told of his earnest wish that those sufferings should, for the protection of the rising generation of parish children, be laid before the world. Thus assured, I went to enquire for him, and was much pleased with his conversation. If this young man had not been consigned to a cotton-factory, he would probably have been strong, healthy, and well grown; instead of which, he is diminutive as to stature, and his knees are grievously distorted. In his manners, he appeared remarkably gentle ; in his language, temperate; in his statements, cautious and consistent. If, in any part of the ensuing narrative, there are falsehoods and misrepresentations, the fault rests solely with himself; for, repeatedly and earnestly, I admonished him to beware, lest a too keen remembrance of the injustice he had suffered should lead him to transgres the limits of truth. After I had taken down his communications, I tested them, by reading the same to other persons, with whom Blincoe had not had any intercourse on the subject, and who had partaken of the miseries of the same hard servitude, and by whom they were in every point confirmed.

ROBERT BLINCOE commenced his melancholy narrative, by stating, that he was a parish orphan, and knew not either his father or mother. From the age of four years, he says, "till I had completed my seventh, I was supported in Saint Pancras poorhouse, near London." In very pathetic terms, he frequently censured and regretted the remissness of the parish officers, who, when they received him into the workhouse, had, as he seemed to believe, neglected to make any entry, or, at least, any to which he could obtain access, of his mother's and father's name, occupation, age, or residence. Blincoe argued, and plausibly too, that those officers would not have received him, if his mother had not proved her settlement; and he considered it inhuman in the extreme, either to neglect to record the names of his parents, or, if recorded, to refuse to give him that information, which, after his attaining his freedom, he had requested at their hands. His lamentations, on this head, were truely touching, and evinced a far higher degree of susceptibility of heart, than could have been expected from the extreme and long continued wretchedness he had endured in the den of vice and misery, where he was so long immured. Experience often evinces, that, whilst moderate adversity mollifies and expands the human heart, extreme and long continued wretchedness has a direct and powerful contrary tendency, and renders it impenetrably callous.

In one of our early interviews, tears trickling down his pallid cheeks, and his voice tremulous and faltering, Blincoe said, "I am worse off than a child reared in the Foundling Hospital. Those orphans have a name given them by the heads of that institution, at the time of baptism, to which they are legally entitled. But I have no name I can call my own." He said he perfectly recollected riding in a coach to the workhouse, accompanied by some female, that he did not however think this female was his mother, for he had not the least consciousness of having felt either sorrow or uneasiness at being separated from her, as he very naturally supposed he should have felt, if that person had been his mother. Blincoe also appeared to think he had not been nursed by his mother, but had passed through many hands before he arrived at the workhouse; because he had no recollection of ever having experienced a mother's caresses. It seems, young as he was, he often enquired of the nurses, when the parents and relations of other children came to see his young associates, *why no one came to him*, and used to weep, when he was told, that *no one had ever owned him*, after his being placed in that house. Some of the nurses stated, that a female, who called soon after his arrival, inquired for him by the name of "Saint; and, when he was produced, gave him a penny-piece, and told him his mother was dead. If this report were well founded, his mother's illness was the cause of his being removed and sent to the workhouse. According to his own description, he felt with extreme sensibility the loneliness of his condition, and, at each stage of his future sufferings, during his severe cotton-mill servitude, it pressed on his heart the heaviest of all his sorrows—an impassable barrier, "a wall of brass," cut him off from all mankind. The sad consciousness, that he stood alone ' *a waif on the world's wide common;*' that he had no acknowledged claim of kindred with any human being, rich or poor—that he stood apparently for ever excluded from every social circle, so constantly occupied his thoughts, that, together with his sufferings, they imprinted a pensive character on his features, which probably neither change of fortune, nor time itself, would ever entirely obliterate. When he was six years old, and, as the workhouse children were saying their Catechism, it was his turn to repeat the Fifth Commandment—"Honour thy father and thy mother, &c.," he recollects having suddenly burst into tears, and felt greatly agitated and distressed—his voice faltering, and his limbs trembling. According to his statement, and his pathetic eloquence, in reciting his misfortunes, strongly corroborated his assertion, he was a very ready scholar, and the source of this sudden burst of grief being inquired into by some of his superiors, he said, "I cry, because I *cannot* obey one of God's commandments, I know not either my father or my mother, I cannot therefore be a good child and honour my parents."

It was rumoured, in the ward where Robert Blincoe was placed, that he owed his existence to the mutual frailties of his mother and a reverend divine, and was called the young Saint, in allusion to his priestly descent. This name or appellation he did not long retain, for he was afterwards called Parson; often, *the young Parson*; and he recollected hearing it said in his presence, that he was the son of a parson Blincoe. Whether these allusions were founded in truth, or were but the vile effusions of vulgar malice, was not, and is not, in his power to determine, whose bosom they have so painfully agitated. Another remarkable circumstance in his case, was, that when he was sent in August, 1799, with a large number of other children, from Saint Pancras workhouse, to a cotton-mill near Nottingham, he bore amongst his comrades, the name of *Parson*, and retained it afterwards till he had served considerably longer than his FOURTEEN YEARS, and then, when his Indentures were at last relinquished, and not till then, the young man found he had been apprenticed by the name of Robert Blincoe. I urged the probability, that his right indenture might, in the change of masters that took place, or the careless indifference of his last master, have been given to another boy, and that to the one given to him, bearing the name of Blincoe, he had no just claim. This reasoning he repelled, by steadily and consistently asserting, he fully recollected having heard it said his real name was Blincoe, whilst he remained at Saint Pancras workhouse. His indentures were dated the 15th August, 1799. If, at this time, he was seven years of age, which is by no means certain, he was born in 1792, and in 1796, was placed in Pancras workhouse. With these remarks I close this preliminary matter, and happy should I be, if the publication of these facts enables the individual to whom they relate, to remove the veil which has hitherto deprived him of a knowledge of his parentage, a privation which he still appears to feel with undiminished intensity of grief.

Two years have elapsed, since I first began to take notes of Blincoe's
No. 1.

extraordinary narrative. At the close of 1822 and beginning of 1823, I was seized with a serious illness, which wholly prevented my publishing this and other important communications. The testimony of a respectable a surgeon, who attended me, as any in the country, even ocular demonstration of my enfeebled state, failed to convince some of the cotton spinners, that my inability was not feigned, to awnswer some sinister end ; and such attrocious conduct was pursued towards me, as would have fully justified a prosecution for conspiracy. Animated by the most opposite views, the worst of miscreants united to vilify and oppress me ; the one wanting to get my papers, in order, by destroying them, to prevent the enormities of the cotton masters being exposed; and another, traducing my character, and menacing my life, under an impression that I had basely sold the declarations and communications received from oppressed workpeople to their masters. By some of those suspicious, misjudging people, Blincoe was led away. He did not, however, at any time, or under any circumstances, retract or deny any part of his communications, and, on the 18th and 19th of March, 1824, of his own free will, he not only confirmed all that he had communicated in the spring of 1822, with many other traits of suffering, not then recollected, but furnished me with them. It has, therefore, stood the test of this hurricane, without its authenticity being in any one part questioned or impared. The authenticity of this narrative is, therefore, entitled to greater credit, than much of the testimony given by the owners of cotton-factories, or by professional men on their behalf, as will, in the course of this narrative, be fully demonstrated, by evidence wholly incontrovertible. If, therefore, it should be proved, that atrocities to the same extent, exist no longer ; still, its publication, as a preventative remedy, is no less essential to the protection of parish paupers and foundlings. If the gentlemen of Manchester and its vicinity, who acted in 1816, &c., in conjunction with the late Mr. Nathaniel Gould, had not made the selection of witnesses too much in the power of incompetent persons, Robert Blincoe would have been selected in 1819, as the most impressive pleader in behalf of destitute and deserted children.

## CHAP. II.

OF the few adventures of Robert Blincoe, during his residence in old Saint Pancras workhouse, the principal occurred when he had been there about two years. He acknowledges he was well fed, decently clad, and comfortably lodged, and not at all overdone, as regarded work; yet, with all these blessings in possession, this destitute child grew melancholy. He relished none of the humble comforts he enjoyed. It was liberty he wanted. The busy world lay outside the workhouse gates, and those he was seldom, if ever permitted to pass. He was cooped up in a gloomy, though liberal sort of a prison-house. His buoyant spirits longed to rove at large. He was too young to understand the necessity of the restraint to which he was subjected, and too opiniative to admit it could be intended for his good. Of the world he knew nothing, and

No. 2.

the society of a workhouse was not very well calculated to delight the mind of a volatile child. He saw givers, destitute of charity, receivers of insult, instead of gratitude, witnessed little besides sullenness and discontent, and heard little but murmurs or malicious and slanderous whispers. The aged were commonly petulant and miserable—the young demoralized and wholly destitute of gaity of heart. From the top to the bottom, the whole of this motley mass was tainted with dissimulation, and he saw the most abhorrent hypocrisy in constant operation. Like a bird newly caged, that flutters from side to side, and foolishly beats its wings against its prison walls, in hope of obtaining its liberty, so young Blincoe, weary of confinement and resolved, if possible to be free, often watched the outer gates of the house, in the hope, that some favourable opportunity might facilitate his escape. He wistfully measured the height of the wall, and found it too lofty for him to scale, and too well guarded were the gates to admit of his egress unnoticed. His spirits, he says, which were naturally lively and buoyant, sank under this vehement longing after liberty. His appetite declined, and he wholly forsook his usual sports and comrades. It is hard to say how this disease of the mind might have terminated, if an accident had not occurred, which afforded a chance of emerging from the lifeless monotony of a workhouse, and of launching into the busy world, with which he longed to mingle.

Blincoe declares, he was so weary of confinement, he would gladly have exchanged situations with the poorest of the poor children, whom, from the upper windows of the workhouse, he had seen begging from door to door, or, as a subterfuge, offering matches for sale. Even the melancholy note of the sweep-boy, whom, long before day, and in the depths of winter, in frost, in snow, in rain in sleet, he heard pacing behind his surley master, had no terrors for him. So far from it, he envied him his fortune, and, in the fulness of discontent, thought his own state incomparably more wretched. The poor child was suffering under a diseased imagination, from which men [of mature years and elaborate culture are not always free. It filled his heart with perverted feelings— it rendered the little urchen morose and unthankful, and, as undeserving of as he was insensible to, the important benefits extended to him by a humane institution, when helpless, destitue and forlorn.

From this state of early misanthropy, young Blincoe was suddenly diverted, by a rumour, that filled many a heart among his comrades with terror, viz. that a day was appointed, when the master-sweeps of the metropolis were to come and select such a number of boys as apprentices, till they attained the age of 21 years, as they might deign to take into their sable fraternity. These tidings, that struck damp to the heart of the other boys, sounded like heavenly music to the ears of young Blincoe :— he anxiously inquired of the nurses if the news were true, and if so, what chance there was of his being one of the elect. The ancient matrons, amazed at the boy's temerity and folly, told him how bitterly he would rue the day that should consign him to that wretched employment, and bade him pray earnestly to God to protect him from such a destiny. The young adventurer heard these opinions with silent contempt. Finding, on farther inquiry, that the rumour was well founded, he applied to seve-ral menials in the house, whom he thought likely to promote his suit, entreating them to forward his election with all the interest they could command! Although at this time he was a fine grown boy, being fearful he might be deemed too low in stature, he accustomed himself to walk in an erect posture, and went almost a tip-toe;—by a ludicrous conceit, he used to hang by the hands to the rafters and balustrades, supposing that an exercise, which could only lengthen his arms, would produce the same effect on his legs and body. In this course of training for the contingent honour of being chosen by the master-sweeps, as one fit for their use,—with a perseverance truly admirable, his tender age considered, young Blincoe continued till the important day arrived. The boys were brought forth, many of them in tears, and all except Blincoe, very sorrowful. Amongst them, by an act unauthorised by his guardians, young Blincoe contrived to intrude his person. His deportment formed a striking con-trast to that of all his comrades; his seemed unusually high : he smiled as the grim looking fellows approached him ; held his head as high as he could, and, by every little artifice in his power, strove to attract their notice, and obtain the honour of their preference. While this fatherless and motherless child, with an intrepid step, and firm countenance, thus courted the smiles of the sooty tribe, the rest of the boys conducted them-selves as if they nothing so much dreaded, as to become the objects of their choice, and shrunk back from their touch as if they had been tainted by the most deadly contagion. Boy after boy was taken, in preference to Blincoe, who was often handled, examined, and rejected. At the close of the show, the number required was elected, and Blincoe was not among them! He declared, that his chagrin was inexpressible, when his failure was apparent.

Some of the sweeps complimented him for his spirit, and, to console him, said, if he made a good use of his time, and contrived to grow a head taller, he might do very well for a fag, at the end of a couple of years. This disappointment gave a severe blow to the aspiring ambition of young Blincoe, whose love of liberty was so ardent, that he cared little about the sufferings by which, if attained, it was likely to be alloyed. The boys that were chosen, were not immediately taken away. Mingling with these, some of them said to our hero, the tears standing in their eyes :—"why, Parson, can you endure the thoughts of going to be a chimney-sweep ? I wish they would take you instead of me." "So do I, with all my heart," said Blincoe, "for I would rather be any where than here " At night, as Blincoe lay tossing about, unable to sleep; because he had been rejected, his unhappy associates were weeping and wailing, because they had been accepted ! Yet, his heart was not so cold as to be unaffected by the wailings of those poor children, who, mournfully antici-pating the horrors of their new calling, deplored their misfortune in the most touching terms. They called upon their parents, who, living or dead, were alike unable to hear them, to come and save them ! What a difference of feeling amongst children of the same unfortunate class. The confinement that was so wearisome to young Blincoe, must have been equally irksome to some of his young associates; therefore, the love of

liberty could not have been its sole cause,—there was another and a
stronger reason—all his comrades had friends, parents, or relations:
poor Blincoe stood alone ! no ties of consanguinity or kindred bound him
to any particular portion of society, or to any place—he had no friend to
soothe his troubled mind—no domestic circle to which, though excluded
for a time, he might hope to be reunited. As he stood thus estranged
from the common ties of nature, it is the less to be wondered at, that, pro-
pelled by a violent inclination to a rambling life, and loathing the restraint
imposed by his then condition, he should indulge so preposterous a
notion, as to prefer the wretched state of a sweeping-boy. Speaking
on this subject, Blincoe said to me, "If I could penetrate the source
of my exemption from the sorrow and consternation so forcibly
expressed by my companions, it would probably have been resolved by
the peculiarity of my destiny, and the privation of those endearing ties
and ligatures which cement family circles. When the friends, relatives,
parents of other children came to visit them, the caresses that were sometimes exchanged, the joy that beamed on the faces of those so favoured,
went as daggers to my heart ; not that I cherished a feeling of envy at
their good fortune ; but that it taught me more keenly to feel my own
forlorn condition. Sensations, thus, excited, clouded every festive hour,
and, young as I was, the voice of nature, instinct, if you will, forced me
to consider myself as a moral outcast, as a scathed and blighted tree, in
the midst of a verdant lawn.

I dare not aver, that such were the very words Blincoe used, but they
faithfully convey the spirit and tendency of his language and sentiments.
Blincoe is by no means deficient in understanding : he can be witty,
satirical, and pathetic, by turns, and he never showed himself to such
advantage, as when expatiating upon the desolate state to which his utter
ignorance of his parentage had reduced him.

During Blincoe's abode at St. Pancras, he was inoculated at the Small
Pox Hospital. He retained a vivid remembrance of the copious doses of
salts he had to swallow, and that his heart heaved, and his hand shook
as the nauseous potion approached his lips. The old nurse seemed to
consider such conduct as being wholly unbecoming a *pauper child ;* and
chiding young Blincoe, told him, he ought to "lick his lips," and say
thank you, for the good and wholesome medicine provided for him at the
public expense; at the same time, very coarsely reminding him of the
care that was taken to save him from an untimely death by catching the
small-pox in the natural way. In the midst of his subsequent afflictions,
in Litton Mill, Blincoe, declared, he often lamented having, by this
inoculation, lost a chance of escaping by an early death, the horrible destiny for which he was preserved.

From the period of Blincoe's disappointment, in being rejected by the
sweeps, a sudden calm seems to have succeeded, which lasted till a
rumour ran through the house, that a treaty was on foot between the
Churchwardens and Overseers of St. Pancras, and the owner of a great
cotton factory, in the vicinity of Nottingham, for the disposal of a large
number of children, as apprentices, till they become twenty-one years of
age. This occurred about a twelvemonth after his chimney-sweep mis-

carriage. The rumour itself inspired Blincoe with new life and spirits ;
he was in a manner intoxicated with joy, when he found, it was not only
confirmed, but that the number required was so considerable, that it
would take off the greater part of the children in the house,—poor infatu-
ated boy ! delighted with the hope of obtaining a greater degree of liberty
than he was allowed in the workhouse,—he dreamed not of the misery
that impended, in the midst of which he could look back to Pancras as
to an Elysium, and bitterly reproach himself for his ingratitude and folly.

Prior to the show-day of the pauper children to the purveyor or cotton
master, the most illusive and artfully contrived falsehoods were spread, to
fill the minds of those poor infants with the most absurd and ridiculous
errors, as to the real nature of the servitude, to which they were to be
consigned. It was gravely stated to them, according to Blincoe's statement, made in the most positive and solemn manner, that they were all,
when they arrived at the cotton-mill, to be transformed into ladies and
gentlemen : that they would be fed on roast beef and plum-pudding—be
allowed to ride their masters' horses, and have silver watches, and plenty
of cash in their pockets. Nor was it the nurses, or other inferior persons
of the workhouse, with whom this vile deception originated ; but with
the parish officers themselves. From the statement of the victims of
cotton-mill bondage, it seems to have been a constant rule, with those
who had the disposal of parish children, prior to sending them off to
cotton-mills, to fill their minds with the same delusion. Their hopes being
thus excited, and their imaginations inflamed, it was next stated, amongst
the innocent victims of fraud and deception, that no one could be *compelled*
to go, nor any but volunteers accepted.

When it was supposed at St. Pancras, that these excitements had operated sufficiently powerful to induce a ready acquiescence in the proposed
migration, all the children, male and female, who were seven years old, or
considered to be of that age, were assembled in the committee-room, for the
purpose of being publicly examined, touching their health, and capacity,
and what is almost incredible touching their *willingness* to go and serve as
apprentices, in the way and manner required ! There is something so detestable, in this proceeding, that any one might conclude, that Blincoe had
been misled in his recollections of the particulars ; but so many other sufferers have corroborated his statement, that I can entertain no doubt of the
fact. This exhibition took place in August 1799, and eighty boys and
girls as parish apprentices, and till they had respectively acquired the age
of twenty-one years, were made over by the churchwardens and overseers
of Saint Pancras parish, to Messers. Lamberts', cotton-spinners, hosiers
and lace-men, of St. Mary's parish, Nottingham, the owners of Lowdam
Mill. The boys, during the latter part of their time, were to be instructed
in the trade of stocking weaving—the girls in lace-making. There was no
specification whatever, as to the time their masters were to be allowed to
work these poor children, although, at this period, the most abhorrent
cruelties were notoriously known to be exercised, by the owners of cotton-
mills, upon parish apprentices. According to Blincoe's testimony, so
powerfully had the illusions, purposely spread to entrap these poor children,
operated, and so completely were their feeble minds excited, by the blan-

dishments held out to them, that they almost lost their wits.  The thought and talked of nothing but the scenes of luxury and grandeur, in which they were to move.  Nor will the reflecting reader feel surprised at this credulity, however gross, when he considers the poor infants  imagined there were no greater personages than the superiors, to whom  they were, as paupers, subjected, and that, it was those identical persons, by whom their weak and feeble intellects had thus been imposed upon.  Blincoe describes his conduct to have been marked by peculiar extravagance.  Such was his impatience, he could scarcely eat or sleep, so anxiously did he wait the hour of emancipation.  The poor deluded young cratures were so inflated with pride and vanity, that they strutted about like so many  dwarfish and  silly kings and queens, in a  mock  tragedy.  "We began" said  Blincoe " to treat our old nurses with airs of insolence and disdain—refused to associate with children, who, from  sickness, or  being  under age,  had not been accepted ; they were commanded to keep their distance ; told to know their betters ; forbidden to mingle in our exalted circle ! Our little coterie was a complete epitome of the effects of prosperity in the great world.  No sooner were our hearts cheered by a prospect of good fortune, than its influence produced  the  sad  effects  recited.  The  germ of those hateful vices, arrogance, selfishness and  ingratitude, began to display themselves even  before we had tasted  the intoxicating cup.  But our illusion soon vanished, and we were suddenly awakened from the flattering dream, which consigned  the  greater part of us to a fate more  severe  than  that  of the West Indian slaves, who have the good fortune  to serve humane owners. Such  were  Blincoe's reflections in  May  1822.

It appears that the interval was not long, which filled up  the  space between their examination, acceptance, and departure from St.  Pancras work-house, upon their way to Nottingham ; but short  as it was, it left room for dissension.  The  boys could not  agree who should have the *first ride* on their masters' horses, and violent disputes arose  amongst the girls, on subjects equally ludicrous.  It was afterwards whispered at Lowdam Mill, that the elder girls, previous to leaving Pancras, began to feel scruples, whether their dignity would allow them  to drop the usual bob-curtsey to the master or matron of the house, or to the governess by whom they had been instructed to read, or work by the needle.  Supposing all these follies to have been displayed to the very letter, the poor children were still objects of pity ; the guilt rests upon those by whom they had been so  wickedly  deceived !

Happy, no doubt, in the thought of transferring  the burthen of the future support of fourscore young  paupers to other parishes,  the churchwardens and overseers distinguished the departure of this  juvenile colony by acts of munificence.  The children were completely  new  clothed, and each had two suits, one for their working, the other for their holiday dress— a shilling in money, was  given to each—a new pocket handkerchief—and a large piece of gingerbread.  As Blincoe had no relative of whom to take leave, all his anxiety was to get outside the door.  According to his own account, he was the first at the gate, one of the foremost who mounted the waggon, and the loudest in his cheering.  In how far the parents or relatives of the rest of the children consented  to this migration ; if they were at all consulted, or even apprised of its being in contemplation, formed no part of Blincoe's communications. All he stated was, that the whole of the party seemed to start in very high spirits. As to his own personal conduct, Blincoe asserts, he strutted along dressed in party-coloured parish clothing, on his way to the waggon, no less filled with vanity than with delusion : he imagined he was free, when he was in fact legally converted into a slave ; he exulted in the imaginary possession of personal liberty, when he was in reality a prisoner. The whole convoy were well guarded by the parish beadles on their way to the waggons; but those officers, bearing their staves, the children were taught to consider as a guard of *honour*. In addition to the beadles, there was an active young man or two, appointed to look after the passengers of the two large waggons, in their conveyance to Nottingham. Those vehicles, and very properly too, were so secured, that when once the grated doors were locked, no one could escape. Plenty of clean straw was strewed in the beds, and no sooner were the young fry *safely lodged* within, than they began throwing it over one another and seemed delighted with the commencement of their jouryney. A few hours progress considerably damped this exultation. The inequality of the road, and the heavy jolts of the waggon, occasioned them many a bruise. Although it was the middle of August, the children felt very uncomfortable. The motion of the heavy clumsey vehicle, and so many children cooped up in so small a space, produced nausea and other results, such as sometimes occur in Margate hoys. Of the country they passed through, the young travellers saw very little.—Blincoe thinks the children were suffered to come out of the waggon to walk through St. Alban's. After having passed one night in the waggon, many of the children began to repent, and express a wish to return. They were told to have patience, till they arrived at Messrs. Lamberts, when, *no doubt*, those gentlemen would pay every attention to their wishes, and send back to St. Pancras, those who might wish to return. Blincoe, as might have been expected, was not one of those *back-sliders*—he remained steady to his purpose, exulting in the thought, that every step he advanced brought him nearer to the desired spot, where so many enviable enjoyments awaited him, and conveyed him farther and farther from the detested workhouse ! Blincoe being so overjoyed with the fine expectations he was to receive at Lowdam Mill, he spent his shilling at Leicester in apples.

The greater part of the children were much exhausted, and not a few of them seriously indisposed, before they arrived at Nottingham. When the waggons drew up near the dwelling and warehouse of their future master, a crowd collected to see the *live stock* that was just imported from the metropolis, who were pitied, admired, and compared to lambs, led by butchers to slaughter ! Care was taken that they should not hear or understand much of this sort of discourse. The boys and girls were distributed, some in the kitchen, others in a large ware-room, washed, combed and supplied with refreshments ; but there were no plum-pudding—no roast beef, no talk of the horses they were to ride, nor of the watches and fine clothing that they had been promised. Many looked very mournful ; they had been four days travelling to Nottingham : at a more advanced period of their lives, a travel to the East Indies might not have been estimated as

a much more important or hazardous undertaking. After having been
well refreshed, the whole of the boys and girls were drawn up in rows, to
be *reviewed by their masters*, their friends and neighbours. In Blincoe's
estimation, their masters, Messrs. Lamberts', were " stately sort of
men." They looked over the children and finding them all right, according to the INVOICE, exhorted them to behave with proper humility and
decorum. To pay the most prompt and submissive respects to the orders
of those who would be appointed to instruct and superintend them at
Lowdam Mill, and to be diligent and careful, each one to execute his or
her task, and thereby avoid the punishment and disgrace which awaited
idleness, insolence, or disobedience. This harangue, which was delivered
in a severe and dictatorial tone, increased their apprehensions, but not
one durst open a mouth to complain. The masters and their servants
talked of the various sorts of labour to which the children were to apply
themselves, and to the consternation and dismay of Blincoe and his associates, not the least allusion was made to the many fine things which had so
positively been promised them whilst in London. The conversation
which Blincoe heard, seemed to look forward to close, if not to unremitting toil, and the poor boy had been filled with expectations, that he was to
work only when it pleased him ; to have abundance of money and fine
clothes—a watch in his pocket, to feast on roast beef and plum-pudding,
and to ride his masters horses. His hopes, however were, not wholly
extinguished, because Nottingham was not Lowdam Mill, but his confidence was greatly reduced, and his tone of exultation much lowered.

The children rested one night at Nottingham in the warehouses of their
new masters—the next day they were led out to see the castle, Mortimer-
hole and other local curiosities, in the forest of Sherwood, which are so
celebrated by bards of ancient times. Many shoes, bonnets, and many
other articles of clothing having been lost upon the journey, others were
supplied—but withal Blincoe found himself treated as a parish orphan,
and he calculated on being received and treated as if he had been a gentleman's son sent on a visit to the house of a friend or relative. By the
concurring testimony of other persons who had been entrapped by similar
artifices, it appears certain, that the *purveyors* of infant labourers to
supply the masters of cotton and silk factories with cheap labourers,
adopted this vile, unmanly expedient, in most of their transactions. It
will be seen, by the evidence of Sir Robert Peel, Baronet, David Owen,
Esq. and other witnesses examined in 1816, that, when children were
first wanted to attend machinery in cotton-factories, such was the aversion
of parents and guardians to this noxious employment, that scarcely any
would submit to consign their off-spring to those mills, the owners of
which, under the specious pretext of diminishing the burdens occasioned
by poor-rates, prevailed on churchwardens and overseers, to put their
infant paupers into their hands. Since then, by a gradual progress of
poverty and depravity, in the county of Lancashire alone, there are
some thousand fathers, mothers, and relatives, who live upon the produce
of infant labour, though alloyed by the dreadful certainty, that their gain
is acquired by the sacrifice of their children's health and morals, and too
frequently of their lives, whereby the fable of Saturn devouring his children, seems realised in modern times.

# CHAP. III.

Lowdham Cotton-Mill, situated near a village of that name, stood ten miles distant from Nottingham, on the Surhill road; thither Robert Blincoe and his associates were conveyed the next day in carts, and it was rather late when they arrived. The mill, a large and lofty edifice, being surmounted by a cupola, Blincoe, at first, mistook for a church, which raised a laugh at his expense, and some jeering remarks, that he would soon know what sort of service was performed there. Another said, he did not doubt but the young cocknies would be very *regular* in their *attendance*. When he came in view of the apprentice-house, which was half a mile distant from the mill, and was told that was *to be his home for fourteen years to come*, he was not greatly delighted, so closely did it resemble a workhouse. There was one source of consolation, however, remaining—it was not surrounded by lofty walls, nor secured by strong gates, as was the case at Pancras. When the first cart, in which was young Blincoe, drove up to the door, a number of villagers flocked round, some of whom exclaimed, " God help the poor wretches."—Eh !" said another, " what a fine collection of children, little do they know to what a life of slavery they are doomed."—" The Lord have mercy upon them," said a third.—" They'll find little mercy here," said a fourth. The speakers were mostly of the female sex, who, shaking their heads, said,— " Ah! what fine clear complexions !"—" The roses will soon be out of bloom in the mill." Such were a part of the remarks which saluted the ears of these children, as they entered the Lowdham Mill. In common with his comrades, Blincoe was greatly dismayed, by the gloomy prognostications, which their guardians did all they could to check, or prevent the children from hearing, hurrying them, as rapidly as they could, inside the house.

The young strangers were conducted into a spacious room, fitted up in the style of the dinner-room, in Pancras old workhouse, viz: with long, narrow deal tables, and wooden benches. Although the rooms seemed tolerably clean, there was a certain rank, oily, smell, which Blincoe did not very much admire. They were ordered to sit down at these tables— the boys and girls apart. The other apprentices had not left work, when this supply of children arrived. The supper set before them consisted of milk-porridge, of a very blue complexion ! The bread was partly made of rye—very black, and so soft, they could scarcely swallow it, as it stuck like bird-lime to their teeth. Poor Blincoe stared, recollecting this was not so good a fare as they had been used to at Saint Pancras. Where is our roast beef and plum-pudding, he said to himself. He contrived, with some difficulty, to eat about one half of his allowance. As the young strangers gazed mournfully at each other, the governor and governess, as the master and mistress of the apprentices were styled, kept walking round them, and making very coarse remarks. Just as they had passed Blincoe, some of the girls began making faces, and one flung a dab of bread against the wall, where it stuck fast, as if it had been plaister. This caught the eye of the governor—a huge raw-boned man, who had served in the army, and had been a drill serjeant, unexpectedly, he produced a large horse-whip, which he clanged in such a sonorous manner, that it made the house re-echo. In a moment, the face-makers and bread throwers were reduced to solemn silence and abject submission. Even young Blincoe was daunted—he had been one of the ring-leaders in these seditious proceedings; but so powerful was the shock to his nerves, sustained from the tremendous clang of the horse-whip, it bereft him of all his gaity, and he sat as demure as a truant-scholar, just previous to his flogging. Yet the master of the house had not uttered a single threat; nor indeed had he occasion; his carbuncled nose—his stern and forbidding aspect and his terrible horse-whip, inspired quite as much terror as was requisite. Knowing that the apprentices from the mill were coming, this formidable being retired, to the great relief of the young strangers, but so deep an impression had he created, they sat erect and formal, scarcely daring to look beyond the nose. Whilst they were in this subbued and neutralised state, their attention was suddenly and powerfully attracted by the loud shouting of many voices, almost instantly the stoneroom filled, spacious as it was, with a multitude of young persons of both sexes; from young women down to mere children. Their presence was accompanied by a scent of no very agreeable nature, arising from the grease and dirt acquired in the avocation.

The boys, generally speaking, had nothing on, but a shirt and trousers. Some few, and but a few, had jackets and hats. Their coarse shirts were entirely open at the neck, and their hair looked, as if a comb had seldom, if ever, been applied! The girls, as well as Blincoe could recollect, were, like the boys, destitute of shoes and stockings. Their locks were pinned up, and they were without caps; very few had on, either jacket or gown; but wore, what, in London, are called pinafores; in Lancashire, bishops!—that is, long aprons with sleeves, made of coarse linen, that reached from the neck to the heels. Blincoe was no less terrified at the sight of the pale, lean, sallow-looking multitude, than his nostrils were offended by a dense and heavy smell of rank oil or grease, that arose at their appearance! By comparison, the new comers appeared like so many ladies and gentlemen. On their first entrance, some of the old apprentices took a view of the strangers; but the great bulk first looked after their supper, which consisted of new potatoes, distributed at a hatch door, that opened into the common room from the kitchen. At a signal given, the apprentices rushed to this door, and each, as he made way, received his portion, and withdrew to his place at the table. Blincoe was startled, seeing the boys pull out the fore-part of their shirts, and holding it up with both hands, received the hot boiled potatoes allotted for their supper. The girls, less indecently, if not less filthily, held up their dirty greasy bishops or aprons, that were saturated with grease and dirt, and having received their allowance, scampered off as hard as they could, to their respective places, where, with a keen appetite, each apprentice devoured her allowance. and seemed anxiously to look about for more. Next, the hungry crew ran to the tables of the new comers, and voraciously devoured every crust of bread and every drop of porridge they had left, and put or answered interrogatories as occasion required."

Thus unfavourable were the impressions produced by the scene that presented itself on his first entrance into a cotton-factory. Blincoe was forcibly struck by the absence of that personal cleanliness which had been so rigidly enforced at St. Pancras. The apprentices were required to wash night and morning ; but no soap was allowed, and without it, no dirt could be removed. Their tangled locks covered with cotton flue, hung about their persons in long wreaths, floating with every movement. There was no cloth laid on the tables, to which the new comers had been accustomed in the workhouse—no plates, nor knives, nor forks—to be sure the latter utensils were not absolutely necessary with a potatoe-supper. Instead of salt-cellars, as had been allowed at Pancras, a very stingy allowance of salt was laid on the table, and Blincoe saw no other beverage drunk, by the old hands, than pump water.

The supper being devoured, in the midst of the gossiping that ensued, the bell rang, that gave the signal to go to bed. The grim governor entered to take the charge of the newly arrived boys, and his wife, acting the same part by the girls, appeared every way suitable to so rough and unpolished a mate. She was a large grown, robust woman, remarkable for a rough hoarse voice and ferocious aspect. In a surly, heart-chilling tone, she bade the girls follow her. Tremblingly and despondingly the little creatures obeyed, scarcely daring to cast a look at their fellow travellers, or bid them good night. As Blincoe marked the tear to start in their eyes and silently trickle down their cheeks, his heart responsive sank within him. They separated in mournful silence, scarcely a sigh being heard, nor a word of complaint being uttered.

The room in which Blincoe and several of the boys were deposited, was up two pair of stairs. The bed places were a sort of cribs, built in a double tier, all round the chamber. The apprentices slept two in a bed. The beds were of flock. From the quantity of oil imbibed in the apprentices' clothes, and the impurities that accumulated from the oiled cotton, a most disagreeable odour saluted his nostrils. The governor called the strangers to him and allotted to each his bed-place and bed-fellow, not allowing any two of the newly arrived inmates to sleep together. The boy, with whom Blincoe was to chum, sprang nimbly into his birth, and without saying a prayer, or any thing else, fell asleep before Blincoe could undress himself. So completely was he cowed, he could not restrain his tears, He could not forbear execrating the vile treachery of which he felt himself the victim ; but still he declared, it never struck him, at least, not till long afterwards, that the *superiors* of St. Pancras had deceived him. The fault, he thought, lay with Messrs. Lamberts, their new masters. When he crept into bed, the stench of the oily clothes and greasy hide of his sleeping comrade, almost turned his stomach.— What, between grief and dismay, and this nauseous smell, it was dawn of day before Blincoe dropt asleep. Over and over again, the poor child repeated every prayer he had been taught, and strove, by unfeigned piety, to recommend himself to the friend of the friendless, and the father of the fatherless. At last, sleep sealed his weary eye-lids—but short was the repose he was allowed to enjoy—before five o'clock, he was awakened by his bed-fellow, who springing upright, at the loud tolling

of a bell, told Blincoe to dress with all speed, or the governor would
flog him and deprive him of his breakfast. Before Blincoe had time to
perform this office, the iron door of the chamber, creaking upon its
hinges, was opened, and in came the terrific governor, with the horse-
whip in his hand, and every boy hastily tumbled out of his crib, and hud-
dled on his clothes with all possible haste! Blincoe and his fellow travellers were the slowest, not being rightly awake. Blincoe said " bless
me, have you *church-service* so soon?" " church-service, you fool, said
one of the larger apprentices, it is to the mill *service* you are called, and
you had better look sharp, or you'll catch it!" saying this, off he scampered. Blincoe, who was at first amazed at the trepidation, that appeared
in the apprentices, soon understood the cause. The grim-looking governor, with the carbuncled nose, bearing the emblem of arbitrary rule,
a horse-whip in his hand, made his appearance, and stalking round the
chamber, looked in every bed-place; as he passed Blincoe and his young
comrades, he bestowed a withering look upon them, which, fully understanding, they hastened below; arrived there, Blincoe saw some of the
boys washing themselves at a pump, and was directed to do the same.—
The whole mass sat down to breakfast at five o'clock in the morning. The
meal consisted of *black bread* and *blue milk-porridge.* Blincoe and his
fellow strangers took their places, mingled with the rest of the apprentices, who, marking their dislike of the bread, eagerly seized every opportunity of eating it themselves. Blincoe and his comrades looked wistfully at each other. Consternation sat deeply imprinted on their features;
but every tongue was silent; young as they were, they had sense enough
to perceive the necessity of submission and the prudence of reserve.

They reached the mill about half past five.—The water was on, from
the bottom to the top, in all the floors, in full movement. Blincoe heard
the burring sound before he reached the portals and smelt the fumes of the
oil with which the axles of twenty thousand wheels and spindles were
bathed. The moment he entered the doors, the noise appalled him, and
the stench seemed intolerable.

He did not recollect that either of the Messrs. Lamberts' were present
at the mill, on his first entrance. The newly arrived were received by
Mr. Baker, the head manager, and by the overlookers of the respective
rooms. They were mustered in the making-up room; the boys and girls
in separate divisions. After being looked at, and laughed at, they were
dispersed in the various floors of the mill, and set to various tasks.—
Blincoe was assigned to a room, over which a man named *Smith presided.*
The task first allotted to him was, to pick up the loose cotton, that fell
upon the floor. Apparently, nothing could be easier, and he set to with
diligence, although much terrified by the whirling motion and noise of
the machiney, and not a little affected by the dust and flue with which
he was half suffocated. They span coarse numbers; unused to the stench,
he soon felt sick, and by constantly stooping, his back ached. Blincoe,
therefore, took the liberty to sit down; but this attitude, he soon found,
was strictly forbidden in cotton mills. His task-master (Smith) gave
him to understand, he must keep on his legs. He did so, till twelve
o'clock, being six hours and a half, without the least intermission.—

Blincoe suffered at once by thirst and hunger—the moment the bell rang, to announce dinner, all were in motion to get out as expeditiously as possible. Blincoe ran out amongst the crowd, who were allowed to go—never, in his life, before did he know the value of wholesome air so perfectly. He had been sick almost to fainting, and it revived him instantaneously! The cocknies mingled together, as they made progress towards the apprentice-house! Such as were playsome made to each other! and the melancholy seemed to mingle their tears! When they reached the apprentice-room, each of them had a place assigned at the homely board! Blincoe does not remember of what his dinner consisted; but is perfectly sure, that neither roast beef nor plum-pudding made its appearance—and that the provisions, the cookery, and the mode of serving it out, were all very much below the standard of the ordinary fare of the workhouse in which he had been reared.

During the space of a week or ten days, that Blincoe was kept picking up cotton, he felt at night very great weariness, pains in his back and ancles; and he heard similar complaints from his associates. They might have suffered less had they been taken to the mill at five o'clock, been worked till eight, and then allowed time to eat their breakfast; but six hours' confinement, to close work, no matter of what kind, in an atmosphere as foul as that which circulated in a cotton-mill, is certainly injurious to the health and growth of children of tender years. Even in mills worked by water, and where the temperature of the air is nearly the same within the mill as without, this is the case; but incomparably more so in mills, such as are found in Manchester, where, in many, the average heat is from 70 to 90 degrees of Farenheit's scale. After Blincoe had been employed in the way described, he was *promoted* to the more important employment of a roving winder. Being too short of stature, to reach to his work, standing on the floor, he was placed on a block; but this expedient only remedied a part of the evil; for he was not able by any possible exertion, to keep pace with the machinery. In vain, the poor child declared it was not in his power to move quicker. He was beaten by the overlooker, with great severity, and cursed and reviled from morning till night, till his life become a burthen to him, and his body discoloured by bruises. In common, with his fellow apprentices, Blincoe was wholly dependent upon the mercy of the overlookers, whom he found, generally speaking, a set of brutal, ferocious, illiterate ruffians, alike void of understanding, as of humanity! Blincoe complained to Mr. Baker, the manager, and all he said to him was :—" *do your work well, and you'll not be beaten.*"— It was but seldom, either of the masters visited the mill, and when they did, Blincoe found it was useless to complain. The overlooker, who had charge of him, had a certain quantity of work to perform in a given time. If every child did not perform his allotted task, the fault was imputed to his overlooker, and he was discharged.—on the other hand, a premium was given, if the full quantity of work was done, and not otherwise. If, therefore, Messrs. Lamberts had remonstrated, or had reprimanded the task-masters, by whom the children were thus mercilessly treated, those taskmasters could, and most probably would have said, that if the owners insisted upon so much work being extracted from the apprentices, and a greater quantity of yarn produced, than it was possible to effect by fair and moderate labour, *they must allow them* severity of punishment, to keep the children in a state of continual exertion. Blincoe had not, of course, sense to understand this, the principal, if not the sole cause of the ferocity of the overlookers—but such was, and is the inhuman policy prevailing in cotton-mills, and whilst that cause remains unchanged, the effect inevitably must be the same. Each of the task-masters, to acquire favour and emolument, urged the poor children to the very utmost!—Such is the driving system, which still holds its course, and which leads to the exhaustion and destruction of annual myriads, and to the utmost frightful crimes;—and such is the force of avorice, there are plenty of spinners, so depraved. as not only to sacrifice other people's children, but even *their own*. Blincoe, was not treated with that sanguinary and murderous ferocity in this mill which these pages will soon delineate; but from morning till night, he was continually being beaten, pulled by the hair of his head, kicked or cursed.

It was the custom, in Lowdham Mills, as it is in most water-mills, to make the apprentices work up lost time, by working over hours! a custom, that might not be deemed unreasonable, or found oppressive, if the regular hours were of moderate duration. Blincoe did not say, that this custom was abused at Lowdham Mill, in an equal degree, to what it was in others; but when children of seven years of age, or, by probability, younger, and to work fourteen hours every day in the week, Sundays excepted, any addition was severely felt, and they had to stop at the mill during dinner time, to clean the frames every other day. Once in ten days, or a fortnight, the whole of the finer machinery used to be taken to pieces and cleaned, and then they had to remain at the mill from morning till night, and frequently have been unable to find time to get any food from this early breakfast till night, after they had left off, a term frequently extended from fifteen to sixteen hours incessant labour.

As an inducement to the children to volunteer to work, the whole dinner-hour, a premium of a halfpenny was allowed! Small as was the bribe, it induced many, and Blincoe amongst the number! On such occasions, the dinner was brought up in tin cans, and often has Blincoe's allowance stood till night, whilst he was almost famished with hunger, and he has often carried it back. or rather eaten it on the road, cold, nauseous, and covered with flue.

Being half starved, and cruelly treated by his task-masters—being spotted as a leopard with bruises: and still believing his ill-treatment arose from causes beyond the controul of the parish officers, by whom he had been disposed of to Messrs. Lamberts, Blincoe resolved to attempt an escape,—to beg his way to London,—to lay his case before the overseers and churchwardens of Saint Pancras, and not only claim redress of injuries, but the fulfilment of the grand promises that had been made to him. "I cannot deny," said Blincoe, "that I feel a glow of pride, when I reflect that, at the age of seven years and a half. I had courage to resent and to resist oppression, and generosity to feel for the sufferings of my helpless associates, not one of whom durst venture to share the peril of the enterprise —On the other hand," said he, "I must give them the credit for sincerity; for, if any one had been unguarded or perfidious, who knew of my *intended* expedition, I should have been put under such restraint, as would have effectually prevented a successful attempt to run away! I considered my situation so deplorable, and my state of thraldom so intolerable, that death appeared as a lesser evil. I was not wholly ignorant of the sufferings I might have had to encounter, nor that I might perish on the way, from want of food or shelter, and yet I persevered in an effort, in which, of forty fellow-sufferers, not one had courage to join, although many had parents or relatives, to whom to flee for succour, and I had none! So far, young as I was, I calculated upon difficulty, danger and sufferings.—In one thing, only, was I deceived ; that error consisted in thinking the evils of my situation intolerable ! I had no recollection of calamities so severe, and consequently no standard by which to regulate my judgment. I therefore, rashly determined in my own mind, that my condition admitted of no aggravation,—I was indeed, soon undeceived! I lived, within the short space of four years, to look back with regret to the comparative degree of ease, plenty of food, and of all other good things enjoyed at Lowdham Mill! This sort of knowledge, is, I believe, commonly taught" said Blincoe, " to all the children of misery, as they sink deeper and deeper in woe! The first stage appears the most intolerable ; but as they descend, like me, they sink so profoundly in the depths of wretchedness, that in their melancholy progress, those stages and degrees, which, at first, appeared as intolerable, lose all their terrors, in accumulated misery, and the desponding heart, when it takes a retrospective glance at past sufferings, often arraigns its want of patience and fortitude, for murmurings measured by present calamities. Their former condition appeared comfortable ! Such was my condition, at a later period, when, to be released from the greater and heavier misery, which I endured at Lowdham, with all its evils, and in the very worst shape, I should have esteemed it as a positive state of happiness." Such was the philosophical reasoning of Robert Blincoe, in 1822. But, to proceed,—steady to his purpose, he embraced the first favourable opportunity of making the projected attempt to escape ! He considered his great danger to lie in being retaken on the road between Lowdham and Nottingham ; but he knew no other way, and was afraid to make inquiry! When the manager and overlooker of the room he worked in were busy, Blincoe set off, dressed in his working clothes. His progress began in a sort of canter, looking behind him every fifty yards for the first half mile, when, finding he had not been seen or pursued, he continued his rapid flight till he reached Burton, and there, as fete decreed, that flight suddenly terminated ; for, as he trotted onwards, a long-shanged, slip-shod tailor, who worked for Lowdham Mill, slid nimbly from his shop-board, which, unfortunately for Blincoe, faced the road, and, placing himself full in the way, with a malicious kind of grin upon his long, lank visage, said "O ! young Parson, where art thou running so fast this way ?" saying this, he seized him by the hand, and led him very loath into his cottage, and, giving him a seat in the back part of the room, placed himself between his captive and the door.

Blincoe saw, at one glance, by these precautions, that he was caught. His indignation was so great at first, he would not give any answer ;

noticing which, his false and artful host said to his wife, " Give the young
Parson something to eat and drink,—he is weary, and will be better able
to pursue his journey, after he has rested and refreshed himself! The Lord
commands us to give food to the hungry, and I dare say," addressing
himself to him, " thou art not so full, but thou canst eat a bowl of bread
and milk." " I must own, to my shame," said Blincoe, " the carnal man,
the man of flesh was caught by the bait! I hungered and I ate, and he gave
me so much, and I drank so heartily, that my teeth disabled my legs! To
be sure, my fare was not very costly:—it consisted of some oaten bread
and butter-milk !"

When this sly fox of a tailor found he could eat no more, still blockading
the door, to question Blincoe as to the object of his journey, which the latter
frankly explained,—Aye, I thought so," said the detestable hypocrite,
" young parson, I thought so,—I saw Satan behind thee, jobbing his
prong into thy * * * *!—I saw thee running headlong into h—ll, when I
stept forth to save thee !" This avowal aroused all Blincoe's indignation,
and he was determined to have a scuffle with his perfidious host; but he had
swallowed so large a portion of butter-milk, and eaten so much oaten bread,
he felt he had lost half his speed ! Disdainful, however, of fraud or denial,
he again avowed his intention, and its cause. The tailor then commenced
an harangue upon the deadly sin of a breach of covenant,—assured Blincoe
he was acting under the influence of Satan! that he was liable to be sent
to Bridewell, to be flogged, and, when sent back to his work, to be
debarerd of all liberty, and led to and from the mill with a halter round
his neck ! Blincoe was neither convinced by this reasoning, nor intimidated by these denunciations—but, alas ! his gluttonous appetite had
disabled him for flight, and being thus disabled, and thus doubly a captive,
he made a merit of necessity, and agreed to go back. if his host would be
his mediator with Mr. Baker, the manager. This was the precise point to
which the jesuitical tailor wished to bring him. Without relinquishing
his seat, the treacherous knave doffed his paper cap, and skeins of thread
that still hung round his long, shaggy neck,—he combed his black, greasy
locks, that hung straight as candles round his lanthorn jaws,—tied a yellow
cotton handkerchief round his neck,—put on a pair of shoes,—took a *crab-
tree* stick, full of knots, in his right hand, and grasping Blincoe's very
tight in his left, he sallied forth on a *work of charity*, as the loathsome
hypocrite called his having entrapped and betrayed a poor oppressed
orphan child, fleeing from slavery and oppression. " In my heart," said
Blincoe, " I detested the wretch with greater bitterness than my task-
master ; but he held me so tight, I could not escape—and the sight of the
bit of crab-tree which he brandished, as he chaunted hymns of thanks-
giving, had also no small share of influence in overawing me,—in short,
into the counting-house this second Judas led me. After an admonition to
beware how again I made an attempt of the kind, the manager gave me a
severe but not cruel chastisement." As to the *hospitable* tailor, when he
had delivered him up, he slung away, not waiting to receive Blincoe's
thanks. Whether he took the *five shillings*, which Blincoe was afterwards
told was the standing reward of those who brought back run-away apprentices, or let it stand till he had five pounds to receive for such services, he

No, 3.

cannot ascertain ; but he was told, this peeping Tom of Burton, had rendered many a poor child the same sort of kindness. " In consequence of this scurvy trick," said Blincoe, " I have never been able to conquer the aversion it created against Methodists ; although I am bound to believe, the wretch was one of the myriads of *counterfeits*, who flock to their standard from venal and corrupt motives."

After Blincoe had received his punishment, every weal and bruise with which he had started found a fellow. He was handed back to Smith, his task-master, by whom he was laughed at and jeered unmercifully, and worked with an increase of severity. When Blincoe left work, his old associates flocked around him, condoling his misfortune, and offering him half-pence and bits of bread that they had saved ! When they heard how *godly* had caught him, their indignation swelled to such a height, they declared they would drown him in the mill-dam, if ever they had an opportunity. These condolements were grateful to his wounded pride and disappointed hopes. As he retired to his miserable bed, the governor, grinning horribly, made him a low bow in the military style, and gave him a hearty kick on his *seat of honour* at the same instant. In this manner, was he ushered to his bed, laughed at by that portion of the elder apprentices, who had made similar attempts, and had undergone a similar or more vindictive punishment. Having abandoned all thoughts of escape, Blincoe submitted sullenly and patiently to his fate ;—he worked according to his age and stature, as hard as any one in the mill. When his strength failed, and his limbs refused their office, he endured the strap or the stick, the cuff or the kick, with as much resignation as any of his fellow-sufferers. In the faded complexions, and sallow looks of his associates, he could see, as, in a mirror, his own altered condition ! Many of his comrades had, by this time, been more or less injured by the machinery. Some had the skin scraped off the knuckles, clean to the bone, by the fliers ; others a finger crushed, a joint or two nipped off in the cogs of the spinning-frame wheels ! When his turn to suffer came, the fore-finger of his left hand was caught, and almost before he could cry out, off was the first joint—his lamentations excited no manner of emotion in the spectators, except a coarse joke—he clapped the mangled joint, streaming with blood, to the finger, and ran off to Burton, to the surgeon, who, very composedly put the parts together again, and sent him back to the mill. Though the pain was so intense, he could scarcely help crying out every minute, he was not allowed to leave the frame. He said but little to any one ; but was almost continually bemoaning in secret the cruelty of his fate. Before he was eight years old, Blincoe declared, that many a time he had been tempted to throw himself out of one of the upper windows of the factory—but when he came to look at the leap he purposed taking, his courage failed him—a propensity, he mentioned not as thinking it evinced any commendable feeling, but as an illustration of the natural and unavoidable consequences of working children too hard, and subjecting them to so many severe privations.

About the second year of his servitude, when the whole of the eighty children sent from Pancras Workhouse, had lost their plump and fresh appearance, and acquired the pale and sickly hue which distinguished factory children from all others, a most deplorable accident happened in

Lowdham Mill, and in Blincoe's presence. A girl, named Mary Richards! who was thought remarkably handsome when she left the workhouse, and, who might be nearly or quite ten years of age, attended a drawing frame, below which, and about a foot from the floor, was a horizontal shaft, by which the frames above were turned. It happened, one evening, when most of her comrades had left the mill, and just as she was taking off the weights, her apron was caught by the shaft. In an instant the poor girl was drawn by an irresistable force and dashed on the floor. She uttered the most heart rending shrieks! Blincoe ran towards her, an agonized and helpless beholder of a scene of horror that exceeds the power of my pen to delineate! He saw her whirled round and round with the shaft—he heard the bones of her arms, legs, thighs, &c. successively snap asunder, crushed, seemingly, to atoms, as the machinery whirled her round, and drew tighter and tighter her body within the works, her blood was scattered over the frame and streamed upon the floor, her head appeared dashed to pieces—at last, her mangled body was jammed in so fast, between the shafts and the floor, that the water being low and the wheels off the gear, it stopped the main shaft! When she was extricated, every bone was found broken!—her head dreadfully crushed!—her clothes and mangled flesh were, apparently inextricably mixed together, and she was carried off, as supposed, quite lifeless. " I cannot describe," said Blincoe, " my sensations at this appalling scene. I shouted out aloud for them to stop the wheels! When I saw her blood thrown about like water from a twirled mop, I fainted. But neither the spine of her back was broken, nor were her brains injured, and to the amazement of every one, who beheld her mangled and horrible state, by the skill of the surgeon, and the excellence of her constitution, she was saved!—Saved to what end? the philosopher might ask—to be sent back to the same mill, to pursue her labours upon crutches, made a cripple for life, without a shilling indemnity from the parish, or the owners of the mill! Such was the fate of this poor girl, but, dismal as it was, it will be seen by the succeeding parts of this narrative, that a lot still more horrible awaited many of her fellow-sufferers, whom the parish officers of St. Pancras, pursuant to Acts of Parliament authority. had apprenticed for fourteen years to the masters of Lowdham Cotton Mill. The dreadful spectacle Blincoe had witnessed in the racking of Mary Richards, rendered his employment more odious than ever.

It is already stated, that the food was very ordinary and not very plentiful; the apprentices were so oppressed by hunger, that the oldest and most daring sallied out at night and plundered the fields, and frequent complaints were made, and the apprentices got a very bad name, which belonged rather to the masters, in whose parsimony it originated!

When Blincoe had served about three years of his time, an event happened at Lowdham Mill, arising out of the manner in which apprentices were treated, that wrought a complete revolution there, and led to a new era in Blincoe's biography! Among the girls, who were bound apprentices to Messrs. Lamberts of Nottingham and Lowdham, were two sisters, named Fanny and Mary Collier, who had a mother residing in London. These young girls finding their health declining from excess of labour, bad provisions, and want of wholesome air and exercise, found means to write a letter to their mother, full of complaints, upon which, the widow undertook a journey to Lowdham, where she resided a fortnight, during which time, she was a reserved and shrewd observer of the condition of her own and of other children, and then returned to the metropolis. As far as Blincoe remembers these circumstances, Mrs. Collier did not make any complaints to Messrs. Lamberts, or to the manager! She reserved such representations for the parish officers of Saint Pancras, which induced them to send down a parochial committee, to inquire into the state and condition of the apprentices. One day, just as the dinner was being served out in the *usual* slovenly manner, without the least notice of the intended visit having been previously given, the Committee arrived, without asking or waiting for permission, they walked into the common room, and tasting the viands upon the table, they found them such as had been described. Whether *conscience* had any concern in the effort to discover and reform abuses in the mill, said Blincoe, I know not; but this I do know, that, if they had had a spark of shame, pity or remorse, the sallow, and sickly appearance of the eighty victims, saying nothing of Mary Richards, who was for ever rendered a cripple, ought to have filled them with sorrow and shame, on account of the base and cruel imposition, that had been practised in 1799. It is more probable, however. that the atrocious treatment experienced by the thousands and tens of thousands of orphan children, poured forth from our charitable institutions, and from parish workhouses, and the dreadful rapidity with which they were consumed in the various cotton-mills, to which they were transported, and the sad spectacle exhibited by most of the survivors, were the real causes, which, in 1802, produced Sir Robert Peel's Bill, for the relief and protection of infant paupers employed in cotton-mills. Hence, the extraordinary liveliness evinced by the overseers and churchwardens of Saint Pancras might have been occasioned by the dreadful scenes of cruelty and oppression developed during the progress of that Bill, which Blincoe never heard of, nor ever saw, till eleven or twelve years after it had passed into a law. It would be difficult to produce a more striking instance of the utter contempt. in which the upstart owners of great establishments treated an act, purposely enacted to restrain their unparalled cruelty and waste of human life. The act itself declared the masters, owners, or occupiers of every cotton-mill in Great Britain and Wales should have a legible copy of the act, placed in some conspicuous and public part of each mill, and accessible to every one; yet, Blincoe, who was reared in the cotton-mill, never saw or heard of any such law, till eleven or twelve years after it had been enacted! When the committee began their investigation, as to the treatment and condition of the children sent from St. Pancras Workhouse, Blincoe was called up among others and admonished to speak the truth and nothing but the truth! So great however was the terror of the stick and strap, being applied to their persons, after these great dons should be at a great distance, it rendered him, and no doubt the great majority of his fellow sufferers extremely cautious and timid. It is however, likely, that their looks bespoke their sufferings, and told a tale not to be misunderstood. The visitors saw their food, dress, bedding, and they caused, in conjunction with the local magistrates, very great alterations to be made. A new house was ordered to be erected near the mill, for the use of the apprentices, in which there were fewer beds to a given space. The quantity of good and wholesome animal food to be dressed and distributed in a more decent way, was specified. A much more cleanly and decorous mode of cookery and serving up the dinner and other meals was ordered. The apprentices were divided into six classes, and a new set of tin cans, numbered 1, 2, 3, 4, 5, and 6, were made, to be served up to each individual, according to the class to which he or she may belong, to hold the soup or porridge ! The old governor was discharged, who had given them all such a fright on their first arrival, and several of the overlookers were dismissed and new ones introduced ;—among the latter description of persons was a man, who seemed wholly destitute of humanity—his name was William Woodward—born, I believe, at Cromford, in Derbyshire. The appearance of this ferocious tyrant at Lowdham Mill proved a much heavier curse, scourge and affliction to Blincoe, than all the grievances which had existed, or were removed ! As Woodward's amusement, in tormenting these poor apprentices, will occupy a large space in the next chapter, I shall say little of him in this.

It was the ill fortune of Blincoe and his associates, that, shortly after the reforms specified were introduced, and the hours of labour reduced, so that their situation became every way incomparably more eligible, Lowdam Mill stopped working.

At this period, Blincoe had served about four years of his time, and had learnt to wind rovings, and spin at the throstle, and certainly earned as much money for his master in the week, as would suffice to keep him a month or longer, in meat, drink and clothes ; but he had not been instructed in any part of the stocking-trade, nor had he acquired such a degree of knowledge of the cotton-spinning, as might enable him to gain his bread elsewhere.

At this juncture, if justice had been done, the apprentices would have reverted to Saint Pancras parish, and not been abandoned as they were, and turned over to a new master, without any care being taken, that he should, if he took them, abide by the condition specified in their first indentures, and act up to the regulations introduced at Lowdham Mill.

Blincoe said, he believed the Messrs. Lamberts wrote to the parish officers of Saint Pancras, informing them of the situation of the children, in order that their friends might take back whom they pleased to claim, and if, in this conclusion. Blincoe is right, and these officers neglected to take proper measures for the safety and protection of so large a body of children, as they had sent to Lowdham Mill, all healthy and straight limbed, they are morally responsible for the unparalled sufferings to which they were afterwards exposed. When the subject shall again come before parliament, it will be requisite to have the conduct of the parish officers on this occasion thoroughly investigated, not so much from a wish to have their offences visited with any legal penalty, if such were practicable, as to shew the necessity of abrogating the power invested in them by act of parliament, to place children beyond a given distance from the place of their birth or settlement :—and secondly, to deprive them altogether of the power of tearing away children from their parents, and sending them into any manufactories whatever, without the knowledge and consent of their parents, or next of kin. If the parish officers think proper to apprentice them to any of the ordinary and established trades, they ought to have that power independently of their parents. In the mill, where Blincoe was next consigned, the *parish children* were considered, treated, and *consumed as a part of the raw materials;* their strength, their marrow, their lives, were consumed and converted into money! and as their live stock consisting of parish apprentices, diminished, new flocks of victims arrived from various quarters, without the cost of purchase to supply their place!

It is within the compass of probability, that there have been, and are yet, instances, wherein the overseers of the poor, and more especially the *assistant* overseers, who are mere mercenaries, and serve for pay, have been, and are, some of them at least, *bribed* by the owners of mills for spinning silk, cotton or wollen yarn, to visit the habitation of the persons receiving parochial aid, and to compel them, when children are wanting, utterly regardless of education, health, or inclination, to deliver up their offspring, or by cutting off the parish allowance leave them to perish for want!

When Messrs. Lamberts gave up the cotton-yarn establishment, carried on at Lowdham Mill, they permitted all their apprentices who wished to leave their employment in a cotton-mill, to write to their parents and friends, and some few found redeemers; the great bulk were, unhappily left to their fate! Being a foundling, and knowing no soul on earth to whom he could look up for succour, Robert Blincoe was one of the unhappy wretches, abandoned to as dismal a destiny as ever befel *a parish apprentice.* It was his evil fortune, with a multitude of fellow sufferers, to be turned over *en masse* to Mr. ELLICE NEEDHAM, of Highgate Wall, Derbyshire, the master and owner of Litton Mill, near Tideswell.

Before, however, I close this delineation of the character and conduct of the owners of Lowdham Cotton-Mill—Messrs. William, Charles, and Thomas Lambert—it is due to them, if living, whatever may be their fortune, and to their memory, if deceased, to state, that, with the exception of Mary Richards, who was so dreadfully racked upon a shaft, and her bones mostly broken, not one of the children sent to their mill by St. Pancras parish, were injured as to be made a cripple, nor were they deformed in their knees and ancles. That there were deficiencies as to food and an excess of labour exacted, is clear, by the alterations which were introduced; but still, compared with what they soon afterwards suffered, they were humanely treated.

They were kept decently clad, had a bettermost suit reserved for Sundays and holidays—were occasionally allowed a little time for play, in the open air, and upon *Goose fair-day*, which is, or then was, a great festival at Nottingham—the whole of them were conveyed in carts to that celebrated place, and regaled with furmety, and sixpence in money was allowed to the very youngest! They went pretty regularly to Lowdham Church on Sundays; were not confined within gates and walls, as was the case at most other mills, where parish apprentices were immured! nor were there any iron-bars before the windows! They were *worked hard*; but not so hard as to distort their limbs, nor occasion declines or deaths! Their food latterly was good, and cleanly cooked. Their bedding, though coarse, was clean! When they had meat, they were allowed trenchers, knives, forks and spoons. It will presently be seen, when carried away from Lowdham Mill, into what a den of vice. disease and famine, filth and slavery, they were plunged; by what hellions they were worried, and all in defiance of a positive, and recently made law, on purpose for their protection, and in the face of the VISITING MAGISTRATE whose visits were, according to Blincoe's assertion, too frequently directed to the luxurious table of the master, to admit even a chance of justice to the apprentices. May this exposition of crimes and sufferings inflicted upon the friendless, the orphan, the widow's son, induce honest and upright men, senators and legislators, effectually to curb the barbarous propensities of hard-hearted masters, and rescue their nation from a worse stain, than even the African Slave Trade, horrible as was that odious traffic, ever inflicted.

---

## CHAP. IV.

The next cotton mill to which poor Blincoe was consigned, together, with those of his companions in tribulation, who had no friend to redeem them from impending misery, belonged to a Mr. Ellice Needham. Like most of his fraternity, his origin was obscure. He is said to have arisen from an abject state of poverty, and had it been by honourable industry, his prosperous fortune had redounded to his credit. Of his primeval state of poverty, it was is weakness to be ashamed. By the profusion of his table, and the splendour and frequency of his entertainments, he seemed to wish to cover and conceal his mean descent. His house, lawns, equipage, and style of living, completely eclipsed the neighbouring gentry; yet, boundless was his ostentation, he was in his heart sordidly mean and parsimonious. His cruelty, in wringing from poor friendless orphans, the means of supporting his guilty and unbecoming pomp, sufficiently evinces the baseness of his heart! His mansion, in 1803, and years later, was at Highgate Wall, near Buxton in Derbyshire.

To this arrogant and unfeeling master, Messrs. Lambert made over the unexpired term of years for which the greater part of the parish apprentices had been bound by their respective indentures. What premium was paid, or, if any, I know not. As this master was neither a hosier, nor a lace manufacturer, he had not the power to fulfil the conditions imposed on Messrs. Lamberts, viz. to instruct the girls, during the last three years of their time, in lace-knitting, and the boys in stocking-weaving. The consequence was, the poor children lost those important advantages, and those who survived the term of their apprenticeship to Ellice Needham, found themselves without that degree of skill which was requisite to enable them to gain their bread, in almost any other cotton-mill, and could touch none but the very coarsest work.

As Messrs. Lamberts were constrained, by circumstances, to stop their works, it might be, that they had not means to support the apprentices; but were forced to get rid of them with the utmost expedition    There have been instances, where, in case of Bankruptcy, parish apprentices bound to cotton-masters, have been put into carts, driven to the verge of the parish, and there turned adrift without money—without a friend or a place to shelter them.  According to Blincoe's account, although Messrs. Lamberts' informed the guardians of the poor of St. Pancras parish of the necessity they were under of giving up their apprentices, or turning them over to their masters, no steps were taken for the protection of the friendless children, an imputation, the more extraordinary, when the promptitude and decision with which they had acted in the case recited, is considered. It is, therefore, probable, that their activity might be owing to the horrid tales, that had then burst upon the public, descriptive of the cruelty and misery, of which parish children placed out in cotton-mills were the victims.  It was in 1802, that Sir Robert Peel, of Bury, who had the largest number of parish and foundling children, employed in his cotton-mills, of any cotton-master in Great Britain, brought forward his bill for their protection.  According to Blincoe's narrative, the committee from St. Pancras arrived at Lowdham Mill, at this juncture, and the reforms introduced at Lowdham Mill, were, therefore, likely to have been owing to the parliamentary agitation of that question; and nothing can be more highly illustrative of the force of public opinion, than this proof of its potent effect on the officers of St. Pancras parish!—Supposing the conjecture to be well founded, at the time the apprentices were removed from Lowdham Mill, this humane act had passed into a law, and had become all but a dead-letter!—It may also have been a reliance upon the effect of that law which induced the parish officers to leave the children to their fate—what THAT fate was will presently appear!

It seems, that Mr. Ellice Needham, the master of Litton Mill, went to Lowdham, to inspect the condition of the apprentices, who had improved very materially after the introduction of the new regulations.  Nothing could be more kind or condescending than Ellice Needham's deportment at Lowdham.  To some, he gave money—to all, he promised most liberal and kind usage—he promised like a Titus—but he performed like a Caligula.

Blincoe could not recollect, with precision, the number of apprentices, male and female, who were removed in carts from Lowdham to Litton Mill.  The first day's progress brought them to Cromford, where they halted for the night.  The girls were lodged in dwelling-houses; the boys, on straw, in a barn or stable!  The next morning, the whole party were marched on foot through the village, as far as Matlock toll-bar, so proud was Woodward (their conductor) of their healthy appearance! Here they again mounted their carts!  But this improvement is not imputable to the wholesomeness of cotton-factory employment; but to the effect of the recent modifications introduced at Lowdham Mill, and to their diminished hours of toil.

It was in the gloomy month of November, when this removal took place! On the evening of the second day's journey, the devoted children reached Litton Mill. Its situation, at the bottom of a sequestered glen, and surrounded by rugged rocks, remote from any human habitation, marked a place fitted for the foul crimes of frequent occurrence which hurried so many of the friendless victims of insatiate avarice, to an untimely grave.

The savage features of the adjacent scenery impressed a general gloom upon the convoy, when Woodward pointed out to them the lonely mill to which they were travelling. As the hands were then at work, all of whom, except the overlookers, were parish children, the conductor of the new comers led them through the mill. The effect of the review filled the mind of Blincoe, and perhaps his unhappy associates, with deep dismay. The pallied, sickly complexions—the meagre, haggard appearance of the Litton Mill apprentices, with their filthy and ragged condition, gave him a sorrowful foretaste of the dismal fate that apparently awaited him. From the mill, they were escorted to the 'prentice-house, where every thing wore a discouraging aspect. Their first meal was water-porridge and oaten cakes—the former thin and ill-made—the latter, baked in flat cakes, on iron griddles, about an inch thick—and being piled up in heaps, was liable to heat, ferment and grow mouldy. This was a new and not a very palatable diet. Whilst Blincoe and many of his comrades went supperless to bed, their half-starved comrades, the Litton Mill apprentices, ravenously devoured what the more dainty Lowdham children turned from with loathing, and told them *their stomachs* would come to in a few days, and that they would be glad to pick from a dunghill, the mouldiest pieces, then so disdainfully flung away.

The lodging-room, the bedding, every thing was inferior to what it was at Lowdham; and the smell, from oil and filth, incomparably more offensive. Blincoe passed a restless night, bitterly deploring his hard destiny, and trembling at the thought of greater sufferings! Soon after four in the morning, they were summoned to the work, by the ringing of a bell. Blincoe was put to wind rovings. He soon found an immense difference, in his situation, having much more work to perform, and being treated with a brutal severity, hitherto unknown to him.

Blincoe remarked, that few of the apprentices had either knife, fork, or spoon, to use at table, or hats, shoes, or stockings. At Lowdham, particularly during the latter part of their stay there, the children used to wash at the pump, night and day, and were allowed soap! At Litton mill, they were called out so early, and worked so late, that little or no attention was given to personal cleanliness! On Friday night, the apprentices were washed, combed, and shirted! Blincoe found his companions in a woeful condition—their bodies were literally covered with weals and contusions—their heads full of wounds, and, in many cases, lamentably, infested with vermin! The eldest girls had to comb and wash the younger apprentices—an irksome task, which was carelessly and partially performed. No soap was allowed—a small quantity of meal was given as a

No. 4.

substitute; and this from the effects of keen hunger, was generally eaten.
The first day's labour at Litton Mill, convinced Blincoe, into what a den
of vice and misery he was cast. The overlookers were fierce and brutal,
beyond any thing he had ever witnessed at Lowdham Mill; to which servitude, terrible as it once appeared, he looked back with regret. In the
retrospect of his own conduct, he felt shame and sorrow—for, compared
with what he had to perform and to endure, he now considered that he had
lived in idleness and luxury at Lowdham. The custom of washing and
shifting on Friday night, arose, he said from a notion, that it was more
*profitable* to allow those ablutions to be then performed, that the apprentices might be kept to work till *midnight* on Saturday, or even beyond
that hour. The apprentices slept about fifty in a room. The governor
used to unlock the door of each room when the first bell rang : having unlocked the last room door, he went back to the first, with a switch stick in
his hand, and if he found any one in bed, or slowly dressing, he used to
lay on without mercy; by which severity, the rooms were soon empty.
The apprentices had their breakfast generally of water-porridge, called in
this part of Derbyshire " stir-pudding," and oaten cake, which they took
in the mill. The breakfast hour was eight o'clock; but the machinery
did not stop, and so irregular were their meals, it sometimes did not
arrive till ten or eleven o'clock. At other times, the overlookers would
not allow the apprentices to eat it, and it stood till it grew cold and covered with flue! Skim-milk, or butter-milk was allowed; but very sparingly,
and often in a stinking state, when it was served out. Forty minutes were
allowed for dinner; of which time, full one half was absorbed in cleaning
the frames. Sometimes the overlookers detained them in the mill the
whole dinner-time, on which occasion, a halfpenny was given, or rather
promised. On those occasions, they had to work the whole day through,
generally *sixteen hours, without rest or food !* These excessive labours,
accompanied by comparative starvation, may appear to my reader, as, at
first, it did to me, almost *incredible ;* but Blincoe's relations, marvellous
as it may appear, was afterwards confirmed by individuals, whose narra-
tives *will be given,* and with whom no sort of acquaintance or intercourse
had latterly subsisted. Owing to this shamefully protracted time of labour,
to the ferocity with which the children were driven by stripes, cuffs, and
kicks, and to the insufficiency of food, no less than its bad and unwholesome quality. Blincoe, in common with his fellow-sufferers has often
dropped down at the frames, and been so weary, when, at last, he left
work, he has given a stronger boy a halfpenny, or a part of his supper,
to allow him to lean upon him on his way back to the 'prentice-house.
  Bad as was the food, the cookery was still worse.—The most inferior
sort of Irish-fed bacon was purchased for the consumption of these children,
and this boiled with turnips, put into the water, I cannot say without
washing; but certainly without paring!—Such was the *Sunday* fare of
the parish children at Litton Mill. When first Blincoe, and the rest of
the children arrived from Lowdham, they noticed many of the other
apprentices had neither spoon nor knife; but had to eat as they could,
meat, thick-porridge, or broth, nor were the new comers long allowed any
such implements. On Sunday, bacon-broth and turnips were served out,

which they eat with oaten-cake, in dirty wooden bowls. It could not be otherwise, than unpalatable; for the portion of water to be converted into *broth,* was very ample. In this, rusty, half putrid, fish-fed bacon, and unpaired turnips were boiled!—A portion of this broth, with coarse oaten-cake was served out, as the first course of a frequent Sunday's dinner. Next, the rusty bacon was portioned out with the boiled unpared turnips!—There was generally, a large quantity of broth to spare, which often became very fetid before it was cold. Into this stuff, no better than hog-wash, a few pails more of water were poured and some meal stirred in, and the disgusting mess was served out for supper or the next day's breakfast, as circumstances required. Blincoe declared, that the stench of this broth was often so powerful as to turn his stomach, and yet, bad as it was, keen hunger forced him to eat it. From all these and other sources of sickness and disease, no one will be surprised that contagious fevers arose in the mill; nor that the number of deaths should be such as to require frequent supplies of parish children, to fill up the vacancies. That such numerous draughts made from mills, where there was no increase of building or of machinery, or apparent call for more infant labourers should not have caused parish officers to institute inquiry, as to the fate of their predecessors, goes far toward confirming the worst imputations cast by the surviving sufferers, upon their parochial guardians. The evidence given by Sir Robert Peel and others, before parliamentary committees, will throw still further light on this important subject, and prove how generally the offspring of the poor have been abandoned by their legal guardians, and left at the disposal of greedy and unfeeling sons of traffic. This neglect on the part of parish officers, was the producing cause of many of the avaricious cotton-masters escaping punishment, for offences which richly merited the gallows. Contagious disease, fatal to the apprentices, and dangerous to society, was the degree of magnitude, at which, the independent rich, more, perhaps, from selfish than social feelings, took alarm, and the public prints exposed a part of the existing abuses in cotton-mills, of which parish children were the victims. So horrid were these recitals, and so general and loud the indignation which they excited, that it reached the inmost recesses of the flinty hearts of the great cotton-masters. Their fears taught them mercy, when no longer able to withstand, nor to silence the accusations brought against them by public-spirited and disinterested opponents. Some of the greatest delinquents yielded, and even became advocates for the interference of the legislative power, between themselves and their servants. A reference to the Appendix will shew that they were accused by the genuine friends of humanity of aiming, by this concession, to insinuate themselves into the confidence of their opponents, and thereby neutralize and subdue the fine spirit by which they found their grasping, vile, insatiate avarice controlled. Be this as it may, those individuals who took so much pains to obtain the act of 1802, seem to have given themselves no manner of trouble, to see it enforced. Almost before the first year expired, it was considered a dead-letter. Just at this crisis, the cruelties, exercised on apprentices at Litton Mill, were at their height. Excess of toil, of filth, and of hunger, led to the poor children being visited by contagious fevers. This calamity, which often broke, by premature death, the bands of this vile thraldom, prevailed to such an extent, as to stop the works. At last, such was Blincoe's declaration, he had known forty boys sick at once, being a fourth of the whole number employed in the mill.   From the combined testimony of many apprentices, none were considered sick, till it was found impossible, by menaces or by corporeal punishment, to keep them to their work. The medical gentlemen, who sometimes attended the sick, aware of the cause of the deaths, used to say, and like a sensible man he spoke :—" It is not drugs, but kitchen physic they want:" and his general prescription was plenty of good bread, beef, soup and mutton broth.   When I questioned Blincoe and others, why this medical man did not represent the horrid plight they were in to the magistrates, he said, the surgeon and magistrates were friends and guests of the master, and in the frequent habit of feasting with him !   Blincoe was among the number of the sick, and remembers pitch, tobacco, &c. being burnt in the chamber, and vinegar sprinkled on their beds and on the floor.   Circumstances which sufficiently denote the malignity of the disease, and the serious apprehensions that were entertained.   So great has the mortality been, that Mr. Needham felt it adviseable to divide the burials, and a part of the dead were buried in Tadington Church-yard, although the burial fees were double the charge of those at Tideswell.   Notwithstanding this extraordinary degree of sickness and mortality, Blincoe declares that the local magistracy took no manner of notice of these occurrences !!!

It might be hazardous to trust so far to the memory, the integrity, or the judgment of Blincoe, or to affirm that the conduct of the local magistrates really was thus culpable—but the imputation is corroborated by the total silence of the magistrates of this part of Derbyshire, as to the character and conduct of the owners of Litton Mill, during the parliamentary investigation of 1816, 17, 18, 19.   The concurrent testimony of Blincoe and several of his fellow-sufferers confirm the fact of contagious fevers having occurred in this mill; of the numerous deaths it occasioned ; of the consequent division of the funerals ; and of the remarks of the clergyman, by whom the last sad rites were performed ; and also, that, *once*, there was a Coroner's inquest held ! there exists some difference of opinion, as to the material fact, whether the body had not been first deposited in the earth, and afterwards taken up.) Not a spark of pity was shewn to the sick of either sex : they were worked to the very last moment it was possible for them to work : and when it was no longer possible, if they dropped down, they were put into a wheel-barrow, and wheeled to the 'prentice-house. According to Blincoe's statement, they were left in the common room below, or carried to their birth in the bed-room, and there left to live or die ! In this melancholy state, all the change that took place in the diet, was an allowance of some *treacle-tea*, that is, hot water sweetened with treacle. The doctor was seldom called, till the patient was in the agonies of death. Generally speaking, the dying experienced less attention than a sheep or a hog !   The owner of Litton Mill was more tender to [those animals; because they cost money, and the anxiety of a character like Mr. Needham's could only be excited by the prospect of a loss of capital ! This solicitude was proportioned to the extent of that risk ; and as parish children and destitute orphans could be had at a less price than sheep or pigs, to supply the place of those that died, it followed, that they were less thought of. I would not willingly exaggerate the atrocities I am depicting. I would not act so unwisely as to overcharge the picture I am drawing; and it is with some degree of diffidence, I state, in consequence of combined and positive testimony, that no nurses or *nursing* was allowed to the sick, further than what one invalid could do for another! That neither candle nor lamp-light was allowed, nor the least sign of sympathy or regret manifested! These facts I admit, are so repugnant to every feeling of Christian charity, that they wear the aspect of greatly embellished truths, or what is but little worse, of malignant fabrications. If they are such, the fault is not mine; for repeatedly, and in the most impressive manner in my power, I admonished Blincoe and his fellow-sufferers, to abstain from falsehood, telling him and them, it would be sure to be detected and lead to their disgrace. What I thought might have more influence with such persons, I also urged the triumph, such baseness on their part, could confer on the master cotton spinners, most distinguished by cruelty and tyranny; yet, still Blincoe and the whole of his former comrades perseveringly and consistently adhered to the truth of the horrid imputations, and declared, if they were called upon, they would at any time confirm their statement. I was bound to give them publicity—if they are founded in truth. If their great features are correctly delineated, no lapse of time ought to be allowed to shelter the delinquents. They should be brought to a public trial; for the imputations extend to too many acts of torture and of wilful deliberate murder; and to the indulgence of propensities, as to overpower scepticism. They embrace atrocities exercised upon poor and friendless boys and girls, of a nature no less abominable than the worst of those which apply to that disgrace to womanhood, Elizabeth Brownrig, or more recently, to the unhappy culprit, Governor Wall. There are yet living, perhaps a hundred witnesses who have been partakers of these ferocious inflictions. Many of them, though in the prime of life, are reduced to such a state of decrepitude, as to flash conviction upon the most incredulous, that it could have resulted from nothing but the most unexampled and long continued cruelty. From the continued and rentless exercise of unlimited despotism upon the truly insulted and most friendless of human beings, upon those, for whose especial protection, a law had been then recently enacted, which, had it been enforced, would have efficiently prevented the occurrence of these crimes, and if I were to assert, that it would be difficult, if not impossible, from the record of sufferings inflicted upon Negro slaves, to quote instances of greater atrocity, than what I have, or am about to develope, I should not exaggerate; nor should I be guilty of bombast, were I to affirm, that the national character has been, and is seriously dishonoured by that system of boundless commercial avarice, in which these detestable crimes originated. It will continue thus shaded, till a full and fair investigation takes place. There never yet was a crisis, when, in the commercial world, the march of avarice was so rapid, or its devastations so extensive upon the morals and well being of society, as within the period embraced by this narrative; a march that seems to acquire celerity in proportion to the increasing spread of its malific *influence*, and to derive *impunity* from the prodigious wealth it accumulates in the hands of a few great and unfeeling capitalists, at the expence of the individual happiness, health, and morals of the million. This iniquitous system is the prolific parent of that tremendous flood of vice, which has saturated the manufacturing populace, with the most appalling depravity. This has reduced those many hundred thousand weavers, to a state of destitution so extréme, as to render the condition of the most destitute portion, incomparably worse than that of the field-slave in the West India plantations, who has the good fortune to belong to a humane proprietor. This baleful and wide wasting system throws upon the crown the unde-served odium of being the cause or the abettor of these dreadful evils, by which the poor weaver is oppressed—an impression that has neutralized tne loyalty of myriads, and fitted them to become, in the hands of unprin-cipled demagogues, the source of popular commotions, of foul and iniquitous conspiracies, of deep and radical disloyalty. So indurated, so inveterate, is the loathing and aversion cherished towards the executive government, in all its ramifications, by a large portion of weavers, that it has induced multitudes wholly to renounce, to vilify in every practicable manner, to degrade christianity! I do not, in this declamation, indulge in light, personal, or selfish motives; for whatever I assert, as positive matter of fact, I hold myself morally responsible, and stand publicly pledged to substantiate my assertion, by adducing, if requisite, not alone the authorities on which I make them, but also to *prove* the validity of those authorities.

With this digression, I close the present chapter.—In those that follow there will be found a narrative of crimes which cannot fail to excite, in an equal degree, horror and incredulity :—at the recital of acts of wanton, premeditated, gross, and brutal cruelty, scarcely to be equalled in the annals of the Inquisitorial tribunals of Portugal or Spain ; yet all those acts of murder and wanton cruelties, have been perpetrated by a solitary master cotton-spinner, who, though perhaps one of the worst of his tribe, did not stand alone; as will be shewn by evidence that it cannot be success-fully rebutted. Nor was it to be expected that the criminality of that master spinner could fail to produce corresponding depravity amongst the wretched apprentices subjected to his rude and savage dominion. In the eventful life of W— Pitt, the depth and extent of that depravity will be strikingly illustrated !—It will be seen that acts of felony were committed in the vicinity of Litton Mill, by the parish apprentices, not, if I am rightly informed, from *dishonest intention ;* but from a desire to be transported to Botany Bay ; deeming even that alternative preferable to the endurance of the horrors of the servitude, to which, as parish apprentices, they had been consigned.

## CHAP. V.

RECURRING to the description, given to me by Robert Blincoe, of the dreadful state of thraldom, to which, with a multitude of juvenile companions, he was involved at Litton Mill, I am instructed to say, that as excessive toil, the want of proper time for rest, and of nourishing wholesome food, gave rise to contagious disease, so a liberal supply of good provisions and a cessation from toil, quickly restored many to health; instead of taking warning by the results of these terrible examples, no sooner were the invalids sent back to the mill, than the system of overtoil, of boundless cruelty, starvation and torture, was at once resumed. Let it not however be supposed, that 'any thing in the shape of dainties had been dispensed to the sick. Wheaten bread, coarse pieces of beef boiled down in soup, or mutton for broth, with good milk or butter-milk, sparingly distributed, formed the extent of those indulgences. This diet, luxurious as it was considered in Litton Mill, did not surpass the ordinary standard of the daily fare, that Blincoe had enjoyed at St. Pancras workhouse, and also, during he latter period of his stay at Lowdham Mill.

I have not yet done more than to mention the cuffs, kicks, or scourging, to which, in common with many other of his unhappy comrades, Blincoe stood exposed, since, by his account, almost from the first hour in which he entered the Mill, till he arrived at a state of manhood, it was one continued round of cruel and arbitrary punishment. Blincoe declared, he was so frequently and immoderately beaten, it became quite familiar; and if its frequency did not extinguish the sense of feeling, it took away the terror it excited on his first entrance into this den of ignorance and crime. I asked him if he could state an average number of times in which he thought he might in safety say, he had suffered corporeal punishment in a week. His answer invariably was, that his punishments were so various and so frequent, it was impossible to state with any thing approaching to accuracy. If he is to be credited, during his ten years of hard servitude, his body was never free from contusions, and from wounds inflicted by the cruel master whom he served, by his sons, or his brutal and ferocious and merciless overlookers.

It is already stated, that he was put to the back of a stretching-frame, when he was about eleven years of age, and that often, owing to the idleness, or the absence of the stretcher, he had his master's work, as well as his own to perform. The work being very coarse, the motion was rapid, and he could not keep up to the ends. For this he was sure to be unmercifully punished, although, they who punished him knew the task assigned was beyond what he could perform. There were different stretchers in the mill; but, according to Blincoe's account, they were all of them base and ferocious ruffians Robert Woodward, who had escorted the apprentices from Lowdham Mill, was considered the worst of those illiterate vulgar tyrants. If he made a kick at Blincoe, so great was his strength, it commonly lifted him off the floor. If he struck him, even a flat-handed blow, it floored him; If, with a stick, it not only bruised him,

but cut his flesh.  It was not enough to use his feet or his hands, but a
stick, a bobby or a rope's-end.  He and others used to throw rollers one
after another, at the poor boy, aiming at his head, which, of course was
uncovered while at work, and nothing delighted the savages more, than
to see Blincoe stagger, and to see the blood gushing out in a stream !  So
far were such results from deterring the monsters, that long before one
wound had healed, similar acts of cruelty produced others, so that, on
many occasions, his head was excoriated and bruised to a degree, that
rendered him offensive to himself and others, and so intolerably painful,
as to deprive him of rest at night, however weary he might be.  In consequence of such wounds, his head was over-run by vermin.  Being reduced to this deplorable state, some brute of a quack doctor used to apply
a pitch cap, or plaister to his head.  After it had been on a given time,
and when its adhesion was supposed to be complete, the *terrible doctor*
used to lay forcibly hold of one corner and tear the whole scalp from off
his head at once !  This was the common remedy; I should not exaggerate the agonies it occasioned, were I to affirm, that it must be equal
to any thing inflicted by the American savages, on helpless prisoners,
with their scalping knives and tomahawks.

This same ruffian, (Robert Woodward) who, by the concurrent testimony of many sufferers, stands depicted, as possessing that innate love of
cruelty which marked a Nero, a Caligula, or a Robespierre, used when
Blincoe could not, or did not keep pace with the machinery, to tie him up
by the wrists to a cross beam and keep him suspended over the machinery
till his agony was extreme.  To avoid the machinery, he had to draw up
his legs every time it came out or returned.  If he did not lift them up, he
was cruelly beaten over the shins, which were bare ;  nor was he released,
till growing black in the face, and his head falling over his shoulder, the
wretch thought his victim was near expiring.  Then after some gratuitous
knocks and cuffs, he was released and instantly driven to his toil, and
forced to commence, with every appearance of strength and vigour, though
he were so much crippled, as to be scarcely able to stand.  To lift the
apprentices up by their ears, shake them violently, and then dash them
down upon the floor with the utmost fury, was one of the many inhuman
sports in Litton Mill, in which the overlookers appeared to take delight.
Frequently has Blincoe been thus treated, till he thought his ears were
torn from his head, and this for very trivial offences, or omissions.  Another of these diabolical amusements consisted in filing the apprentices'
teeth !  Blincoe was once constrained to open his mouth to receive this
punishment, and Robert Woodward applied the file with great vigour !
Having punished him as much as he pleased ;  the brute said with a sneer ;
" I do this to sharpen thy teeth, that thou may'st eat thy Sunday dinner
the better."

Blincoe declared, that he had often been compelled, on a cold winter's
day, to work *naked*, except his trousers, and loaded with two half hundred
weights slung behind him, hanging one at each shoulder.  Under this
cruel torture, he soon sunk ;  when, to make the sport last the longer,
Woodward substituted quarter of hundred weights, and thus loaded, by
every painful effort, Blincoe could not lift his arm to the roller.  Wood-

ward has forced him to wear these weights for hours together, and still to
continue at his work !   Sometimes, he has been commanded to pull off his
shirt and get into a large square skip, when,  the savage, being sure of his
mark, and that, not a blow would  be  lost, used to beat him till he  was
tired ! At other times, Blincoe has been hoisted upon other boys' shoulders,
and beaten with sticks till he has been shockingly  discoloured and covered
with contusions and wounds.

What spinners call, a *draw off*, at one of those frames at which Blincoe
worked, required about forty seconds.   Woodward has often insisted
upon Blincoe cleaning all  the cotton away under the  whole  frame, in a
single draw, and to go out at the further end, under pain of a severe beating.
On one of these occasions, Blincoe had nearly lost his life, being caught
between the faller and the head piece, his head was jammed between them.
Both his temples were cut open and the blood  poured down  each side of
his face, the marks to  be seen !   It was considered next to a miracle,
that he escaped with his life !   So far from feeling the least compassion,
Woodward beat him cruelly, because he had not made *more haste !*  Blincoe
says, to the best of  his recollection,  he was twelve years of age, when this
accident happened

It is a fact, too notorious to be denied, that the most brutal and ferocious
of the spinners, stretchers, rovers, &c. have been in the habit, from mere
wantonness, of inflicting severe punishments upon piecers, scavengers,
frame-tenters, winders, and others of  the  juvenile class, subjected to their
power, compelling them to eat  dirty pieces of candle,  to lick  up tobacco
spittle, to open their mouths for the filthy wretches to spit into ;  all which
beastialities  have been practised upon the apprentices at Litton Mill !
Among the rest, Blincoe has often suffered these indignities.   What has a
tendency to display human nature in its  worst state,  is, that most of  the
overlookers,  who acted  thus cruelly,  had arrived in the mill as parish
apprentices, and, as such, had undergone all these offensive inflictions !

There was, however, one diversion, which, in all my enquiries as to
cotton-mill *amusements,* I never found paralleled.   Of this Robert Woodward, if I mistake not, has a claim  to the honour of  being  the *original
inventor.*   It was thus executed.—A tin can or cylinder, about three feet
high, to receive the rovings, and about nine or ten inches in diameter, was
placed in the midst of  the alley or wheel-house, as the space is called, over
which the frames travel at every draw, and pretty close to the race.  Upon
this can or hollow cylinder, Blincoe  had to  mount ;  and  there to stand
upon one foot, holding  a long brush extended in the opposite hand, until
the  frame came out, about three times in two minutes, invariably knocking
the  can from under  him, both fell to the  floor.   The villian used to
place the can so near  the race, that there was  considerable  danger of
Blincoe falling on it, and, if so,  it would  probably  have  lamed him for
life if it had not killed him  on the spot ; and  he  had, with the utmost
possible celerity,  to throw himself flat upon the floor, that the frame
might pass  over him !   During  this short interval, the amateurs, i. e.
Robert Woodward, Charnock, Merrick, &c. used to set the can upright
again, and it required  no small share of ingenuity, in them, to keep time.
The frame being returned, poor Blincoe  had  to  leap on his feet, and

No.  5.

again to mount nimbly on the hollow column of tin, again to extend his arm, holding the long hair brush, and again sustain a fall, amidst the shouts and yells of these fiends. Thus would the villians continue to persecute and torment him, till they were tired, notwithstanding the *sport* might have been his death. He ran the risk of a broken bone, or the dislocation of a limb, every time he was thus thrown down ; and the time the monsters thus wasted, they afterwards made up by additional labour wrung from their wretched victims !

Another of their diversions consisted in tying Blincoe's hands behind him and one of his legs up to his hands. He had then only one leg left free to hop upon, and no use left of his hands to guard him, if he chanced to fall, and if Blincoe did not move with activity, the overlooker would strike a blow with his clenched fist, or cut his head open by flinging rollers. If he fell, he was liable to have his leg or arm broken dislocated. Every one conversant with cotton-spinning machinery knows the danger of such *diversions*, and of their cruelty, every one can judge.

There seemed to exist a spirit of emulation, and infernal spirit, it might with justice be designated, among the overlookers of Litton Mill, of inventing and inflicting the most novel and singular punishments. For the sake of being the better able, and more effectually to torment their victims, the overlookers allowed their thumb and fore-finger nails to grow to an extreme length, in order that, when they *pinched their ears*, they might make their nails meet, *marks to be seen.*

Needham himself the owner of the Mill, stands arrainged of having the cruelty to act thus, very frequently, till their blood ran down their necks, and so common was the sport, it was scarcely noticed. As regarded Blincoe, one set of wounds had not seldom time to heal, before another set was inflicted ; the general remedy that Blincoe applied was, the oil used to keep the machinery in order. The despicable wretches, who thus revelled in acts of lawless oppression, would often, to indulge the whim of a moment, fling a roller at a boy's head. and inflict deep wounds, and this, frequently, without even a shadow of a fault to allege, or even a plausible reason to assign in justification ! At another time, if the apprentices stood fair for the infliction of a stripe, with a twig or the whip, the overlookers would apply it, with the utmost vigour, and then, bursting into laughter, call it a———-*good hit !* Blincoe declared he had, times innumerable been thus assailed, and has had his head cut severely, without daring to complain of the cause. Woodward and others of the overlookers used to beat him with pieces of the thick leathern straps made supple by oil, and having an iron buckle at the end, which drew blood almost every time it was applied, or caused severe contusions.

Among Blincoe's comrades in affliction, was an orphan boy, who came from St. Pancras workhouse, whose proper name was James Nottingham; but better known as "*blackey,*" a nick name that was given to him, on account of his black hair, eyes, and complexion. According to Blincoe's testimony, this poor boy suffered even greater cruelties, than fell to his own share ! by an innumerable number of blows, chiefly inflicted on his head !—by wounds and contusions, his head swelled enormously. and he became stupid ! To use Blincoe's significant expression, " his head was as soft as a boiled turnip," the scalp on the crown, pitting every where on the least compression. This poor boy, being reduced to this most pitiable condition, by unrestrained cruelty, was exposed to innumerable outrages, and was, at last, incapable of work, and often plundered of his food !— melancholy and weeping, he used to creep into holes and corners, to avoid his tormentors. From mere debility, he was inflicted by incontinency of stools and urine ! To punish this infirmity, conformably as Blincoe declared, to the will of Ellice Needham, the master, his allowance of broth, butter-milk, porridge, &c. was withheld ! During the summer time, he was mercilessly scourged ! In winter, stripped quite naked, and he was slung, with a rope tied round his shoulders, into the dam, and dragged to and fro, till he was nearly suffocated. They would then draw him out, and sit him on a stone, under a pump, and pump upon his head, in a copious stream, while some stout fellow was employed to sluice the poor wretch with pails of water, flung with all possible fury into his face. According to the account I received, not alone Blincoe, but several other of the Litton Mill apprentices, when these horrid inflictions had reduced the poor boy to a state of idiotism,—his wrongs and sufferings,—his dismal condition, —far, from exciting sympathy, but increased the mirth of these vulgar tyrants ! His wasted and debilitated frame was seldom, if ever, free from wounds and contusions, and his head covered with running sores and swarming with lice, exhibited a loathsome object ! In consequence of this miserable state of filth and disease, poor Nottingham has many times had to endure the excruciating torture of the pitch and scalping cap already named !

Having learnt, in 1822, that this forlorn child of misery was then at work in a cotton factory, near Oldfield Lane, I went in search of and found him. At first, he seemed much embarrassed, and when I made enquiries as to his treatment at Litton Mill, to my surprise, he told me "he knew nothing whatever about it." I then, related what Blincoe and others had named to me, of the horrid tortures he endured. "I dare say," said he mildly, "he told you truth, but I have no distinct recollection of any thing that happened to me during the greater part of the time I was there ! I believe," said he, "my sufferings was most dreadful, and that I nearly lost my senses. From his appearance, I guessed he had not been so severely worked as others of the poor crippled children whom I had seen ! As well as I can recollect, his knees were not deformed, or if at all, but very little ! He is much below the middle size, as to stature. His countenance round, and his small and regular features, bore the character of former sufferings and present tranquility of mind.

In the course of my enquiries respecting this young man, I was much gratified, by hearing the excellent character given him in the vicinity of his lodging. Several persons spoke of him as being serious and well inclined, and his life and conduct irreproachable.

We frequently had our best dinner in the week on a Sunday, and it was generally broth, meat and turnips, with a little oat-cake, the meat was of as coarse a sort as could be bought. This being our extra dinner, we did not wish to part with it too soon, therefore it was a general practice amongst the 'prentices to save some of it until Monday, in the care of the governor of the 'prentice house, and for each one to know their own. The practice was to cut in their oat-cake, some mark or other, and lay it on their wooden trenchers. It happened one Sunday we had our dinner of bacon broth and turnips with a little oat-cake. This Sunday, one Thomas Linsey, a fellow 'prentice thought he could like a snack, early in the morning, therefore he took a slice of bacon between two pieces of oat-cake to bed with him, and put it under his head I cannot say, under his pillow, because we never was allowed any. The next morning about three or four o'clock, as it was a usual practice in the summer time when short of water, for a part of the hands to begin their work sooner, by this contrivance we was able to work our full time or near. Linsey was found dead in bed, and as soon as some of the 'prentices knew of his death, as they slept about 50 in a room, there was a great scuffle who should have the bacon and oat-cake from under his head, some began to search his pockets for his tin, this tin he used to eat his victuals with; some had pieces of broken pots, as no spoons was allowed. It was reported this Sunday that this pig had died in the Lees, a place so called at the back of the 'prentice-house. There was no coroner's inquest held over Linsey to know the cause of his death. I shall leave the reader to judge for himself this distressing sight, at so early an hour in the morning.—This occurred at Litton Mill.

It might be supposed, that these horrid inflictions had been practised, in this cotton-factory, unknown to the master and proprietor of Litton Mill; but the testimony, not of Blincoe alone, but of many of his former associates unknown to him, gave similar statements, and like Blincoe, described Ellice Needham the master, as equalling the very worst of his servants in cruelty of heart! So far from having taken any care to stop their career, he used to animate them by his own example to inflict punishment in any and every way they pleased. Mr. Needham stands accused of having been in the habit of knocking down the apprentices with his clenched fists ;— kicking them about when down, beating them to excess with sticks, or flogging them with horse-whips; of seizing them by the ears, lifting them from the ground and forcibly dashing them down on the floor, or pinching them till his nails met ! Blincoe declares his oppressors used to seize him by the hair of his head and tear it off by a handful at a time, till the crown of his head had become as bald as the back of his hand! John Needham, following the example of his father, and possessing unlimited power over the apprentices, lies under the imputation of crimes of the blackest hue, exercised upon the wretched creatures, from whose laborious toil, the means of supporting the pomp and luxury in which he lived were drawn. To boys, he was a tyrant and an oppressor! To the girls the same, with the additional odium of treating them with an indecency as disgusting as his cruelty was terrific. Those unhappy creatures were at once the victims of his ferocity and his lust.

For some trivial offence, Robert Woodward once kicked and beat Robert Blincoe, till his body was covered with wheals and bruises. Being tired, or desirous of affording his young master the luxury of amusing himself on the same subject, he took Blincoe to the counting-house, and accused him of wilfully spoiling his work. Without waiting

to hear what Blincoe might have to urge in his defence, young Needham
eagerly looked about for a stick ; not finding one at hand, he sent Woodward to an adjacent coppice, called the Twitchell, to cut a supply, and
laughingly bade Blincoe strip naked, and prepare himself for a good
*flanking !* Blincoe obeyed, but to his agreeable surprise, young Needham abstained from giving him the promised flanking. The fact was, the
poor boy's body was so dreadfully discoloured and inflamed by contusions, its appearance terrified the young despot, and he spared him,
thinking that mortification and death might ensue, if he laid on an other
" flanking." Hence his unexpected order to Blincoe to put on his things !
There was not, at the time, a free spot on which to inflict a blow ! His
ears were swollen and excoriated ; his head, in the most deplorable state
imaginable ; many of the bruises on his body had suppurated ! and so
excessive was his soreness, he was forced to sleep on his face, if sleep he
could obtain, in so wretched a condition !

Once a week, and generally after sixteen hours of incessant toil, the
eldest girls had to comb the boys' heads ; an operation, that being alike
painful to the sufferer, as disgusting to the girls, was reluctantly endured,
and inefficiently performed. Hence arose the frequency of scald-heads
and the terrible scalping remedy ! Upon an average, the children were
kept to work during a great part, if not all, the time Blincoe was at Litton
Mill, sixteen hours in the day. The result of this excessive toil, super-
added to hunger and torture, and was the death of many of apprentices,
and the entailment of incurable lameness and disease on many others.

The store pigs and the apprentices used to fare pretty much alike ; but
when the swine were hungry, they used to speak and grunt so loud,
they obtained the wash first, to quiet them. The apprentices could be
intimidated, and made to keep still. The fatting pigs fared luxuriously,
compared with the apprentices ! They were often regaled with meal-
balls made into dough, and given in the shape of dumplings ! Blincoe
and others, who worked in a part of the Mill. whence they could see the
swine served, used to say to one another—" *The pigs are served ; it will
be our turn next.*" Blincoe and those who were in a part of the building contiguous to the pigsties, used to keep a sharp eye upon the fatting
pigs, and their meal-balls, and, as soon as he saw the swineherd withdraw, he used to slip down stairs, and, stealing slyly towards the trough,
plunge his hand in at the loop holes, and steal as many dumplings as he
could grasp ! The food thus obtained from a pigs trough, and, perhaps,
defiled by their filthy chops, was exultingly conveyed to the privy or the
duck-hole, and there devoured with a much keener appetite, than it would
have been by the pigs; but the pigs, though generally esteemed the most
stupid of animals, soon hit upon an expedient, that baffled the hungry
boys ; for the instant the meal-balls were put into their troughs, they
voraciously seized them, threw them into the dirt, out of the reach of the
boys ! Not this alone ; but, made wise by repeated losses, they kept a
sharp look out, and the moment they ascertained the approach of the half-
famished apprentices, they set up so loud a chorus of snorts and grunts,
it was heard in the kitchen, when out rushed the swine-herd, armed with
a whip, from which combined means of protection for the swine, this ac-

cidental source of obtaining a *good dinner* was soon lost ! Such was the
contest carried on for a time at Litton Mill, between the half-famished
apprentices, and the well-fed swine.

I observed to Blincoe, it was not very rational, to rob the pigs, when
they were destined to bleed to supply them with food, as soon as they
grew sufficiently fat ! " Oh ! you're mistaken," said he, " these pigs
were fatted for master's own table, or were sold at Buxton ! We were
fed upon the very worst and cheapest of Irish-fed bacon." There was,
it seems, a small dairy at Litton Mill ; but the butter was all sent to his
house. The butter-milk alone was dispensed, and but very scantily, to
the apprentices. About a table-spoonful of meal was distributed once a
week to the apprentices, with which to wash themselves, instead of soap ;
but in nine cases out of ten, it was greedily devoured, and a piece of clay
or sand, or some such thing, substituted : such was the dreadful state of
hunger in which these poor children were kept in this mill.

To attempt a specific statement, how often Blincoe has been kept to
work from five in the morning till midnight, during his period of servitude,
would be hazardous ! According to his own testimony, supported by
that of many others, it was, at times of common occurrence, more especially on the Saturday ! In most mills, the adult spinners left off on
that day at *four* in the afternoon, whilst in these, were parish apprentices were employed, it was often continued, not only till midnight ;
but till six o'clock on the Sunday morning !

Exertion so incessant could not fail to reduce the majority of apprentices
to a state of exhaustion and lassitude, so great as nearly to disqualify
them to benefit by such instructions as an illiterate clown could afford,
who officiated on Sundays as schoolmasters, or by divine worship, when
they were allowed to attend. Nothing could be more cheerless, than the
aspect of these juvenile sufferers, these helpless outcasts, nor more piteous
than the wailings and lamentations of that portion, chiefly of the tenderest
years, whom long familiarity with vice and misery had not rendered
wholly callous.

A blacksmith or mechanic, named William Palfrey, who resided at
Litton, worked in a room under that where Blincoe was employed. He
used to be much disturbed by the shrieks and cries of the boys, whom the
manager and overlookers were almost continually punishing. According
to Blincoe's declaration, and that of others, human blood has often run
from an upper to a lower floor, shed by these merciless taskmasters.
Unable to hear the shrieks of the children, Palfrey used to knock against
the floor, so violently, as to force the boards up, and call out " for
shame ! for shame ! are you murdering the children ?" He spoke to Mr.
Needham, and said, he would not stay in the mill, if such doings were
allowed. By this sort of conduct, the humane blacksmith was a check on
the cruelty of the brutal overlookers, as long as he continued in his shop ;
but he went away home at seven o'clock, and as soon as Woodward,
Merrick, and Charnock knew that Palfrey was gone, they used to pay off
the day's score, and to beat and knock the apprentices about without mo-
deration or provocation, giving them black eyes, broken heads ; saying,
I'll let you know old Palfrey is not here now !" To protract the

evil hour, the boys, when they used to go down stairs for rovings, would
come back and say—"Palfrey and the joiner are going to work all night,"
and sometimes by this manœuvre, they have escaped punishment.

It happened one day, when Blincoe was about twelve years old, he
went to the counting-house with a cop, such being the custom at every
doffing. While Blincoe was there, another apprentice, named Isaac Moss,
came in on the same errand. Upon the floor stood the tin treacle can,
with about 14 pounds of treacle. The sight arrested the attention of
Blincoe, who said softly, " Moss, there is the treacle can come from
'Tideswell !"—" Eh," Moss exclaimed, " so it is." Blincoe said, " I
have no spoon." Moss rejoined, " I have two." Putting his hand to his
bosom and pulling out the bowl of an iron spoon and another which he
kept for another person, down they sat on the floor opposite to each other,
with the can between them, and began operations, lading away as fast as
they could !  Blincoe had a large sized mouth, and in good condition, but
the ruffian, William Woodward the manager, brother to Robert Woodward, having struck Moss a severe blow on the mouth, with a large stick,
it had swollen so much, that the poor lad had the mortification of hardly
being able to use it, and Blincoe could stow away at least three spoonsful
to Moss's one !  While the conscious pair were thus employed, the
enemy, unheard and unperceived, stole upon them.  It was a dark night;
but there was a fire in the counting-house, by the light of which, over
some glass above the top of the door, that grim spectre, the terror and
the curse of these poor boys, Woodward, saw their diversion !  He stood
viewing them some time, when suddenly rushing upon them, he seized
upon them as a cat pounces upon cheese-eating mice !  Blincoe being
most active with his feet, as well as with his spoon, after receiving a few
kicks and cuffs, ran off to the factory, leaving Moss in the power, and at
at the mercy of William Woodward.

At ten o'clock the factory bell rang, and Blincoe went off to the apprentice-house, trembling with apprehension and looking wildly around
amongst the apprentices, in hope of seeing his comrade Moss ; but Moss
was not to be seen !  Presently, an order arrived from Woodward, for
the master of the apprentices to bring down Blincoe !  Richard Milner,
the then governor of the apprentices, a corpulent old man, said, " Parson,
what hast thou been doing ?"—" Nothing," said the parson ; his tremulous voice and shaking limbs contradicting his laconic reply ; and away
they trudged.  When they got to the counting-house, they found Moss
stuck erect in a corner, looking very poorly, his mouth and cheeks all over
treacle.  William Woodward, in a gruff voice, " said, " So you have
been helping to eat this treacle ?"—" I have only eaten a little, Sir.'
Upon which, he hit Blincoe one of his flat-handed slaps, fetching fire from
his eyes, and presently another, another, and another, till Blincoe began to
vociferate for mercy, promising never to eat forbidden treacle any more !
Woodward was full six feet high, with long arms, huge raw bones and
immense sized hands, and when he had tired himself with beating Blincoe,
he exclaimed : " Damn your bloods, you rascals, if you don't lap up the
whole can of treacle, I'll murder you on the spot."  This denunciation was
music to Blincoe's ears, who had never before received such an invitation

To accommodate the young gentlemen, the governor sent to his own
kitchen for two long spoons, and then, with renewed execrations, Woodward bade them set to. Moss then crept softly and soilently out of his
corner, having been cruelly beaten in Blincoe's absence! Looking rue-
fully at each other, down the culprits knelt a second time, one on each side
of the treacle can! Blincoe had still the best of the sport; for poor Moss's
mouth remained deprived of half its external dimensions, and being so
excessively sore, he could hardly get in a tea-spoon, where Blincoe could
shovel in large table-spoonsful! Moss kept fumbling at his lame mouth,
and looking rather spitefully at Blincoe, as if he thought he would eat all
the treacle. Meanwhile Milner and Woodward sat laughing an chatting
by the fire side, often looking at the treacle-eaters, and anxiously waiting
an outcry for quarters! Blincoe eat in a masterly style; but poor Moss
could not acquit himself half as well, the treacle trickling down his chin,
on both sides of his mouth, seeing which, Woodward suddenly roared out,
"Damn you, you villian, if you don't open your mouth wider, I'll open it
for you.' Poor Moss trembled; but made no reply, and Blincoe being
willing to make hay while the sun shone, instead of falling off, seemed,
at every mouthful, to acquire fresh vigour! This surprised and mortified
Woodward not a little, who seeing no signs of sickness, hearing no cry
for quarter, and being apprehensive of an application for another can, got
up to reconnoitre, and, to his amazement, found that the *little Parson,*
who was not a vast deal higher than the can, had almost reached the bottom, and displayed no visible loss or diminution of appetite!

Inexpressibly vexed at being thus outwitted before the governor, he
roared out in a tremendous voice to Milner, "Why damn their bloods,
they'll eat the whole! Halt, you damned rascals, or, I'll kill you on the
spot!" In a moment, Blincoe ceased his play, and licked his lips and
spoon, to shew how keen his stomach still was! Milner and Woodward
then took stock, and found, that, out of fourteen pounds, not three remained; Milner laughed immoderately at Woodward, to think what a
luscious mode of punishment he had found out for treacle stealers!—
Woodward being extremely exasperated, ordered Samuel Brickleton, an
overlooker, to fasten Moss and Blincoe together with handcuffs, of which
as well as of *fetters,* there were plenty at Litton Mill, and then forced
them to carry the can to the apprentice-house between them. When they
arrived at the door, his hand being small, Blincoe contrived to withdraw it
from the handcuff, and ran nimbly off into the room amongst the apprentices,
leaving the treacle can in Moss's hand. Brickleton, unconscious of Blincoe's
escape, arrived in the kitchen, where the Governor and his family resided,
looked round, and seeing only one prisoner, cried out, "Eh! where's
Parson gone." Moss said, he believed he was gone into the apprentice-
house. Brickleton examined the handcuffs and finding they were locked,
was much puzzled to think how the parson had contrived to get his hand
out. The kind and careful Mrs. Milner, knowing there was money due
to Blincoe, for working his dinner-hour, viz. a farthing a day, proposed to
have it stopped, to pay for the treacle which Woodward had compelled
him to eat, on pain of putting him instantly to death. Such was the law
and equity, which prevailed at Litton Mill! That night, in consequence

of his sumptuous supper, Blincoe was forbidden to enter his bed, and he laid all night, in the depth of winter, on the hard cold floor.

This part of the subject requires an explanation, as to the equivalent given by the owner to the apprentices, in lieu of their dinner hour. This hour consisted, in general, of forty minutes, and not always so many. The master, to induce the apprentices to work all day long, promised each three-pence per week, if they worked the whole of the dinner hour, and they had to eat it, *bite and sup*, at their work, without, spoon, knife, or fork, and with their dirty oily fingers! They were thus kept on their feet, from five o'clock in the morning, till nine, ten, and even eleven o'clock at night, and on Saturdays, sometimes till twelve ; because Sunday was a *day of rest !* Frequently, though almost famishing, the apprentices could not find time to eat their food at all ; but carried it back with them at night, covered with flue and filth. This liberality did not last long. The halfpenny was reduced to a farthing, and this farthing was withheld till it amounted to several shillings, and then, when the master *pleased*, he would give a shilling or two, and none dare ask for more. Those whom the overlookers pleased to order so to do, had to work their dinner hour for nothing, and their comrades used to fetch their dinners, who, not unfrequently, pilfered a part. The money thus earned, the poor 'prentices used to reserve, to buy wheaten cakes, and red herrings, to them, luxuries of the most delicious kind. Such was the miserable manner in which they were fed, that, when they gave the pence to Palfrey (the smith,) to bring the tempting cake of wheaten flour, and the herring, in the morning, they used to say to their comrades. " Old Palfrey is to bring me a cake and herring in the morning. Oh ! how greedily I shall devour them." They commonly dreamt of these anticipated feasts, and talked of their expected luxuries in their sleep. When Palfrey arrived, they would, if they dared, have met him on the stairs, or have followed him to the smithy) ; but, in an eager whisper, enquired " have you brought my cake and herring ?" " Aye, lad," said Palfrey, holding out the expected provisions. Eagerly they seized the herring and the cake, and the first full bite generally took off head or tail, as it came first to hand, while the cake was thrust inside their bosom ; for they worked with their shirt collar open and generally without jackets. The poor souls, who, having no pence, could have no dainties, would try to snatch a piece slyly, if it were possible, and if that failed, they would try to beg a morsel If the possessor gave a taste, he held the herring so tight, that only a very small portion could be bitten off, without biting off the ends of the owner's fingers, and their whole feast was quickly finished, without greatly diminishing their appetite. It happened, by some extraordinary stroke of good fortune, that Blincoe became possessed of a shilling, and he determined to have what he termed, a proper blow out ; he, therefore, requested Palfry to bring him six penny wheaten cakes, and half a pound of butter. Blincoe was then a stretcher, and had, as such, a better opportunity to receive and eat his dainties unobserved. The cakes he pulled one by one, from his bosom, and laying them upon the frame, spread the butter on them with a piece of flat iron. and giving his two comrades a small part each, he set to and devoured all the rest ; but the unusual quantity and

No. 6.

quality nearly made him ill. Blincoe had no appetite for his dinner or supper, and, he, therefore, let another comrade eat it, who engaged to give Blincoe his when he happened to lose his appetite Such were the prospective and contingent negotiations carried on by these wretched children, relative to their miserable food.

If Blincoe happened to see any fresh cabbage leaves, potato or turnip parings, thrown out upon the dunghill, he has ran down with a can full of sweepings, as an excuse, and as he threw that dirt on the dunghill, he would eagerly pick the other up, and carry it in his shirt, or in his can, into the mill, wipe the dirt off as well as he could, and greedily eat them up. At other times, when they had rice puddings boiled in bags for dinner—the rice being very bad and full of large maggots, Blincoe not being able to endure such food, used to go into one of the woods near the factory, and get what the boys called *bread and cheese*, that is, hips and hipleaves, clover, or other vegetable, and filling his bosom, run back to the mill, and eat his trash, instead of fowl rice, with which neither butter-milk, milk, treacle, nor even a morsel of salt, was allowed.

Amongst the most singular punishments inflicted upon Blincoe, was that of screwing small hand-vices of a pound weight, more or less, to his nose and ears, one to each part; and these have been kept on, as he worked, for hours together! This was principally done by Robert Woodward, Merrick and Charnock. Of these petty despots, Merrick was the most unpardonable, as he had been a parish apprentice himself, and ought to have had more compassion This Merrick was a stretcher, and Blincoe when about 11 or 12 years old, used to stretch for him, while he, Merrick, ate his dinner. Out of kindness, or because he could not eat it himself, Merrick used occasionally to leave a small part of his allowance, and tell Blincoe to go and eat it. On Mondays, it was the custom to give the boys bread and treacle, and turnip *broth* made the day before, which generally stunk to such a degree, that most of the poor creatures could only pick out the oat bread, the broth being loathsome. Whenever Merrick left a bit of bread and treacle in the window, Blincoe used to run eagerly at the prize, and devour it voraciously. On Monday, this overlooker, who was a most inhuman taskmaster, sent Blincoe down to the card-room for a basket of rovings, a descent of four or five stories deep, for this burthen of considerable weight. During the time he was gone, Merrick rubbed tar upon the oat cake, and laid it in the window as usual. When Blincoe returned, the brute said, "go and eat what lies in the window." Blincoe seeing as he supposed, so much treacle upon the bread, was surprised ; for Merrick usually licked it clean off, and to his bitter mortification, found, instead of treacle, it was TAR. Unable to endure the nauseous mouthful, Blincoe spat it out, whilst Merrick, laughing at him, said, What the devil are you spitting it out for." Poor Blincoe, shaking his head, said, You know, mon," and Blincoe left the remainder of the tarred cake in the window, when his comrade, Bill Fletcher, a poor lad since dead, who came from Peak Forest, took up the bread, and scraping off the tar as clean as he could, ate it up, apparently with a good appetite ! To such dreadful straights were they driven by hunger, the apprentices have been known to *pick turnips out of the necessary*, which others, who had stolen them, had thrown there to conceal, and washing them, have devoured the whole, thinking it too extravagant even to waste the peeling.

Palfry, the Smith, had the task of rivetting irons upon any of the apprentices, whom the masters ordered, and those were much like the irons usually put upon felons! Even young women, if suspected of intending to run away, had irons riveted on their ancles, and reaching by long links and rings up to the hips, and in these they were compelled to walk to and from the mill to work and to sleep! Blincoe asserts, he has known many girls served in this manner. A handsome-looking girl about the age of twenty years, who came from the neighbourhood of Cromford, whose name was Phebe Rag, being driven to desperation by ill-treatment, took the opportunity, one dinner-time, when she was alone, and when she supposed no one saw her, to take off her shoes and throw herself into the dam, at the end of the bridge, next the apprentice house. Some one passing along, and seeing a pair of shoes, stopped. The poor girl had sunk once, and just as she rose above the water he seized her by the hair! Blincoe thinks it was Thomas Fox, the governor, who succeeded Milner, who rescued her! She was nearly gone, and it was with some difficulty her life was saved! When Mr. Needham heard of this, and *being afraid the example might be contagious*, he ordered James Durant, a journeyman spinner, who had been apprenticed there, to take her away to her relations at Cromford, and thus she escaped!

When Blincoe's time of servitude was near expiring, he and three others, namely, William Haley, Thomas Gully, and John Emery, the overlookers, took a resolution, to go out of the factory, at a fixed hour, meaning not to work so many hours: but, according to Blincoe's account, neither he nor his comrades had ever heard up to that time, of any law which regulated the hours of apprentices working in cotton-mills, nor did they know what an act of parliament meant, so profound was the ignorance in which they had been reared! Blincoe and his mutinous comrades, having left work at the expiration of fourteen hours labour, went off to the apprentice house. Upon this, the manager, William Woodward, sent off an express to the master, (Mr. Needham), at Highgate Wall, a lone and large mansion about four miles distant. Orders came back, to turn all four out of the apprentice-house that night; but not to give them any provisions! Being thus turned out, Blincoe got lodging with Samuel Brickleton! One or two of his comrades slept in the woods, which luckily was hay time.— Brickleton's hospitality did not include provisions, and having had no food since twelve o'clock the day before, Blincoe was sorely hungry in the morning, but still he had nought to eat! About nine o'clock, all four, agreeable to the orders they received the night before, went to the counting-house at the mill. Mr. Needham was there in a terrible ill-humour — As soon as he saw Blincoe come in, he took from his body, his waistcoat and jacket, and fell upon him with his thick walking-stick, which he quickly broke by the heavy blows laid on poor Blincoe's head and shoulders, and he kept on swearing the while, " *I'll run you out, you damned rascal.*" As soon as he could escape, Blincoe ran off to his work, when Haley and Emery, who were apprentices, like Blincoe, caught their share of his fury! At noon, Blincoe went eager enough to the apprentice house, having had no food for twenty-four hours. Having in a few minutes, devoured his portion, he ran off at full speed, without hat, jacket, or waistcoat, his head and body greatly bruised, towards the residence of a magistrate, named Thornelly, who resided at Stanton-Hall, a place about six miles beyond Bakewell, and eleven from Litton-Mill! There, resided, at this time, at Ashford, about four miles from Litton-Mill, a man named Johnny Wild, a stocking-weaver, who had been his (Blincoe's) overlooker, when first he went to Lowdham Mill. Filled with the fond hope of being made at once a gentleman, thither, poor Blincoe, now twenty years of age, directed his course. Johnny Wild was sitting at his frame, weaving stockings, and was surprised to see Blincoe run up to the door like a wild creature, terror in his looks and reeking with perspiration, without hat, coat, or waistcoat. To him, Blincoe told the cruel usage he had met with, and the wounds and bruises he had just received, which were sufficiently visible! Wild and his wife seemed touched with compassion, at the sad plight Blincoe was in, gave him a bowl of bread and milk, lent him a hat, and directed him his way. Thus refreshed, the fugitive set off again, running as fast as he could, looking often behind him. As he passed through Bakewell, Blincoe thought it best to slacken his pace, lest some mercenary wretch, suspecting him to be a Litton Mill apprentice running away, should, in the hope of receiving a reward of a half-crown piece, seize him and send him back to prison! As he passed along many seemed to eye him intently; but no one stopped him. About six o'clock in the evening, being heartily jaded, he arrived at the house of Mr. Thornelly. It happened, that the magistrate was at dinner—but some person, in his employ, understanding that Blincoe came to seek redress for alleged violence, went to the supplicant in the yard, saying, " Who do you want ?—" Mr. Thornelly."—What for ?—" I am an apprentice at Litton Mill, master has beat me cruelly, do look at my shirt ?"—" Never mind, never mind," said this person, " you cannot see Mr. Thornelly to-day ; he is at dinner; there will be a bench of justices to-morrow, about eleven in the morning, at the Sign of the Bull's Head, facing the church at Heam ; you must go there." This place lay about five miles from Litton Mill, on the Sheffield road. Finding there was nothing to be done at Stanton-Hall, poor Blincoe began to measure back his weary steps to Litton Mill! He called at Johnny Wild's, as he returned, who allowed him to rest; but, of food, he could not offer any ; having a large family, and being but a poor man, he had none to spare ! Blincoe gave back his hat, and arrived at the apprentice-house between nine and ten, being then giving-over time ! William Woodward, the manager, whose heavy hand had inflicted blows and cuffs beyond calculation on poor Blincoe, was about the first person by whom he was accosted ! In a tone, about as gentle as that of a baited-bear, and an aspect much more savage, said, " Where have you been ?"—" To Mr. Thornelly."—" I'll Thornelly you to-morrow," said he, and turned away. Not knowing what the next day might bring forth, Blincoe applied for his mess of water-porridge, which, after a journey of two and twenty miles, tasted highly savory, and then he retired to his bed, praying God to end his life, or mitigate its severity—a prayer that was common at Litton Mill!—Sore as he was, he slept; but it was on his face, his back being too much bruised, to lie in that position, or even on his side ! In the morning, he

rose and went to his stretching frame. Between seven and eight o'clock
Blincoe saw Woodward going to the apprentice-house, from the window
of the factory. Seeing this opportunity, without waiting for breakfast,
Blincoe again made a start, still without hat, waistcoat or coat, towards
Heam, to state to the magistrates the cruel treatment he had received.—
The day was fine. The hay was about, and miserable as was poor Blincoe, he could not but feel delighted with the sweet air and romantic scenery. Having been thus expeditious, Blincoe was at Heam, an hour and
a half too soon. To amuse himself, he went into the Church-yard. As
soon as the magistrates arrived, from whose hands he came to supplicate
for justice, Blincoe went to the Bull's Head. The officiating clerk was an
attorney named Cheek, who resided at Whetstone-Hall, a mansion situated
within half a mile of Tideswell. To this person, Blincoe began unbosom-
ing his grief, and in the earnestness of his harrangue, and fearful, lest the
attorney did not catch every syllable, the half-naked Blincoe crept nearer
and nearer; but Mr. Cheek not relishing the dense, foul scent of oil,
grease, and filth, said, " Well, well, I can hear you, you need not come
so near; stand back." Poor Blincoe, not a little mortified, obeyed his
command, and, by the time Blincoe's piteous tale was ended, the magistrates had mostly arrived, to whom Mr. Cheek, the clerk to the magistrates, read the paper, which Blincoe supposed contained his intended de-
position. Blincoe was then sworn. One of the magistrates, Blincoe believes it was a Mr. Middleton, of Leam Hall, said, " Where is Mr.
Needham ?"—Blincoe replied, "He's gone to-day (Tuesday) to Manchester Market" This prevented their sending a man and horse to fetch
him. One of the magistrates then said to Blincoe, " Go strait to the mill,
to your work."—Oh! Sir, he'll leather me," meaning, Mr. Needham
would beat him again. " Oh. no ! he durst na'—he durst na`," said one
of the magistrates in reply. Upon this, some one advised, that a letter
should be sent to Mr. Needham, in whose much dreaded presence, Blincoe
had no inclination to appear ! Blincoe cannot recollect who wrote the
letter, but thinks it was Mr. Middleton, who said, " If he leathers you,
come to me." This gentleman resided at a distance of about eight miles
from Litton Mill. Having this powerful talisman in his possession, Blincoe
returned direct to the mill, and, advancing boldly to Woodward, the manager,
said, " Here's a letter for Mr. John Needham," the son of the old master,
who is now resident in Tideswell ! Blincoe informed Woodward, he had
been at a justice-meeting at Heam. and as a justice had sent this letter,
Woodward did not dare to lay violent-hands upon him. This day, poor
Blincoe had to fast till night, making a complete round of another
twenty-four hours of fasting ! On Wednesday, John Needham returned from Manchester market, and appeared, as usual, at Litton Mill.
—The letter, from which Blincoe anticipated such beneficial results, was
handed to the young Squire, by William Woodward, the manager. He
broke the seal, read it through, and ordered Blincoe to be called out of
the factory, from his work. Obedient to the summons, and not a little
alarmed, he appeared before his young master, whose savage looks
shewed, ere he spoke a word, a savage purpose. The first words were,
" Take off your shirt, you damned rascal !" Blincoe obeyed, his head
and back being still very sore. John Needham instantly began flogging
him with a heavy horsewhip, striking him with his utmost force, wherever

he could get a blow. It was in vain Blincoe cried for quarters—in vain he promised never again to go to a Magistrate, in any case whatever. John Needham kept on flogging, swearing horribly and threatening furiously, resting between while, till he had fully satisfied his sense of justice! He then unlocked the door, and, saying, " You'll go again, will you?" bade Blincoe put on his shirt, and go to his work. Away went Blincoe, scarcely able to stand, and covered with additional bruises from head to foot. Even this horrid flogging did not deprive Blincoe of his appetite, nor of his determination to seek redress of the Magistrates, and accordingly, the next Sunday night, when some of the time-outs were let out of the prison, Blincoe, availing himself of the darkness of the night, watched the opening of the yard door, and crouching almost on his hands and knees, crept out unseen. Shortly after the order was given to set down to supper. Every 'prentice, male and female, knew their own places. In about two minutes, two hundred half-famished creatures were seated. Their names were called over, to see that none were missing, when, little parson could not be found. Governor Thomas Fox, on learning of this event, ordered the door warder to be called, who declared most vehemently, he had not let Blincoe out, and further, he had not passed the door ; upon this, a general search was made in all the rooms and offices, high and low; but no where was little parson to be found. Meanwhile, as soon as Blincoe found himself outside the hated walls, he set off again up Slack, a very steep hill close to the mill, and made the best of his way to Litton, and going to the house of one Joseph Robinson, a joiner, who worked in Litton Mill, who had known Blincoe at Lowdham Mill, was well acquainted with the horrid cruelties he had suffered, and heartily compassionating Blincoe's miserable state, gave him a good supper, and let him sleep with his sons. In the morning, Robinson, who was really a humane man, and a friend to the poor children, gave Blincoe some bread and meat, and giving him a strict injunction not to own *where* he had slept, Blincoe set off, about six o'clock in the morning, to Mr. Middleton's house. The morning was showery, and Blincoe had neither hat, coat, or waistcoat, and he had about eight miles to go, in search of justice. He arrived at Mr. Middleton's long before his hour of appearance. At last, Mr. Middleton got up, and Blincoe approaching, crawling like a spaniel dog, said, Sir, I have come again, Mr. Needham has been beating me worse than ever, as soon as he read your letter over." Seeing the miserable state Blincoe was in, drenched with the rain and half naked, Mr. Middleton said, " go into the kitchen and rest yourself—you should not have come here first ; you should have gone to Mr. Cheek, of Whetstone Hall, and he would have given you a summons ;" upon this, poor Blincoe said mournfully, " Eh, Sir, he will do nought for me—he is so thick with my master—they are often drinking together." " Pshaw, pshaw," said the Justice, "he's like to listen to you—he must;" but then, as if recollecting himself, he said, " Stop, I'll write you a letter to Mr. Cheek." In the Justice's kitchen, poor Blincoe got some bread and cheese, which was indeed a luxurious food, though unaccompanied with any beer. Blincoe thus refreshed, again set off to Mr. Cheek, a distance of about eleven or twelve miles, bareheaded and dressed only in trowsers and shoes. The rain continuing pouring in torrents. When Blincoe

reached Whetstone Hall, one of the first persons he saw, was a woman of
the name of Sally Oldfield, her husband, Thomas Oldfield, then dead,
had been governor of the 'prentices of Litton Mill. She was then house-
keeper to Messrs. Shore and Cheek, at Whetstone Hall. Those gentlemen were amongst the most intimate friends and visitors of Mr. Needham,
and Sally Oldfield, who recollected Blincoe, alias parson, said; " Eh,
Parson ! what do you want here ?" " I have a letter from Mr. Middleton
to Mr. Cheek." " Eh !" said little old sally again, Are you going
against your master?" Blincoe told her he was, and how cruelly he had
been treated. Sally could not comprehend any right Blincoe had to complain, and said, " Eh ! thou should'st not go against thy master." Saying this, she took him to the kitchen, gave him some bread and cheese,
and plenty too, and some good beer, and then said, " Parson, thou mun
never go against thy master ; what do you have for dinner on Monday ?
—do you have treacle now ?" " No, we have dry bread and broth."
" Ah," continued she, " *Treacle is too dear.*' Blincoe could scarce
refrain from smiling, recollecting the feast of the treacle can ; but he said
nothing, and not a soul came near him. There Blincoe sat until night,
when he began to think the magistrates were hoaxing him, and he thought
there was no utility in waiting for justice, or a possibility of obtaining
redress ! he would never more complain ! seven hours sat Blincoe in Lawyer Cheek's kitchen, and not the least notice being taken of him or his
letter, he made his solitary way back to the mill, and arrived there just as
the mill had loosed, and going direct to Woodward, told him where he had
been, and concealing the conviction he felt, that it was not possible to obtain redress ; he assured the tyrant, with tears and lamentations, that if he
would intercede to prevent his being flogged again, he would never run away
more. " On these conditions," said Woodward, " I will, if I can," and
from that day Blincoe cannot recollect, that he was either flogged or
beaten ; but, *still* Blincoe had no knowledge, that there was any
Act of Parliament for the protection of poor orphans like himself.
—He knew of the magistrates coming to the mill ; but he had no distinct
idea that they came to *redress grievances !* So great was the terror of
the poor ignorant apprentices, no one dared complain, and he cannot recollect that they ever gave themselves any other trouble, than merely
going over the mill ! Every thing was previously prepared and made
ready. The worst of the cripples were put out of the way, The magistrates saw them not. The magistrates could never *find out* any thing
wrong, nor hear of a single individual who had any complaint to make !
—When Blincoe was about twelve or thirteen years of age, he well remembers an apprentice, almost grown up, who lost is life in an attempt
to escape. He had tied several blankets or sheets together, to reach the
ground from the chamber window, where he slept, which was three or
four stories high. The line broke, he fell to the ground, and he was so
much hurt at the fall, he died soon after. Blincoe thinks some surgeon or
doctor came to him ; but he has not the least recollection of any Coroner's
inquest being held ! In addition to the punishments already stated,
Robert Woodward and other overlookers have kicked him down a whole
flight of stairs ; at other times, he has been seized by the hair of his head
and dragged up and down the room, tearing off his hair by handsful, till

he was almost bald !  All the punishments he suffered, were inflicted upon others, and, in some cases, even to a worse degree than on himself.  He even considers he came off tolerably well, compared with others, many of whom, he believes, in his conscience, lost their lives, and died at the ap- prentice-house, from the effects of hard usage, bad and scanty food, and excessive labour.

—◆—

## CHAP. VI.

BLINCOE remained in Litton Mill a year after he had received his inden- tures, not from inclination ; but to get a little money to start with.  His wages were only four shillings and sixpence weekly, and this was to have been paid monthly ; but, month after month elapsed, and, instead of an honest settlement, there was nothing but shuffling! The first money he received was eighteen and sixpence, and being in possession of that sum, he thought himself incalculably rich ! He scarcely knew what to do with it ! It took away his appetite.—After he was a little composed, he devoted a few shillings to the purchase of some dainties, such as wheaten cakes and herrings! He then worked and lived like others, till his master owed him nearly half a years labour.  The pay day came and then he drew nearly thirty shillings, the rest was kept back, so that Blincoe seeing no prospect before him but perpetual slavery for a merciless master, made up his mind to be off; and on Tidswell May fair, which happens on the fifteenth of May, he put his plan in execution ! He knew not where to go; but started the next morning at hazard ! When he came to Chapel-a- Frith, he determined to visit a celebrated fortune-teller, called Old Beckka' ! She lived in a small back-house, a haggard, black, horrid- looking creature, very old, having a long beard, and dressed like a per- son who lived in ages past ! Her name was very influential all over Derbyshire. So very famous was *old Beckka'*, that people came far and near, and she was reputed to be possessed of land and houses.—She never took a smaller fee than a shilling, even from the very poorest of her vota- ries. Her name was well-known at Litton Mill. If any thing was stolen, Woodward, the manager, or Gully, or some *one* of the overlookers, used to go to Chapel-a-Frith, to consult *old Beckka'*. To this sybil, Blincoe repaired, holding a shilling, between his thumb and finger ! Perfectly understanding the object of his visit, she first took the shilling, and then said " Sit down." He felt really frightened, and, if she had bade him stand upon his head, he declared he should have obeyed ! He had been told, that she had really enchanted or bewitched persons, who had endea- voured to cheat or deceive her, or by whom she had been offended, causing them to lose their way, and sent ill fortune in many shapes. Our novice was also told, that ladies and gentlemen of high estate had come in their coaches, all the way from London, to learn their destiny, all which cir- cumstances produced, on his uncultivated mind, the sensations described ! No sooner was Robert Blincoe seated, than the witch of Chapel-a-Frith, put a common tea-cup in his hand, containing a little tea grounds, " Shake it well," said Beckka. Blincoe obeyed, Then the oracle drained away the water, and twirling the cup round and round, she affected, with the utmost gravity, to read his future fortune, in the figures described in the sediment at the bottom. Assuming a wild stare, and standing erect over him, her eyes apparently ready to leap from their sockets, she exclaimed, in a hollow sepulchral tone of voice, "You came from the outside of London, did you not?" "Yea," said the astonished Blincoe, "I did." "You came down in a waggon, and have been at a place surrounded with high rocks and great waters, and you have been used worse than a stumbling stone." Blincoe's mouth, and eyes, and ears, all seemed to open together, at this oracular speech, as he said, "Yea, yea, it is true." Then she said,—"Your troubles are at an end.—You shall rise above those, who have cast you down so low.—You shall see their downfall, and your head shall be higher than theirs.—Poor lad! terrible have been thy sufferings.—Thou shall get up in the world! you'll go to another place, where there'll be a big water, and so go thy way in peace, and may God prosper thy steps!" Filled with amazement, mingled with rising hopes of better fortune, Blincoe arose and departed, making a very low reverence to "old Becka," as he went out, and impressed with the fullest conviction, that she was truely a sorceress; the simpleton, forgetting, that his costume, his wild and pallid looks, and the scent of his garments, tainted as they were with the perfume of a cotton factory, were more than sufficient to point out to the fortune-teller, the past and present, from which she speedily fabricated the future fortune, for her simple visitor! Blincoe thought he got but a very short story for his shilling! On the other hand, he was very well contented with its quality, since it promised him, and in such positive terms, that he should rise above his cruel oppressor and become a great man. Filled with these thoughts, he stepped briskly along, not much encumbered with luggage; for he carried all his wardrobe on his back. When he arrived at a spot called "Orange end," where four ways met, he was perplexed which to take, the oracle of Chapel-a-Frith not having apprised him of this dilemma, nor which road to take! Being quite in an oracular mood, very happy, that he had got so far away from Litton, and fully convinced, that, go where he would, and befall him what would, he could not blunder upon a worse place, nor be oppressed by a more evil fortune, he tossed up a halfpenny in the air, making it spin round its own axis, and waiting its course as it rolled, resolved to follow in that direction. Its course happening to be pointed towards New Mills, Derbyshire, thither he bent his course, but failed in his application for work. Blincoe, therefore, walked on, till he came to Mr. Oldknow's Cotton Factory, at Mellow, and there he crept towards the counting-house, in an humble mood, and said, in a very meek tone of voice, "If you please, Sir, can you give me work?" The manager, Mr. Clayton, a gentleman by no means deficient in self-respect, asked sharply: "Where do you come from?" "From Litton Mill, Sir." "Where are your indentures?" "There they are, Sir," said Blincoe, holding up the papers. There were two or three gentlemen, in the counting-house, and they looked earnestly over the indentures and then at Blincoe, one of them saying, "Did you come from Pancras workhouse?" "Yes, Sir." "Why, we are all come from thence! we brought many children the other

No. 7.

day to this Mill." " Indeed, Sir," said Blincoe, pitying, in his heart, the poor creatures, and thinking it would have been merciful to have killed them outright at once, rather than put them to such a place as Litton Mill had proved to him. Looking at the names of the subscribing officers and overseers, one of the Pancras parish officers said to Mr. Clayton : "Some of these officers are dead." Blincoe again exclaimed " Indeed, Sir,"— recollecting the atrocious lies and cruel deceptions, those men had practised upon him, in his infant years, by telling him to believe that, in sending him to a cotton-factory, he was to be made at once a gentleman ; to live upon roast beef and plum-pudding ; to ride his master's horses ; to have a watch in his pocket and plenty of money, and nothing whatever to do ! Poor Blincoe could not help thinking to himself :—" Where are the souls of these men gone, who, knowing the utter falsehood of their seductive tales, betrayed me to destiny far more cruel than transportation ?" The overseers, looking at the distorted limbs of this victim of parochial economy, said " Why, how came you so lame ? you were not so when you left London, were you ?" No, Sir, I was turned over, with the rest of the unclaimed 'prentices, from Lowdham Mill, to Ellice Needham, of Litton Mill." " How did they keep you ?—what did you live upon ?" " Water porridge—sometimes once, sometimes twice a day— sometimes potatoes and salt for supper: not half enough, and very bad food." " How many hours did you work ?" " From five, or occasionally six o'clock in the morning, till nine, half-past ten, and sometimes eleven, and, on Saturday nights, till twelve o'clock." The person wrote these answers down ; but made no comment, nor ever noticed the material facts ; that Blincoe had not been taught the trade he should have learnt, and that the parish officers of Pancras had utterly neglected him and his miserable comrades, when the Lowdham Mill factory stopped ! The manager then bade a person shew Blincoe where he might get lodgings, and bade him come to work in the morning. Blincoe was too much afraid of giving offence, by asking questions in the counting-house, to venture to enquire as to his parentage ; but, as soon as he had got lodgings, he strove to make out where the officers were to lodge that night, at Mellor, to enquire further ; but hearing they were just then gone, he was deprived of the opportunity ! This occurrence, filling his mind with melancholy reflections, he shed many tears in solitude that night ! The next morning, he went to his work, and found it was as hard as at Litton Mill ; but of more moderate duration—the hours being from six in the morning, till seven in the evening. The 'prentices, whom he saw at work, seemed cheerful and contented—looked healthy and well, compared with those at Litton ! They were well fed, with good milk-porridge and wheaten bread for breakfast, and all their meals were good and sufficient ! They were kept clean, decently dressed, and every Sunday went twice to Marple Church, with Mr. Clayton, their under-master, at their head ! On the whole, it struck Blincoe, that the children were in a Paradise, compared with the unfortunate wretches whom he had left at Litton Mill, and he indulged in the humane hope, that the lot of children just then brought down from London, might escape the dreadful sufferings he had had to endure ! Unfortunately, the trade, which Blincoe had been fourteen or fifteen years articled to learn, was by no means so good as husbandry labour. The wages, Mr. Oldknow offered him, were *eleven shillings per week*, at the time that a good husbandry labourer could earn from sixteen shillings to a pound ! After having been some months in M . Oldknow's factory, Blincoe learnt, that, whilst he did as much work, and as well as any man in the factory, which employed several hundred apprentices, Mr. Clayton had fixed his wages at three or four shillings per week less than any other person's. Blincoe could not impute this to any other cause, than an idea, that he was in so crippled a state, he dared not demand the same as another ! Such is the mean and sordid spirit, that sways almost the whole of those establishments. When a poor creatuue has been crippled at one mill, and applies for work at another, instead of commiserating his condition and giving him the easiest and best work and best pay, it is a common custom, to treat them with the utmost contempt, and though they may be able to do their work as well for their masters, though not with the same ease to themselves, as one who has escaped being crippled, the masters generally make it a rule to screw them down to the very lowest point of depression, and, in many cases, give them only half their wages. On this principle was Blincoe dealt with at Mellor Factory ; but, as the wretched diet on which he had been fed at Litton, enabled him to live upon three shillings per week, he saved money each week. Having an independent spirit and not being willing to work for less than his brethren, he took an opportunity one evening, to go to the counting-house and doffing his hat to Mr. Clayton, said, " Sir, if you please, will you be so good to rise my wages ?" Turning sharp round, he said, " Raise your wages ! why, I took you in upon *charity only !*" " I am sure it was very good of you, Sir," said Blincoe, who well knew that such hands as himself were scarce, therefore, that his charity began at home.— Hearing Blincoe speak in such humble, yet somewhat ironical terms ; for he possessed a rich vein of sarcastic humour, Mr. Clayton said, " Well, go to your work, I'll see." They paid every fortnight at the factory.— The next pay night, Blincoe found himself paid at the rate of thirteen shillings, which was still two shillings under the price of other workmen ! This continued a few weeks, when, an old servant, whom they had employed many years, applied for work, and on the Friday night fortnight, Blincoe's wages were sent up to him, with an order *to depart*. This is what is called *getting the bag*. Blincoe being alike surprised and hurt, and knowing he had done his work well and had never lost a minute, set an enquiry on foot, and he was told, from very good authority, it was because he had applied for an advance of wages, and because Mr. Clayton thought it was taking an advantage of him. Curious logic ! Mr. Clayton seems totally to forget the advantage he had, in the first instance, taken of poor Blincoe, and feeling very sore, when the young fellow applied for redress, he seized this opportunity, and, in this petty way, to wreak his anger ; and as the factory of Mr. Oldknow stood so very high, if compared with that of Ellice Needham, of Litton, these blemishes fully prove, how foul and corrupted is the spirit of traffic, since, in its best shape, it could not resist the temptation of taking a mean advantage of the necessities and the misery of a fellow creature.

Although the treatment of parish pauper apprentices was very liberal, compared to what they had endured at Litton Mill, the journeymen were governed by a very tight hand. If they arrived only two or three minutes after the clock had struck, they were locked out ; and those, who were within, were all locked in, till dinner time, and not only were the outward doors, below, locked ; but every room above, and there was a door-keeper kept, whose duty it was, a few minutes before the respective hours of departure, to unlock the doors, by whom they were again locked, as soon as the work-people arrived ! In every door, there was a small aperture, big enough to let a quart can through, so that the food brought by parents and relations could be handed to them within —no one being permitted to go in or out, and, of course, the necessaries, two or three to each room, were within side the room, where the people worked ! Such was the rigid order and severe discipline of one of the most *lenient* master cotton-spinners ! Mr. Oldknow caused a road to be made from the turnpike to his mill, which saved some length of way, and every stranger, or person not absolutely working in the mill, who used it, had to pay a halfpenny—and, as the road led to New Mills and Mellor, those work-people, in common with all others, had to pay a half-penny. There was a toll-house erected, and also a toll-bar, and the speculation, if not very neighbourly, is said to have been very profitable.

When Blincoe left this establishment, which seemed to vie with some of the largest factories in Manchester, both in its exterior grandeur, and in magnitude, he had contrived to save the greater part of his wages, and having a few pounds in his pocket, he felt less dismay at this harsh and unexpected treatment, than if he had acted with less prudence and been destitute. He had served faithfully and diligently upwards of half-a-year, and a character from so respectable an employer might be serviceable, he, therefore, made his appearance once more before Mr. Clayton, and doffing his hat, and assuming the most lowly and respectful attitude, said, in his usual slow and plaintive tone :—" Will you please, Sir, give me a character ?"—O no ! O no !" replied the manager, " we never give characters here," with an unfriendly aspect ! Blincoe thought it was better to be off and seek his fortune elsewhere, than stop and argue. This circumstance strongly marks the oppressive character of these establishments. It is clear, that Mr. Clayton did not chuse to hire Blincoe without a character, or something equivalent, by requiring to see his indentures ; and, after the young man had served them diligently and honestly, for six months, he surely should have written to certify, that he had done so, and the denial *might* have prevented his getting another employer. However the law might stand at present, upon this point, in any future legislative measure, a clause should be introduced, to *compel* every master to give a written character, except where some positive act of gross misconduct interposed to neutralise the claim !

From Mellor Mill, Blincoe walked to Bollington, in Cheshire, a village not far from Macclesfield, and about 18 miles distance, having a bundle, which, slung upon a stick, he carried upon his shoulder. He passed several road-side houses of entertainment, allaying his thirst from the living fountains, and satisfying his hunger with a penny cake. In this way, he travelled, till he arrived at Bollington, where he obtained work in a factory, situated on the Macclesfield road, belonging to a Mr. Lomax. He was placed in the card-room, which is reckoned the most laborious and unwholesome in the factory, on account of the great quantity of dirt and dust; but Mr. Lomax promised him a stretching frame, at the end of a fortnight. The fortnight having expired, Blincoe saw no signs of being relieved from stripping off the cotton from the cards. He made up his mind to be off, and march on towards Staley Bridge, in the hope of bettering his condition! As he was going along some fields, for a short cut, he was met by a couple of suspicious looking fellows, who, stepping boldly up to Blincoe, said in a stern voice, What have you got in that bundle?" I dunna know, Mester, but if you'll ask the gentleman on horseback, that is coming on the horse road, at the other side of the hedge, he'll tell you." Hearing this, and marking the calm indifference of Blincoe, the interrogators took to their heels, and never once looked behind them, as he could perceive; and thus the poor little wanderer outwitted the marauders, and saved his shirt and stockings, and, by the possibility, the hard-earned treasure he had in his fob. Having thus adroitly got rid of the thieves, Blincoe made the best of his way to the main road, and the best use of his legs, till he got in view of some houses, where he thought himself out of danger. Arrived at Staley Bridge, situate upon a river, which separates Cheshire and Lancashire, and where there are many spinning factories, he applied to a man named William Gamble, who had lived in Yorkshire. This man, twelve or thirteen years before, was one of the overlookers at Lowdham Mill, and very much addicting himself to kicking the apprentices and dragging them about by the hair of the head, up and down the rooms, and then dashing them upon the floor, on account of which propensity, he was reprimanded and removed, when the overseers of Pancras parish arrived. Indeed this man and one Smith, were the terror of the poor children; but Blincoe wanting work and knowing he was an overlooker in Mr. Harrison's factory, which, by way of preeminence, was called the Bastile, poor Blincoe had been so many years accustomed to Bastiles, he was not easily daunted. To Gamble he repaired, and who having bestowed so many marks of his paternal regard upon Blincoe, he recognized him at once and very kindly got him work at ten shillings per week, which he drew for the use of Blincoe, during a few weeks, to whom he acted as caterer, and provided him with a bed, so that Blincoe had nothing whatever to do, but his work, which was tolerably moderate, that is, compared with Litton Mill. Notwithstanding its unseemly appellative, the work-people were not locked up in the rooms, as at Mellor.

The master had another method of restraining his work people from going out, and which saved the pay of a door-keeper, namely, by the counting-house being so placed, the people could not go in or out without being seen! There Blincoe worked some months; but not being perfectly satisfied with the conditions in which the stewardship of William Gamble left him, he took the liberty to remove from his hospitable roof, and the result was, he could live upon and lay up one half of his wages. The wages paid at this mill were very low, and the work very laborious, being the stripping of the top cards ! The fixed quantum was six pounds per day, which is a severe task. After this, the master went up to Blincoe and others, as they were at work, and informed them, he would have more weight of cotton stripped off the top cards, or turn them away, and Blincoe not feeling inclined to perform more work for that pay, asked for his wages and left the Bastile !

Hence, Blincoe went to Mr. Leech, the owner of another factory, at Staley Bridge, by whom he was engaged at nine shillings a week ; but he found the cotton so foul and dirty, and the work so hard, he staid not long; as the owner paid only once in three weeks, it required some privation, before any wages could be got ! After three days toil, Blincoe went to his master and asked him to lend as much silver as his work came to, and, having obtained it, he took French leave, to the great offence of his employer. Blincoe still remained at Staley Bridge, though unemployed. He next obtained work at the mill of a Mr. Bailey, whose father had then recently had one of his arms torn off by the blower, and he died in a few hours from the dreadful effects of that accident. Here Blincoe stopped, stripping of 'cards, for eleven shillings per week, during several months, when, having saved a few pounds, he determined to try his fortune at Manchester, which celebrated town was only seven or eight miles distant. Of London, Blincoe retained only a faint recollection, and he thought Manchester the largest and the grandest place in all the world. He took lodgings in St. George's-road, being attracted by the residence of James Cooper, a parish apprentice from the same workhouse with himself, who had been so cruelly flogged at Litton Mill. By this young man, Blincoe was received in a friendly manner, and he lodged in his house near Shudehill. Blincoe arrived at Manchester at a bad time, just at the return of peace, and he had a difficulty of getting work. His first place was in the factory of Mr. Adam Murray. There the engines worked only four days and a half per week ; for which he received no more than seven shillings and a penny. Blincoe suffered much from the heat of the factories at Staley ; but in this of Mr. Murray's, he found it almost suffocating, and if there had been as great a heat in the factory at Litton, added to the effects of long hours, and bad and scanty food, it is probably it had cut him off in the first year of his servitude ! Blincoe, thinking it was wise to risk the chance of bettering his fortune, left Adam Murray's gigantic factory, at the end of the week, and next went to work in Robinson's factory,* as it is called, which belongs to Mr. Marriet. There he was engaged to strip cards, at half a guinea per week. He worked at this several months, living in a frugal manner, and never going into public-

* Whilst Blincoe worked at Robinson's old factory, Water-street, Manchester, having, by denying himself even a sufficiency of the cheapest diet, clothed himself more respectably than he had ever been—and having two-pound notes in his pocket, he determined to spend a few shillings, and see the diversions of a horse-race, at Kersal-Moor—but not being aware that such beings as pick-pockets were in the world, he put his pocket-book in his outside pocket, whence it was stolen by some of the light-fingered gentry, and poor Blincoe had to lament his want of caution.

houses, or associating with idle company; but, when he was engaged, by the rule of the overlookers, he was forced to pay a couple of shillings, by way of footing, and then he went to a public-house in Bridge-street, where this silly and mischievous custom, let Blincoe into the first and last act of drunkenness, in which he was ever concerned, and he felt ill several days afterwards. At the same time, many of his comrades, who worked in the same room, and who contributed each so much money, got drunk also. This was spent contrary to Blincoe's wishes, who grieved that he was obliged to drink the ale. If he had refused, he would have been despised, and might have lost his employ; and if a poor fellow had been ever so low and wanted this money for the most essential purpose, it must not be refused. This is a pernicious custom, and should be abolished. Blincoe continued several months in this factory, living as it were alone in a crowd, and mixing very little with his fellow work people. From thence Blincoe went to a factory, at Bank Top, called Young's old factory, now occupied by Mr. Ramsbottom, and there, after a time, he was engaged as stoker, or engine man, doing the drudgery for the engineer. Here, he continued three years, sleeping a great part of the time on a flat stone in the fire hole. If it rained in the night he was always drenched! but he had formerly suffered so much by hardships, and the pay was so small, he determined to do his best to save as much money as might suffice to enable him to try to live as a dealer in waste cotton; from which humble state many of the most proud and prosperous of the master cotton-spinners of Manchester have emerged. His employer, liking him, raised his wages to thirteen shillings a week, and, whilst Blincoe was about as black as a chimney sweeper in full powder, the hope of future independence induced him to bear his sable hue. and his master behaved to him with more humanity, than he had been accustomed to experience. He was however disturbed by some petty artifices of the manager, in the year 1817, and an attempt being made to lower his wages, for which, upon an average, he worked sixteen hours in the day. Blincoe resolved to quit such hard, unremitting and unprofitable servitude, and from that period he commenced dealer and chapman. At the end of the first year, he found his little capital reduced full one-half; but on the other hand, he gained, in experience, more than an equivalent, to what he had lost in money, and, being pretty well initiated into the *mysteries of trade*, and having acquired a competent knowledge of raw or waste cottons, he commenced his second year, in much better style, and, at the end of that year, he had not only regained his lost capital, but added £5 to it.

Blincoe hired a warehouse and lived in lodgings. In the year 1819, on Sunday, the 27th. of June, he happened to be, with several other persons, at the christening of a neighbour's child, where several females were present. An acquaintance of Mester Blincoe's (no longer poor Blincoe,) a jolly butcher, began to jest and jeer him, as to his living single. There was a particular female friend present, whose years, though not approaching old age, outnumbered Blincoe's, and the guests ran their jokes upon her, and some of the company said, Blincoe, get married to-morrow, and then we'll have a good wedding, as well as a christening, to-day. Upon which Blincoe, leering a little sideways at the lady, said, "Well, if

Martha will have me, I'll take her and marry her to-morrow." She, demurely, said "Yes." Then, said Blincoe, though taken unawares, now, if you'll stick to your word, "I will." She then said, "I'll not run from mine, if you don't." Hearing this, there was a great shout, and when it had subsided, the butcher offered to bet a leg of mutton, that Blincoe would not get married on Monday, the 28th. of June, and others betted on the same side, when Blincoe determined to win the bets, and a wife in the bargain. Blincoe said to his comrades, "Well, that I may not be disappointed, I'll even go to see for a license to-night." Two of the party went to see all was fair. When Blincoe had got half-way, being fearful of a *hoax* by Martha, he hit on the device of holding back, telling her he could not get the license without her presence, and when she agreed to go, then still more securely to prevent his being laughed at, he said, "I have not money enough in my pocket, will you, Martha, lend me a couple of pounds?" In an instant she produced that sum, giving it to Blincoe, and they proceeded. Blincoe was so bashful he neither took her hand nor saluted her lips; but, accompanied by two of the persons who had laid wagers, went to the house direct, of the very celebrated, though not *very reverend Joshua Brookes*, lately deceased. The next morning they went in a coach from his lodgings in Bank-Top, and were married in the Old Church! Blincoe won his bets and his wife? They have lived together with as great a share of conjugal tranquillity, as falls to the lot of many, who are deemed happy couples, and he has ever since kept upon the advance in worldly prosperity. He has lived to see his tyrannical master brought to adverse fortune, to a state of comparative indigence, and, on his family, the visitation of calamities, so awful, that it looked as if the avenging power of retributive justice had laid its iron hand on him and them. In how short a time Blincoe's career will verify the prediction of the old sybil of Chapel-a-Frith remains to be seen; but it is in the compass of probability, that he may, in the meridian of his life, be carried as high, by the wheel of fortune, as the days of his infancy and youth, he was cast low!!

In the year 1824, Blincoe had accumulated in business that sum of money he thought would be sufficient to keep his family, with the exception of his cotton-waste business; shortly after he gave up a shop which he had occupied for a few years at No. 108, Bank-Top, Manchester, and took a house in Edge-place, Salford, whilst living there, thought proper to place some of the money he had saved by industry to the purchasing of some machinery for spinning of cotton—and took part of a mill of one Mr. Ormrod, near St. Paul's-Church, Tib-street, in this he was engaged six weeks, with the assistance of some mechanics, getting the machinery ready for work—the first day it was at work, an adjoining room of the building caught fire, and burnt Blincoe's machinery to the ground, not being insured, nearly ruined him.— Blincoe declares that he will have nothing to do with the spinning business again—what with the troubles endured when apprentice to it, and the heavy loss sustained by fire, is completely sick of the business altogether.

*End of the Memoir of Robert Blincoe.*

## CONFIRMATIONS OF ITS VERACITY.

Ashton-under Line, Feb. 24, 1828.

DEAR SIR—I have read the narrated sufferings of Robert Blincoe with mingled sorrow and delectation : with sorrow, because I know, from bitter experience, that they have really existed ; with delectation, because they have appeared before the public through the medium of the press, and may, peradventure, be the means of mitigating the misery of the unfortunate apprentices, who are serving an unexpired term of apprenticeship in various parts of Lancashire and Derbyshire. In 1806 or 7, I was bound an apprentice, with twelve others, from the work-house of St James,' Clerkenwell London, to a Mr. J. Oxley, at Arnold-mill, near Nottingham. From thence, after two years and three months' servitude, I was sold to a Mr. Middleton, of Sheffield. The factory being burnt down at this place, I with many others, were sold to Mr. Ellice Needham, of Highgate-wall, the owner and proprietor of Litton Mill ! Here I became acquainted with Robert Blincoe, better known at Litton-mill by the name of Parson. The sufferings of the apprentices were exquisite during Blincoe's servitude, both in point of hunger and acts of severity ; but, subsequent to Blincoe's departure from that place, the privations we had to endure, in point of hunger, exceeded all our former sufferings (if that were possible), having to subsist principally upon woodland sustenance, or, in other words, on such food as we could extract from the woods. What I now write is to corroborate the statement of Blincoe, having heard him relate during my apprenticeship, all, or nearly all, the particulars that are now narrated in his memoir. I may also add, that I worked under Blincoe, at the same machine, in the capacity that he had done under Woodward, without receiving any harsh treatment from him— nay, so far was Blincoe from ill-treating the apprentices employed under him, that he would frequently give part of his allowance of food to those under his care, out of mere commisseration, and conceal all insignificant omissions without a word of reproach — I cannot close this letter without relating an anecdote that occurred about two years ago. Happening to call at a friend's house one day, he asked if I knew Robert Blincoe I replied in the affirmative. Because, added, he, I saw a prospectus of his biography some time past ; and related the same to W. Woodward, who was on a visit here, and who immediately said, "HE'LL GIVE IT MA," and became very dejected during the remainder of his visit.

Your humble servant,

JOHN JOSEPH BETTS.

---

Samuel Davy, a young man, now employed in the Westminster Gas Works, has called on the Publisher of BLINCOE'S MEMOIR, and has said, that his own experience is a confirmation of the general statement in the Memoir. Samuel Davy, when a child of 7 years of age, with 13 others, about the year 1805, was sent from the poor-house of the parish of St. George's, in the Borough of Southwark, to Mr. Watson's mill, at Penny Dam, near Preston, in Lancashire ; and successively turned over to Mr. Burch's mill, at Backborough, near Castmill, and to Messrs. David and Thomas Ainsworth's mill, near Preston. The cruelty towards the children increased at each of those places, and though not quite so bad as that described by Blincoe, approached very near to it. One Richard Goodall, he describes, as entirely beaten to death ! Irons were used, as with felons, in gaols, and these were often fastened on young women, in the most indecent manner from the ancles to the waist ! It was common to punish the children, by keeping them nearly in a state of nudity, in the depth of winter, for several days together. Davy says, that he often thought of stealing, from the desire of getting released from such a wretched condition, by imprisonment or transportation ; and, at last, at nineteen years of age, though followed by men on horseback and on foot, he successfully ran away and got to London For ten years, this child and his brother were kept without knowing any thing of their parents, and without the parents knowing where the children were. All applications to the Parish Officers for information were vain. The supposed loss of her children, so preyed upon the mind of Davy's mother, that, with other troubles, it brought on insanity, and she died in a state of madness ! No savageness in human nature, that has existed on earth, has been paralleled by that which has been associated with the English Cotton-spinning mills.

No. 8.

# A LETTER

TO

## SIR JOHN CAM HOBHOUSE, BART. M.P.

ON

## "THE FACTORIES BILL."

### BY A MANUFACTURER.

> " Signior Antonio, many a time and oft,
> On the Rialto, you have rated me
> About my moneys and my usances.
> Still have I borne it with a patient shrug;
> For suffering is the badge of all our tribe."
> MERCHANT OF VENICE.

LONDON.

PUBLISHED BY LONGMAN, REES, ORME, BROWN AND GREEN,
PATERNOSTER-ROW ;

SOLD ALSO BY BIGGS, PARLIAMENT-STREET ; RIDGWAY, PICCADILLY ;

J. BAINES & CO., ROBINSON, INCHBOLD, HEATON, CROSS, KNIGHT, SPINK,
CULLINGWORTH, BINGLEY, AND HOBSON, LEEDS; INKERSLEY AND STANSFELD,
BRADFORD; WHITLEY AND BOOTH, HARTLEY, AND BIRTWHISTLE, HALIFAX;
MOORE, SMART, AND KEMP, HUDDERSFIELD ; AKED, KEIGHLEY ; BROOKE, DEWS-
BURY ; HARRISON, BARNSLEY; AND ALL OTHER BOOKSELLERS.

ONE SHILLING.

1832.

# PREFACE.

———

The Question of " the Hours of Labor, in Factories," has assumed an altered aspect since the following pages were written, the publication of which was abandoned as unnecessary, when the fate of Sir J. C. Hobhouse's Bill, as affecting Woollen, Worsted, Flax, and Silk Mills, became known. As, however, the Question is again agitated with redoubled violence, I have determined to submit them to the Public.

# A LETTER, &c.

## TO SIR JOHN CAM HOBHOUSE, BART. M.P.

SIR,

  I MAKE no exordium of apologies for addressing you,
as you are the introducer of a Bill into the House of Commons, for the regulation of the hours of labor in cotton,
worsted, and other factories; the provisions of which, as far
as relate to all but cotton factories, although ultimately
abandoned by you, are before the public, in the various
drafts of your bill, as amended in committee.

  Permit me rather to express my surprize and regret on the
occasion ; *surprize*—that you have so unexpectedly embarked
in a branch of legislation of no ordinary difficulty, and with
which the public is not wont to see your name associated ;
and *regret*—that you should place your political reputation
in jeopardy by so gratuitous and ill advised an undertaking.
—That you have spontaneously, and from personal knowledge and conviction, brought forwards your bill to abridge
the hours of labor of the working classes, I cannot believe :—
First, because I am not aware that you are connected with,
or have intimate and extensive acquaintance with the manu-

factories for which you propose to legislate, or that you possess even a general knowledge of the subject, derived from actual observation and correct information. Secondly, because, from your public career, I conceive you anything but prone to the grovelling interests of trade, or the sordid and prolix details of commerce.—For these reasons, and the internal evidence contained in the reports of your speech on the subject, and in a letter which has appeared in the public papers, I believe that you have been imposed upon by the exaggerations and misstatements of parties who conceive it is their interest to procure the passing of the bill, and that your fears and imagination have been more than ordinarily excited. On any other supposition, I cannot account for the circumstance of the " factories bill" having been introduced into Parliament—by the defender of civil freedom at home and abroad—the enlightened advocate of the cause of Greece—the uniform supporter of liberal policy—and the representative of, perhaps, the most enlightened constituency in the empire.

The unexpected opposition which arose at the eleventh hour, was dissolution to the factories bill, as far as it related to all but cotton mills. Would that it were final extinction to it ! Whether or not you propose to revive the subject, the public has yet to learn. Meantime the voice of no manufacturer has broken the silence which that body has kept on this question ; and I therefore feel myself at liberty, as no other opponent has arisen, to state to you and the public, what appear to be the inevitable effects of such a bill : for it appears so repugnant to sound principles of legislation, as to incur every hazard of *failure* in the *beneficial effects* it proposes to secure, but every *certainty* of the *evils* which it aims at *obviating*.

The terms which have been used by those who raise the hue and cry against the " factory system," are so strong and sweeping, that they who are personally unacquainted with the routine and discipline of the manufactories of the country, must conclude, that the practices which are prevalent therein, are cruel, wanton, and easy of removal. Indeed, every artifice and delusion has been put in requisition,* in those parts of the north of England, where the bill, and its notable provisions, have been agitated, to fix upon the employers of the population, the odium of the present condition of the working classes; and they have been represented in the most unscrupulous terms, " as tyrants and oppressors"—the abettors of " infant slavery," and adult bondage.

As might be expected from the impetuosity of the attack, and the blackness of the charges against the mill-owners, there have been found, manufacturers, who have pusillanimously sat down under these gross and foul calumnies, and have thus tacitly acquiesced in the truth of the charge by mute submission.—Others there are, who adopted a middle course, by acquiescing in the popular delusion ; and though disliking the hard names and strong terms applied to themselves, in common with the rest of the trade,—yet, by a timely confession of faith, setting forth their opinions, and very gentle censure of the bad language employed by the ADVOCATE of their cause, gained all the credit due for good intentions, and unabated adherence to their old and repudiated practices !

But a body of the worsted spinners of Yorkshire, above one hundred in number, did not thus mince matters, but they fearlessly declared their opinions upon the bill by petitions to Parliament, both as respected its probable effects on themselves, their trade, and the people employed by them.

* I here instance a poetical production entitled " The Factory Child," and an imaginary Dialogue in the Leeds (supposed) dialect; a more degraded picture of the working classes, than the one—and a more shameless libel, upon them and their employers, than the other—cannot be penned.

The draft of the bill before me, dated 24th March, 1831, which I believe is the last draft of the bill in that shape, briefly states the alleged ground of interference with the present usages of the trade, as follows :—" Whereas, it has, *of* " *late, become* a practice in cotton, woollen, &c. factories, " to employ a great number of young persons, of both sexes, " late at night, and in many instances, all night ; and certain " regulations *have become* necessary, to preserve the health " and morals of such persons. Be it therefore enacted," &c.* I will not stop to enlarge upon the assumption of the whole of the premises of this conclusion ; which, however, I am at present unaware to have been established before the committee, by a single particle of evidence; except, indeed, that be thought evidence, which consists of the bare affirmations of those who have been instrumental in inducing you to undertake this measure ; or the wild charges and violent ravings on the subject, which have appeared in a country newspaper : but I will take the opportunity of making a few remarks on the various branches of industry, which the bill proposed to embrace in its operaion.

With respect to the *actual* moral and physical state of the working classes, it admits of little doubt, that there is very little information to be gathered, which is to be relied on, except as local registers of the few cases reported upon. The fact is, I believe, that there is very little known to the rest of the community, of the general physical and mental condition of the poor; and unless disease and famine be added to poverty, the public at large knows little of the ways of the laboring

---

* The obvious intent of the words " *of late*" and "*become,*" is palpable. As there is no year of our Lord fixed in the preamble, as the era of the commencement of " *night work,*" a convenient and well studied vagueness is adopted, which will suit the 16th century, *if need be*, as well as the 19th. Shade of Arkwright!—Spirit of departed Peel !—custom immemorial—" *of late*" " *become.*" An usage " beyond the memory of man," " *of late*" " *become.*" ! !

classes, either as to their most urgent wants, or prevailing
prejudices.

I believe that in the manufacturing districts of Yorkshire,
which comprise the woollen, worsted, cotton, silk and flax
manufactories, little information respecting the comparative
degrees of influence which these branches of trade exercise
upon the population, has been accumulated, except in a
pamphlet on " The Effects of the Principal Arts, Trades,
and Professions; and of the civic States and Habits of Living,
on Health and Longevity, with particular Reference to the
Trades and Manufactures of Leeds : by C. T. Thackrah:"
a work which contains much general and minute information
on this subject; and which is characterized by benevolent
views and generous feeling, and at the same time, by a deep
conviction of the difficulty of securing the adoption of preventive remedies in general.*

A valuable paper on the effects of cotton factories, has
likewise been published in the North of England Medical and
Surgical Journal, by Dr. Kay, of Manchester, in which the
peculiar influence of that branch of industry appears to be,
chronic inflammation of the membranes of the stomach and
lungs, induced by the minute fibres of cotton-wool, and particles of dust, with which the atmosphere of cotton factories
is impregnated, being inhaled into the lungs. The distinctive

* On this point the author says, (p. 52—3) " But there is a strange
" apathy both among the men and the masters. Though very intelligent,
" and conversant not only with the science of their manufacture, but often
" also with knowledge in general, they are remarkably thoughtless on a
" subject which most deeply concerns them. Man after man dies of decay
" in the prime of life, and no warning is taken by the survivors. Machine-
" makers, indeed, are generally unwilling to admit the fact of excessive
" mortality. They naturally dislike the idea of being more subject than
" their neighbours, to disease and death. They will rarely admit that they
" labor under disorder till consumption is established, and its effects ap-
" parent to every observer. To our general questions they reply, ' we are
" all pretty healthy.' "

characters of the atmosphere of cotton, woollen, worsted, flax and tow, and silk mills, as an element of disease, deserve remark.

Cotton, it is well known, is extremely light in weight, and its fibre is short and buoyant. It is, therefore, from the nature of its staple to be expected, that there will be a considerable portion of the "flyings" of waste of the cotton, held in suspension in the atmosphere of a cotton mill;—and we are told by the medical authority above quoted, that this atmosphere, loaded with particles of cotton and dust, engenders a morbid irritability of the membranes of the throat, lungs, and stomach, and ultimately induces a chronic disease, called GAS-TRAGLIA. In the woollen mills, the peculiarity results from the effluvia arising from the oil, which is profusely used, in addition to the natural animal grease or yolk of the wool; and likewise from the dye, in which, in some branches of that trade the wool is prepared before its processes commence in the mill. The temperature requisite to be maintained in woollen mills, is, I believe, quite immaterial, which is a main point of distinction between them and the cotton factories.— The worsted mills are free from all the peculiarities of the foregoing branches of trade, from the nature of the staple material employed, which consists of the longest parts of the fleece, which *cannot be manufactured into worsted yarn*, unless washed perfectly clean, and rendered as free as possible from the natural animal grease and impurities of the fleece. This, I think, a material point of distinction in favour of the healthiness of the worsted trade; and one which has not been alluded to or considered by those who say that legislation is NECESSARY, as far as I am aware in this question. The short fibres which are disengaged, and fly off as waste, in the various processes of the worsted trade, are not of the injurious nature which the medical authority I have quoted ascribes to the cotton "flyings," as they are too heavy to be held in suspension in the atmosphere; and instead of floating in it, they accordingly fall to the ground. And from the very nature of the material employed, it is self-evident that this is a source of disease which cannot exist in the worsted trade.

The authority I have before quoted,—*(Thackrah on Effects, &c. page* 39,)—says, "spinners of worsted inhale a fine dust; but this is not in such quantity as to produce marked effect." This is *the only passage* in the whole treatise which relates to the worsted trade, and I take it as tolerably conclusive evidence in favour of the superior salubrity of this branch of industry.

Of the silk manufacture, I have no data to offer, and little experience; and it is besides a manufacture of more limited extent. From the nature of the material used, and its value, I think there is no hazard in stating it to be as cleanly an occupation as those I have last mentioned.

The flax and tow manufacture is liable to the same objections as the cotton; which, however, are more limited in degree though of nearly the same kind as in the cotton trade, and is undoubtedly less salubrious than either the manufactures of silk or wool;—as, like cotton, it is a vegetable fibre and partakes of a similar disposition to load the atmosphere with the fine particles thrown off in the manufacturing processes.

On a comparative review of the several branches of manufacture into which "the factory system" divides itself, viz :— The cotton, flax and tow, woollen, worsted, and silk manufactures, I believe it will be found on enquiry, among practical men, who have extensive means of observation, and a general knowledge of these branches of industry, that the silk, worsted, and woollen mills, are the most healthy, and the flax and tow, and cotton, the most unhealthy; and that they rank, in point of salubrity, in pretty nearly the order in which I have enumerated them.

There is one physiological fact which bears upon this
part of the subject, which seems to have been entirely over-
looked by those who contend for the sad ravages produced
upon the constitutions of those employed in factories. I
allude to the well known fact, that the human frame and
constitution will become acclimated to every variety of circumstance, and that if early inured to any particular treatment
or situation, man will live and enjoy existence, wherever
Providence has cast his lot. Now if we apply this well known
fact to the point in question, I think it affords a solution
of many apparent hardships and unfavorable conditions of life.
It is a quaint saying, —" What is one man's food, is another
man's poison." The exposure to the weather, which the
agricultural population and out-door laborers think no hardship, and seldom suffer from, would be death to those who
are inured to the climate of manufactories ; and *vice versa*,
nausea and suffocation would probably be the symptoms of
the country farmer, if translated to a West-Riding woollen
mill. So that all argument respecting the situation and
sensations of the operatives, founded on the supposed nature
of their occupations, and the *nervous imaginings* of those who
think " humanity" consists of roast beef and plum pudding—
country air—a temperature of sixty degrees—south aspect—
dry feet—brawny limbs—and rosy cheeks—is, to say the least
of it, " a most lame and impotent conclusion." There is
health in the factory, as well as in the field.

But when it is considered or known what kind of habita-
tions are in many cases occupied by the poor engaged in
factories, in towns, what the atmosphere they live in, when
emancipated from their labor, and what is the home they
exchange for the factory, I think few will be disposed to admit, that they are gainers in point of fresh air, ventilation,
or salubrity, by retiring to the narrow streets and squalid
abodes, in the vicinity of reeking dunghills, obstructed sewers,

and overflowing sources of pestilential malaria. Indeed, the factory is, to many of its inmates, frequently a palace, in point of every thing which contributes to salubrity.*

I might in this place notice many other trades notoriously injurious and fatal, which would form a curious but appalling detail, were I to collect and compare their mortality with those which form the more strict subject matter of this letter—such as " the Sheffield grinders," " white lead manufacture," &c. and the diseases incident to them : as " painters' cholic," "rupture," "opthalmia," " tubercular consumption," &c. to which few are not victims, and all liable—but though this would form a strong collateral argument against the alleged grounds on which legislative enactments on the subject, and details of manufactures are vindicated, and shew incontestibly that the factory system is not by any means so fatal as many of the employments in which the population of this country is engaged—yet I must neglect to avail myself of this line of argument at present, at whatever loss it may be to my undertaking. I will state my conviction, however, without reserve, that the degree and amount of disease produced by labour in mills and factories, is far exceeded by many other occupations which cause no clamour at the present day, among the sole possessors of " *humanity.*"

But whatever be the evils entailed by the system, there is one striking result of it, which is matter of universal notoriety ; and that is, that the reflection and thought necessary in the management of its occupations, improves the faculties and intellect of the population, to an extent which renders it the most intelligent mass, in the same station of life, which

* The reports made to the various boards of health, recently established throughout the country, attest the correctness of this description of the abodes of the poor, in towns. The reports, in fact, far exceed the sketch here given, of the situation and condition of those districts inhabited by the working classes.

is to be found in the world; and this, I conceive to be, so far, a signal advantage to the cause of civilization and human improvement. Nevertheless it is doubtless a strange and melancholy ordinance, as respects the present state of things, that those inventions of genius in chemical and mechanical science, and those wonderful improvements in the arts of life, the direct tendency of which is to increase the leisure of man, by rendering his labour infinitely more productive, should, under a diseased political constitution, seem to have a directly contrary effect. But without combating for a moment the asserted dreadful evils of the " factory system," and grant- ing for argument's sake, all that is insisted upon (and indeed is required!) by the restrictionists for their case, I will ask, what does it all amount to in point of fact? And putting the question into a tangible shape, as a practical question, I ask, does it form a case for legislative inter- ference, and one which can be removed by such a partial remedy as a specific act, which leaves the causes of the evil still unaffected and active? And I venture to say that it does not; and that so far from the contingent circumstances of " the system" being remedied or annihilated by the proposed nostrum, that they will be, on the contrary, ag- gravated to an extent which you do not contemplate or con- ceive of, and from which I am sure you would revolt, did you anticipate them.

These effects I will state as fully as I am able, and pro- ceed to put you in possession of my reasons, which coincide with the arguments of more than one hundred manufac- turers within the circle of a few miles, as declared in their petitions and resolutions against your " factories bill." Although you expressed high contempt for their opinions upon the subject, (which, however, are practical, and there- fore worth weighing) yet as that occasion is past, and your bill, as respects them, is as it were still-born, I am induced the more on that account, and by my high opinion of your general parliamentary character, to state them again, that you may pause and ponder upon the certain consequences of any such measure.

The last draft of the bill which I have seen, and which is dated 24th March, 1831, proposes to enact "That no " person under nine years of age, be employed in any factory " —no person under eighteen, to work in the night, nor " more than eleven hours and a half any one day, and " only eight hours and a half on Saturday,—not less than " one hour and a half per day to be allowed for meals,—lost " time may be worked up at the rate of half an hour per day, " between January and December of each current year, by " mills driven by water power :" but steam power is excluded from this privilege, though this complicated engine is by its principle, more liable to accident than a water wheel, which is the simplest motive power possible. Such are the main provisions of this bill, if I add summary punishment by fine upon the manufacturer who transgresses the appointed hour, one single minute.

It is not a little curious to trace the manoeuvres of its promoters, who forthwith fell upon the anti-slavery advocates, and charged them with inhumanity and oppression at home, or as it was technically termed, " *white slavery*," by way of set-off against the incessant attacks of the whigs on the system of " negro slavery." Thereupon the whig press waxed violently wrath, and being tender of its reputation, vindicated its humanity with eagerness, blowing hot or cold, according to the aspect of the stars! Even those who appeared at first aware of the difficulty of the question, if meddled with at all by the legislature, fell into the pitfall of their adversaries, in a short time and swelled the clamour for " protection." The dogma that infants are

" not free agents," was the watch-word of the restrictionists. Members of Parliament seeing the ferment, and how matters ran, and that the bill was a "cabinet question" in Leeds, caught the influenza "in the natural way," and seemed to tremble at the hobgoblin " white slavery," more than the grim spectre, " negro slavery." But, whatever lengths the negro emancipationists go on this question, the restrictionists will give them little credit. They have got the start, and will keep the lead till the delusion passes, or the spell is broken by the bodily presence of griping distress and experience.

But to return to the bill. The first and immediate consequence of limiting the ages of children employed, to " under nine years," will be to throw out of employment all that class of hands. This is perhaps the most cruel stroke to the poor man which could have been inflicted. It is inflicted, we are told, because it is necessary—and it is necessary, because children are not "*free agents,*" and their parents thus " prevent the *order of nature,* and live upon the earn-" ings of their children." Now, Sir, what the " order of " nature," which these self-styled philanthropists mean, is, I cannot take upon myself to declare, without making confusion of terms more confounded ; but this I *do* know, that PROVIDENCE ordains at present that children shall con-tribute to the support of their parents and family, in return (shall I say ?) for the care and protection, food and raiment, which their parents have afforded *them,* during the years of helpless infancy. And how such a state of things can be changed or subverted by Act of Parliament, I do *not* know, whilst all the concomitant circumstances of their situa-tion remain unchanged and unalleviated. But I will stop at the threshold, and protest against this threatened invasion of the rights of the parent over the child, as an infringement of the liberty of the subject, and a direct violation of the homes of Englishmen —whether attempted under the thin guise of such jargon as the phrase " free agency" of children, or in the more suspicious and questionable shape of humane consideration for those who are to be imposed upon.

To do justice to the *humanity* which prompted your advocacy of the supposed cause of the poor, as much exceeds my feeble powers of eulogy, as it exceeds the span of my comprehension to enter into your views on what appears to me so straight forward and plain a question. I trust, however, that it will not be deemed superfluous that I should fortify my poor judgment with authority ; especially as the author whom I can call to my aid on this occasion, is the most celebrated who has written upon the subject; and whom both you, and I, and every individual, who has expressed an opinion on the question, have as little pretension to call in question, as has insignificance to compare itself with originality and greatness. " The pro-
" perty which every man has in his own labor, as it is the
" original foundation of all other property, so it is the most
" sacred and inviolable. The patrimony of a poor man lies in
" in the strength and dexterity of his hands, and to hinder
" him from employing this strength and dexterity in what
" manner he thinks proper, without injury to his neighbour,
" is a plain violation of the most sacred property. It is a
" manifest encroachment upon the just liberty of the workman,
" and of those who might be disposed to employ him. As it
" hinders the one from working at what he thinks proper, so it
" hinders the others from employing whom they think proper.
" To judge whether he is fit to be employed, may surely
" be trusted to the discretion of the employer, whose interest
" is so much concerned. The affected anxiety of the lawgiver
" lest they should employ an improper person, is evidently as
" impertinent as it is oppressive."—*Smith's Wealth, &c.*—
*Macculloch's Edit. Vol.* 1, *p.* 201—2.

The right of the parent over the child, is that of nature —it is inalienable and indefeasible. It is a right no law can

call in question, as its exercise is no infringement of the rights
of society, but independent of all social institutions, being
contingent upon, and necessarily flowing from, the parental
relation.   If this right be called in question, then no human
right is worth a sheep-skin.   The bill is, in fact, a reversion
to the rude and barbarous legislation of Lycurgus, who also
took all the children of the state under hand, and enacted all
manner of cruelties under fine names, to fit them for his
purposes : but *the bill* " out-Herods Herod," and is more
unsparing than the savage Spartan legislator's edicts, which
fixed *seven years* to be the age at which children should cease
to be a burden to their parents, whilst the bill saddles the
British operative with an idle, unprofitable family, till they
be *nine years old*.   The veriest serf has as much control
over his offspring, as the English freeman would under
the bill.   And are we to be told that the British operative is
so brutish and degraded as not to be entrusted with that rule
over his family which his employer enjoys, though he be not a
whit more worthy of the privilege, nor its exercise more
endeared to him ?   Are we to be told that the working classes,
as a body, are so far sunk in degradation, and so prone
to oppression towards the children of their own loins, as to call
for the interference of the laws, and to justify the present
attempt against their firesides, and the privileges of their
homes ?   Can it be proved to the satisfaction of any reasonable
man, that the effects of such a measure are justifiable on the
ground, that a few instances of selfish depravity have been
ascertained to exist, or of " parents who prevent the order of
nature, by living upon the labors of their children ?"   And
can you, Sir, consent to be the instrument of such blind
legislation—legislation which deals with the exception in defiance of the great and indisputable rule—that the laboring
classes of this country are not the callous and unfeeling
tyrants over their offspring, which some would represent
them to be ?

If, Sir, you have indeed magnanimity enough to contemplate, unmoved, the wanton bereavement of the means of existence and comfort from hundreds of families; how, let me ask, will the " order of nature," as it is termed, be confirmed or restored by your bill, when the parents cease to receive the wages now earned by their children ? Is industry, manufacturing skill, population, capital, and intellectual progression, to stand still or retrograde " as the act of Parliament directs," because want and improvidence, misery and guilt are in the world ? Is it consistent with equity— with plain reason—with common sense—that every such family as consists of children under the proscribed age, (of which there are hundreds,) shall be subject to want, to distress, and to idleness, because it is an alleged violation of an alleged " order of nature," that many parents have been reduced, by vice and misfortune, to so low a state of poverty, as not to have wherewithal to subsist upon, but the earnings of their children ? And when these families are rendered idle and unprofitable, who will provide those formerly industrious children with their bread—that bread, too, which has been so wilfully and wickedly snatched from out of their mouths ? Oh, what a consolation it will be to such families, that they, forsooth, have time for mental recreation and improvement ! Think you, Sir, that the mechanic, when returned home from his toil to the abode of his miserable family, will be in the vein to induige in intellectual pursuits, or be in a tone of mind to moralize on the political condition of his country, when the reflection is forced upon him by every object before his eyes— that he is compelled to waste those hours in idleness, and unpaid, which were once so heartily devoted to the service of his family, now around him in want ? Think you, that the man with a family of seven or eight children, " under nine years of age" (and there are thousands of such instances) who is a hard working industrious weaver, or a laborious diligent comber, will ply his task the more contentedly, because the factory doors are closed against his children, and they crowd their fireless home in ignorance and rags—ignorance of what they might have learnt—and in rags because they are thus in profitless ignorance? What, if the father of this family be himself out of employment—what, I ask, will be their situation? What avails the aid of the parochial pittance, now "dwindled to its shortest span" in consequence of the unusual calls upon it—calls which have rendered it a grievous burden to the community at large—a burden increased by a special Act of Parliament—an Act of Parliament framed upon the most crude and contradictory principles—although, forsooth, in harmony with a certain imaginary " order of nature !" I will not enlarge farther upon the operation of this part of your bill, on other parts of society; which, however, I firmly believe will be felt most seriously by others than the immediate sufferers; but I will proceed to point out how the next clause I have enumerated, will affect the other classes of work-people employed in factories.

In worsted mills, the departments of spinning, twisting, and winding are performed by those under eighteen years of age. There are exceptions, perhaps, in all these departments, but the statement is correct in general terms. They will be curtailed of half-an-hour's actual attention to business and labour per day, and they will have an hour and a half allowed besides this for meals. What is the practical effect of this provision? Why that the work-people will be actually detained and confined by the labors of the day, thirteen hours instead of twelve as at present. Now without remarking severely upon this provision, I must say that it is the most notable I ever remember to have heard proposed for the improvement of the working classes; and so thoroughly demonstrative of the principles of the bill, as to baffle all parallel, and confound all simile. But let me next shew you, Sir, what is the consequence of reducing the actual term of labor, half an hour per day—and that will be half an hour's wage deducted from the day's wages, that is, half a day's wages per week. This is as certain and inevitable as that to-morrow or wage-day will arrive—and it is, in fact, nothing less than strict justice, according to the present wages of these classes, which, I believe, are equitable, and governed by supply and demand. This may seem very arbitrary and grinding, but, nevertheless, so it will be. For one consequence of the present irrational clamor for protection, by certain Yorkshire spinners, is, that it has produced a strong feeling of disgust and aversion to the bill, among that class of men, by whom alone, the provisions of the bill can be carried into effective operation, and by whom any other measures of amelioration in the general management and details of the factory system can ever be brought into force. To clamour and jargon have been added gross invective and insult, and the aspersions thus cast upon them (I believe most unjustly and falsely,) have tended less to convert them to opinions thus promulgated, than even that lack of argument and practical knowledge which have been brought to bear upon the question. IT IS BEYOND DOUBT, WELL UNDERSTOOD, THAT A PROPORTIONATE REDUCTION OF WAGES WILL BE GENERALLY ADOPTED, WHEN *(if ever)* THE FACTORY BILL BECOMES LAW IN YORKSHIRE. The working classes, who, though often deluded upon points of speculative opinion, on account of their partial information, are generally shrewd and sound in their practical views, will see the cause of the change, and the alleged reasons for it, when their employers put the bill into their hands, and will ultimately, if not immediately, become convinced, that the reduction of their wages *is not from any natural cause*, such as supply and demand, scarcity and superabundance of hands, or the necessities of a bad season of trade,—*but that it is an artificial and wilful visitation upon them*, inflicted by an act of Parliament, which will relieve the situation of neither manufacturer nor laborer; but which has been passed in obedience to the cry originally raised by interested parties, and is converted into a punishment upon those who have been their dupes.

But what will the restrictionist do on the pay-day ? Oh, he of course will pay the old wages for the " *short time*" which he has been exciting his work-people and the whole country to demand, and he will now, doubtless, be in a prosperous state, being afraid of no " needy manufacturer," who pays wages according to the length of the day—and being quite confident of a brisk demand for his goods, which, be it remembered, however, now are rendered dearer by his having artificially increased the value of labor. This is the only course for the restrictionist. Let him never dream of reducing wages to an equivalent standard, as he values his character ! He may, to be sure, *profess* to give the present wages of twelve hours labour, for the hours (whatever they be) which are restricted by the bill—but no other manufacturer will throw away his capital in this manner, whilst there is such a superabundance of labor in the country, but will pay *ad valorem*. The restrictionists, however, will soon be brought to their senses, when they find their rivals paying *ad valorem wages ;* and unless we mistake them, they will contrive to creep out of the dilemma under cover of their favourite pretext, " *competition*," and undoubtedly fall in with the prevalent prejudices in favor of the *depreciated standard of wages,*—wages, let it be remembered, forced upon the population by an act of Parliament, which defies all experience, and violates every sound principle of legislation.

I doubt not, Sir, that you have become, during the deliberations on the bill in committee, acquainted with the many peculiarities of circumstance and locality which embarrass those manufacturers who are dependent upon water power—how that dry seasons on the one hand, and the floods of spring and autumn on the other, arrest the progress of industry in every department of such mills; but there are other circumstances which relate to the usages of this class of manufacturers, which I cannot take for granted you are familiar with; and therefore, I will show how these customs and arrangements are the offspring of experience and necessity, and how they will be deranged by the proposed interference. It is a general custom among them, that when the mill stands, by reason of any casualty above named, that the hands employed go home till the mill begins to work again, and no abatement is made in wages for this stoppage, but the full wages are paid, and the lost time is worked up by degrees. But see the consequences of the bill upon this part of the system. The bill provides " that the abovementioned time of daily labor " shall extend at the rate of half an hour per day, until such lost " time shall have been made good, but no longer. Provided " also, that no time which shall have been so lost during any " year, from the first day of January to the thirty-first day " of December, shall be worked up in the subsequent year;" which indeed very much resembles the tortoise overtaking the hare! After this rate of working up the time, one day lost will require *twenty-three days* to recover it. Now if any spinner is so unfortunate as to lose a week's work in December, it is gone for ever, as the grand and crowning absurdity of the clause, enacts, that what is legal on the thirty-first of December, is illegal on the first of January, and irrecoverable *because* the year of our Lord is no longer 1831 ! Let us see, however, what would be the redress of the spinner if he should lose a week in the summer months—or in August, September, or October. According to the above clause, if it requires twenty-three days under the bill, to work up one day lost, it will require 132 days to recover a week's loss, or thereabouts—but as there remain only about 132 working days between the first of August and the thirty-first of December, he must be a

most excellent manager who can regain what is irrecoverable !
Now the greatest obstructions occur, perhaps, during the
months above-named, varying, of course, indefinitely ac-
according to localities. It follows then, that *all stoppages
after the first of August will be a dead loss of time,* so that the
pretended bonus of working up lost time is all a delusion, and
will not prevent the stoppage of wages; than which event, if
you can imagine any more serious calamity to a poor family,
after a week's idleness, I confess my powers of comprehending
the horrible exceeded.

There is a body of manufacturers of worsted, which consists of individuals who have accumulated a small capital,
which they have invested in machinery, and employ chiefly
by spinning for hire, materials which belong to others.—
They generally occupy a room, or part of a room, in the
small water wheel mills in the valleys of the West-Riding
of Yorkshire, and are provided with as much "*power*" as
they require for their machinery, from the wheel they all
employ in common. These men are, for the most part, fathers,
who employ their own families. They are at once, masters,
bookkeepers, overlookers, and mechanics. Now mark the
injustice of the bill to these honest and industrious men. It
stops their machinery, interdicts the labour of their families,
and throws the younger children a dead burden upon their
hands—and all this evil unmixed with good—because we are
pompously told that " the order of nature is prevented."

But if there be any real ground of charge and complaint—if
indeed these manufacturers are so savage and unfeeling in their
families as to be matter of notoriety, the fair way of remedying
these abominations is to put the charges to the test. There is no
need of factory bills to abate such evils, for the law is sufficient *now* to punish such offences against the person, when sub-

stantiated; and it is a pitiful mockery of society to pretend to remedy the inevitable evils and disadvantages of manufactories, by heaping

" Line upon line, and precept upon precept."

The magistrate will settle the matter at once, if there is any tangible offence proved; and if there be not, then, indeed, no legislatorial specific can be devised, which will not inflict an equivalent evil upon some other part of the patient. As in the natural body, the presence of disease is indicated by the out-breaking of virulent humors and local disorders—so in the social body, the diseased state of society is denoted by the various burdens which harass the productive classes.

Now in the one case as in the other, these disorders are symp-tomtic of the disease, but they are not the disease itself, which is a complication of disorders, and which cannot be cured by plasters and washes applied to the surface of the body, (which, if they produce any effect at all, will only drive the disease to some other perhaps more dangerous and vital part)—but it must be treated with strong and more active means, curative and preventive, such as experience and sound practice suggest and sanction. A broad measure alone will reach the case of trade and population. Isolated Acts of Parliament, like the plasters and washes of the quack practitioner, only heal over the sore at best, if successful,—often inflame it the more—at all times are temporizing and empirical expedients.

Now there are laws against every imaginable crime, from the most atrocious which infringes the personal freedom of the subject, to that which, by even a breath, affects his fair name —laws, whose ponderous mass and perplexing details are a very proverb—the perfect knowledge of which almost sur-passes the powers of any one human mind—which in themselves I believe contain the very essence of civil freedom, and the

spirit of social existence—and still they are too weak—mere
cobweb fabrics—for the detection and apprehension of the
great and wide-spread " tyranny of the factories !" What then
is this undefined and undefinable crime which is unknown to
the laws of this country ?   What is this offence and oppression
which is so subtle as to have evaded the law itself ?

I fear that in answering these questions, I may be charged
with insinuating that there is inequality and injustice in the
laws—that the administration of them is partial and corrupt—
that there is any offence against the person, which can be properly so called, which the law does not overtake.  But I must
state that there is an usage of this realm, which circumstances of POLITICAL MISGOVERNMENT, EMBARRASSED FINANCE,
COMMERCIAL DIFFICULTY AND DENSE POPULATION, have
combined to produce, and which is called in some parts of
this country, by the name of " white slavery." Notwithstanding that I have considered the circumstances to which
the population is subject in the various pursuits of industry ; I find that this " white slavery" is little akin to the
slavery of the negro.  I find *the one* a free man, whose rights
are known to, and defended by, the law of the land, alike against
the oppression of the most powerful, as the vengeance of his
equals :—*the other*, a poor passive slave without an acknowledged right, or will of his own.  I find *the one*, cultivating
the field which is his freehold, or plying the loom at his
will, returning to his " house, which is his castle," with the
wages of his labor, which are at his own absolute disposal :—
*the other*, toiling under a broiling sun, beneath the eye of the
task-master, for a handful of maize, clothed as he is fed, at
the caprice of his owner, who is his absolute lord and master,
and who can dispose of his labor as of that of any beast of burden.  I find *the one* surrounded by a family of which he is the
natural and acknowledged head and guardian, from which no
human law has a right or the power to separate him, whilst

God preserves to him a sane mind. *The other*, a father indeed
of a family—but alas ! their powerless parent and ineffectual
guardian—liable to be snatched from his home and family at a
moment's warning, and without appeal, whenever his owner
shall think fit.—Can this be the same slave, whom the British
operative is said to resemble so closely ?

Now with respect to this " Slavery in Yorkshire," I will
lay before you two statements respecting the length of the
hours of labor in various manufacturing districts abroad,
which have appeared in the public papers, and which, as they
are affirmed upon unquestionable authority, and remain un-
contradicted, I hold to be correct as to the fact stated. *

" There has been much said about the length of the hours
" of labour in factories in this country, which have been repre-
" sented to exceed all that the world ever saw, and to be far
" worse than negro slavery. I will, for the information of the
" public, lay before you an account of the customs of our
" manufacturing neighbours of both continents. The state-
" ment is from the mouth of a man who is practically and
" intimately acquainted with the subject, by a residence of
" some years at the places where the system is pursued, and it
" is confirmed by the evidence and testimony of another who
" has had similar opportunities. ' In the states of New York,
" Ohio, Jersey, Pensylvania, and generally throughout the
" United States of America, which are engaged in manufac-
" tures, the hours of labour in mills (in the summer half
" year) are from sun-rise to sun-set ! The bell rings at three
" o'clock a. m., the mill begins to run at four, and continues
" till eleven a. m. ; they rest two hours during the heat of the
" day, and run from one p. m. to seven p. m., or thirteen
" hours per day. In the winter half-year, they commence at

* See a letter, published a few months ago, in the Halifax and
Huddersfield Express, signed " VINDEX."

" half-past five a. m. and run till twelve o'clock, dinner one
" hour, and run from one p. m. to half-past seven p. m., i. e.
" thirteen hours and a half per day.' This is the routine in
" the land of Liberty and Equality, the chosen land of
" freedom and independence, where personal and public
" liberty are enjoyed in a perhaps greater extent than in any
" other nation in the world.

" In Germany, the Netherlands, and France, the cus-
" toms of manufactories appear to be much alike. In summer
" they begin the day at five a. m. and, with the interval of
" one hour for dinner, run till eight p. m., i. e. fourteen hours
" per day. They receive their wages every fortnight, on
" Saturday afternoon, when they stop at five p. m. On the
" alternate Saturdays, however, they work up the three hours,
" and actually run till ten o'clock at night.* In winter they
" work from daylight, (or about half-past seven) till nine, with
" one hour for dinner, i. e. about twelve hours and a half
" per day. Such is the statement which I am assured on the
" evidence of two persons who have been at, and subject to
" the discipline practised at the places named, and who posi-
" tively affirm that such are the prevailing and general customs.
" I add no comment, but give the statement as I received it,
" leaving it to be weighed by those who assert, ' Yorkshire
" slavery' to be unparalleled."

In corroboration of the accuracy and truth of these
statements, I will make another extract from Dr. Lardner's
Cabinet Cyclopœdia, Vol. xxii ; " Treatise on the Silk
Manufacture :" which bears remarkable testimony to the same
facts, and is entirely independent evidence.

" The French and Italian throwsters are still contented if
" their spindles revolve 300 to 400 times in each minute,

---

* This, let it be noted, is *seventeen hours labor for that day.*

" while ours are performing commonly 1800, and sometimes
" even 3000 gyrations in the same space of time. Our French
" rivals are fully aware how greatly the English throwsters are
" in advance of them in this particular, but have not the same
" inducement that exists in this country, to incur a heavy-first
" expense in alterations, that they might secure a prospective
" advantage. The wages paid in Lyons, to men employed in
" silk-mills, *does not average more than six shillings and six-*
" *pence per week;* and the earnings of women and girls, who
" form five-sixths of the number of hands employed, scarcely
" exceed three shillings per week, for which pittances the
" whole are required to labor fourteen hours *per diem.*"

The following passage from a letter of the celebrated
O. P. Q., the correspondent of the Morning Chronicle, dated
10th December, is confirmatory of the accuracy of the facts
above stated :—" Little did those who made the barricades
" and fought at them, and drove away the Bourbons, and the
" priests, and the jesuits, and the courtiers, and the titled, of
" France,—little did they think that the same budget
" would be proposed—more taxes be laid on the millions—an
" enormous and monstrous civil list be demanded—and the
" public money be expended in altering the gardens of the
" Tuilleries, to make private walks for the citizen king, and
" his sons and daughters ! ! AND THIS AT A TIME WHEN A
" WORKMAN AT LYONS GAINS TENPENCE PER DAY TO
" SUPPORT HIMSELF, HIS WIFE, AND PERHAPS TWO OR
" THREE INFANT CHILDREN unable to work on account of
" their tender years."

It has been insisted upon as a great hardship, that in many
factories, no stoppage has been made for breakfast or tea ; and
at first glance it does appear an oppressive and inconsiderate
regulation. But on examination into this usage, it is found
like all other customs, to be founded upon some good

D

reason. It is true indeed that the machinery runs round, business goes on, and time is saved, (which will be lost under the bill)—and it has hence been hastily concluded that the children, "like beasts of burden, must eat whilst they work." Now what does this formidable charge amount to ? Why, that it is a mere fabrication and extravaganza, and that if it exist in any such cases, it is most rare, and the result of gross mismanagement. There are in every mill, extra hands, called "doffers," who change the bobbins when full, and also sweepers, who clean the floors, machinery, &c. whom it is usual for the overlookers to leave in charge of those machines whose managers are about to take their meals. They are then at liberty to sit down and take their food with comfort, and by this arrangement avoid exposure to the frost and snow, and wet dirty streets, which the bill would compell them to traverse twice a-day, to their expence in comfort, clothing, and waste of time. This arrangement is so natural and practicable, owing to the great variation in the hours at which the parents bring their meals, continuing in some mills from half-past seven o'clock till nine; and at tea-time, from four to half-past five; that it is evident the objection is made by no practical man, most of whom know the aversion which the children who live at a distance show, to leave the mill even during dinner hour, in bad weather. But as it forms a charge of apparent cruelty against the body of worsted spinners, I reply to it in order that those who are unacquainted with the details of that trade, may be in possession of the explanation.

As for the health of the younger branches of those who are employed in factories, I repeat the words of the petitions of the worsted manufacturers to Parliament, viz :—" that the " period between fourteen and twenty-one is the most critical " period of life, in those employed, and that those of the ages " between seven and fourteen are more capable of undergoing " long continued labor, than those of the ages before-named.

" For confirmation of this opinion, we would appeal to all the
" medical men of the district." In support of the soundness
of this practical opinion, I shall not cite the names of a
hundred manufacturers who have daily and hourly experience
of the regularity of attendance and alacrity of their youngest
hands, and who declared this to be their deliberate opinion ;
but I will quote Mr. Thackrah himself once more—an authority, I think it will be granted, not inclined to lead to " self-
interest" and " extortion,"—still less to soften down the case,
or suppress the facts he produces. " The substitution of
" *children* for adults produces less apparent immediate evil—
" *young persons are observed to bear the occupation much better*
" *than those of full age.* They *do not* manifest serious disease
" in the lungs. They are indeed very sickly in appearance,
" and their digestive organs become impaired, but they make
" no urgent complaint, and are able to pursue their labor with
" little interruption. At thirteen or fourteen years of age they
" are dismissed from the mill, or transferred to another depart-
" ment, and thus they avoid the effects of bronchial irritation,
" which at a later period might have led to consumption,
" *a disease known to be most fatal between the ages of eighteen*
" *and thirty;*" p. 44. Again: " Why then, it may be asked,
" is not the effect of the dust in such circumstances marked
" and immediate ? The vis-vitæ, we may reply, the conser-
" vative principle, is particularly active *in children.*" These
quotations, be it remembered, are Mr. Thackrah's opinions on
the influence of the flax manufacture, a branch of labor tenfold
more uncleanly and insalubrious than the occupation of woollen
or worsted spinning.

I ask you then, Sir, is it not the strongest collatteral evidence in support of the truth and accuracy of the fact declared
in those reviled resolutions of the worsted spinners of Yorkshire ; resolutions, let me remind you, which have never yet
been met by sound argument, and uncontroverted as incon-

trovertible by big words and bad language? I repeat, that the health of those employed in worsted manufactories is not surpassed by any class of subjects in the British dominions. But if their hours of labor be restricted, I cannot pretend to say to what extent the effects of inadequate food aad worse clothing, may extend; but this is certain and undeniable, that an impoverished diet and scanty clothing are the very elements of epidemic and active disease, and I respectfully submit this bare, but significant fact, to your further consideration.

But to the point at issue, let me enquire how the health and morals of the population are to be secured by lessening the duration of labor only half an hour per day, or even a whole hour per day, as some restrictionists would curtail them? How is health to be improved, how are evil communications and acquaintances to be counteracted by half an hour's respite from the sources of contagion, whilst the children are still exposed to them all the rest of the day? Is it not self-evident that if either the physical or moral atmosphere be infected, that nothing but strict quarantine can prevent infection. If exposure to the source of infection for a single hour be sufficient to produce disease, how can the effects of ten, eleven, or eleven and a half hours' association with the causes, be counteracted by half an hour's earlier removal, or by anything but total absence from exposure?

Nothing short of this, if there be *malaria* either in the atmosphere of the factory itself, or in the life and conversation of its inmates, will secure exemption, if it be not secured already. Prohibit all labor in factories, and then they cannot be charged with ruining the health and morals of the people; but unless you take this step, you cannot eradicate the inherent evils of manufactories—you cannot change human nature and human infirmity—you cannot overthrow strong and frequent temptations. You may limit the term of labor, and the earnings of the working classes employed—you may reduce the length of the exposure to evil, a twenty-fourth part of a day, or even a twelfth, but this will avail no more than to fix limits to the rolling tide of ocean, or the boundless powers of thought.

It is not a little curious and instructive to review the various attempts which have been made to provide for or counteract the multifarious circumstances of trade, and the various contingencies of industry, by legislative enactment. In fact, the statute book is loaded with abortive and obsolete acts relating to Trades, such as the cotton trade, the hosiery trade, the silk trade, the button-maker's trade, and even the tailor's trade. But what avail all these statutes? why they are a mere dead letter, and no more regarded than so many old ballads. These acts, however, are still in force, and as much part and parcel of the law of the land as the most valuable act of Parliament ever passed; but who ever dreams of enforcing them? The reason is obvious. The law has aimed at too much and attempted what it is not able to do; that is, to control the natural privileges and course of trade, and to adjust by the rule and square of authority, the contracts between master and workman, and the fluctuating details of productive industry. To these venerable relics may be added many modern achievements, which, though they are in their object and intent, worthy and well meant, yet have failed by the inherent weakness and insufficiency of the means employed, to carry them into effect. Such as the famous "smoke burning act," which it was predicted, would purify the manufacturing districts and towns, and make grass grow on the very chimney tops. But what is this in practical effect? all smoke! Then there is "Martin's act," a most humanely intentioned act, but as inadequate to protect brute animals from ill-treatment as it is to make butchers and knacker-men humane and kind, by act of Parliament.

Now these acts are founded upon the same common basis as all other partial interests, and certain greater monopolies, (which shall be nameless in this place,)—they may exist a few months or years at most, and either be repealed by another express act of Parliament, or die the natural death of absurdities; but still they are *fallacious,* dead or alive—and *injurious,* inasmuch as they lead the mass of society to put their trust in quack remedies, and distract the public mind from the great and wasting pestilence which originates and propagates them all.

Various causes have conspired to promote this piecemeal legislation, and none so powerfully as the delay of reform in the constitution of the house of Commons itself,—a cause of evil and an impediment to good, which has been far too faintly estimated by those who suffer under it. Attention has been called to various evils in society, at sundry times, when they have reached the crisis of their fate, and in order to pacify, and in hopes to aleviate, *and by way of getting rid of the subject,* the approved practice has been, (and is to this day) *" to bring in a bill,"* which is duly read and passed, and the subject is dropped pro-tempore, though the real cause of the evil *is untouched* by the bill provided, and to say the truth, is in most instances, quite beyond the reach of any solitary measure unaccompanied by more general means of alleviation. Thus we have " corn law" after " corn law," and " game bill" after " game bill," each approaching with reluctant step nearer than its predecessor to the point, which it ought to have started from, but still at immeasurable distance from those sound principles which ought from the first to have been the foundation and basis of legislative measures. The number and motley variety of these acts is evidence in itself, of the unsound and disordered state of the commonweal, and a convincing instance of the fruitlessness of those patchwork repairs which are effected by " putting new cloth into old garments."

It is now bruited in the ears of the country, that the bill is a popular measure among the working classes themselves— and that they are all in favor of it. The circumstance of the apparent popularity of the bill, however, is, a very sandy foundation for a legislatorial superstructure, though at all times encouraging to architects and contractors. But, be not deceived, Sir John, by addresses of "committees of over-lookers,"—do not imagine that these documents are independent or spontaneous emanations, or that any set of men is so blind as to be really enamoured of reduced wages, and make this calamity the subject of a petition to Parliament. The very circumstance of *this exhibition* of overlookers, and the cut and dried style of their whole proceedings, confirms suspicion of an *underplot,* and that they are mere puppets which facilitate the grand plot. They know the part they are to perform, be assured, and they are, I have not the slightest shadow of doubt, instigated, if not gently compelled by *superior influence.* " The factories bill" is, in fact, a mere political tool of their betters, the fashionable test of " fit and proper persons" to serve in Parliament. Would these men, think you, sell their birth-right for such a mess of pottage, were they unconstrained ? They know little of the *main game,* be contented. The " anti-slavery" party however, have been regularly badgered into the adoption of the Shibboleth.— Two out of the four county members have been forced to open their mouths in perspicuous language, and even the very embryo candidates of " an unrepresented town," have most unmercifully been " put through their facings," by the incessant attacks of " the uncircumcised." The prostitution of this vaunted " measure of humanity" to selfish and sinister purposes, is not an imaginary or conjectural degradation. It is disgustingly notorious and of weekly occurrence, for " the Genius" of the delusion still works the spell after his own fashion, in the same spirit of fanaticism and cunning which presided in council, in the beginning. But as to the mass of the people, I most firmly believe, from all I have been able to gather, that they know as little of the real character of the bill and its practical effects, as they do of the Khan of Tartary. Those who have heard of the bill, have been *told* that it is " a measure of humanity," and that if it passes they will only work eleven hours and a half per day, but every allusion to reduced wages is sedulously avoided, and this part of the question is at once overpowered by hallelujahs, hosannas and exclamations of " glory," " victory over darkness !" &c. &c.—These arts have quashed all reasonings and have superseded the necessity of argument *on this question*, as on many others before it.

It is stated by some restrictionists, that eleven hours and a half per day is long enonugh for children to be kept at work. Others state ten hours to be their favourite maximum. For my own part, I do not scruple to state, that considered as an ABSTRACT QUESTION AND PUTTING ALL THE CIRCUMSTANCES OF THE CASE OUT OF CONSIDERATION as a practical question— that I go beyond them all—and that I should like the hours of labor for children to be reduced to six hours per day. But like most other abstractions, 1 fear that this would be impracticable in daily experience. I should be, indeed, rejoiced to see half the time now engaged by the toil of the body, occupied in the culture of the mind—I should contemplate such a state of society with delight and hope, when the earliest years of the children of the poor, were employed in the expansion of the reason, in the acquirement of knowledge, and in lessons upon all those points which concern rational creatures and accountable moral beings : and I know only *one reason* why the children of the poor *are not* educated like the children of the rich—why *they* learn to work before they learn to read—and why *their superiors* in worldly advantages, learn every thing and anything before they learn the means by which they are one day to shift for themselves in the world. And that reason is, BECAUSE NECESSITY DEMANDS IT OF THEM ; and necessity we know, seldom gives any other reasons for its orders.

The laboring classes know this truth instinctively. They are seriously impressed with it from childhood ; they know it in manhood by experience ; and they think it not a hardship to labor, but a hardship and an imputation on their characters to be idle. It is a reproach among the respectable of the lower classes to live without visible occupation, which is at once an imputation upon their honesty, and a slur upon their character. When, however, I come to reduce these aspirations and benevolent wishes to practise, and when I come to consider the practical consequences of such a measure, even in its most modified application, upon those whom it proposes to benefit, I find such philanthropy as this quite unfit for daily wear—a mere closet system of philosophy—a dreamy abstraction—and as mistaken and galling a kindness as it would be to clothe the working classes in purple velvet, or brocade, and regale them with the elegancies of high life, amidst the calls of want, and the cries of poverty.

I should wonder sometimes at the inconsistencies of the restrictionists, did I forget how mankind differ on plainer questions far than this, and how clamour and wrong names to wrong things have lead men to risk the substance for the shadow, and to endure folly and want, and misgovernment and tyranny, for the mere echo of the *name* of liberty. I am conscious that advice and expostulation, nay even the voice of reason and the very finger of demonstration have failed to convince men on practical questions, long before the factories of England were raised on her wealth-creating streams, or ever the flocks yielded their snowy tribute to the husbandman. Still I do not doubt that a much shorter time than many of the restrictionists would contemplate, as probable, will turn

E

the tide of the delusion, which so many of them, in my opinion, are afloat in. A day has brought about mightier revolutions of opinion than this, and a single season of distress has effected more powerful changes in the popular mind.

Having stated what I believe will be the effects of the factories bill, or any similar measure, upon the working classes themselves, I will turn to the other view of the question, viz. ;—how it will influence trade and capital.

There can be no doubt that the quantum of goods produced in mills and factories, will be diminished in direct proportion to the curtailment of the hours of labour. What are the consequences of such a step ? *Dearer goods,* that is, dearer clothing—*decreased profits,* therefore, *slower* accumulation of *capital,* or of the fund out of which the wages of labor are paid—*diminished trade,* that is, less demand for labor—*less money in circulation,* that is, " bad-times" for the shopkeepers, and want and starvation for their former customers. Now trade depends upon the perfection of the means of production, and the ability of the customer to buy at a remunerating price to the manufacturer. If it is encouraged and promoted by dispatch and rapid execution of orders, which save interest on capital invested, and likewise make a quicker return of profits, it will be checked or injured by every thing which taxes the commodity with delay or expense, as these add to the cost of all articles of commerce, and must ultimately be paid by the consumer—as the manufacturer takes these expenses into his calculation on fixing the price, below which it does not remunerate him to manufacture. Now a bill which renders the hours of labor shorter, makes labor itself dearer, by making it less productive ; and if labor be dearer, the manufactured article will be dearer too, and in proportion as

it is dearer, it will be further out of the reach of ordinary customers, and thus affect the general demand. When trade is
depressed, competition is always felt in its most desperate form.

It is the avowed object and argument of the restrictionists
that the bill is to "*put down*" competition, by shortening
the hours of labour; thus, by decreasing the quantity of goods
produced, "*too many* will not be made," and consequently
goods will always be at a "fair price." *If there be* "a demand
for goods," those who have the power to produce the greatest
quantity, will fare the best; in other words, the *largest and
most wealthy manufacturers.*—for though *they*, like the small
manufacturer, can only work the legal number of hours, yet,
as they can command capital, they will increase their machinery
*ad libitum;* meantime, if a brisk demand arise, prices must
rise with the scarcity of goods, and this too will suit their
case exactly, for their goods will be at a monopoly price. The
bill is as perfect an engine for the purposes of the " monied
interest," as was ever conceived. It gives the capitalist a
grand opportunity to " pull down his barns and build
greater," like the miser in the parable; but to the " little
manufacturer," who has been cajoled into the vulgar error,
that, like the reform bill, it will abolish taxes, make rivers of
milk and honey flow through the land, and mend trade and
wages—to him, it will say, in a voice of thunder, " EXCLU-
SION—EMBARRASSMENT—RUIN." There is, indeed, ample
provision in store, for those who can command as much capital
as they can wield, but gradual exclusion to that class of
manufacturers, whose industry constitutes their main capital,
and all which they can command.

Yet, in the face of the notorious fact, that large
concerns can manufacture cheaper than small ones, the
restrictionists clamour for "*protection*," (as the wolf in the
fable protested against the lamb, which was on the other side

of the stream,) and attempts to pin down his inconsiderable competitor, by the strong arm of legislative restriction. Now competition arises from some necessity. What creates the necessity? I answer, Taxation, Monopoly, and Population. The "gluts of the market" are effects of the same necessity, and they will not be stopped by reducing the productive powers of labor, and the price of wages, till the above causes of obstruction to trade be also removed—or till hundreds of manufacturers are ruined—and till goods are at such a famous price as to be out of the reach of Dutch, Belgians, and Russians alike.

I have pointed out; in another place, whom and what description of manufacturers the bill will injure the most, and I now add, that they are the only effectual agents in keeping down the price of the manufactured article, from their limited means and moderate expectations of profit. If this class of manufacturers be sacrificed to the avaricious and narrow minded cry of the more wealthy, the trade will become as clean a monopoly as the East India Company's trade with the East; and it will run the risk of being driven out of the country, by the extortion of those who can afford to hold stocks of goods, so that the English merchant may probably be in no long time superseded by foreigners. This may be ridiculed as impossible—it may be scoffed at as preposterous, by those who put their trust in "Parliaments," but I would remind them and you, Sir, that England owes the very "woollen trade itself," to the tyranny and intolerance of a foreign legislature; and that America first commenced her career in manufactures under the guidance of those artisans whose skill has been rendered profitless, and whose home has been made a disgrace to a civilized nation, by British misgovernment and taxation.

And what, let me ask, will be the state of the Working Classes during these revolutions in business, with Rates and

Taxes, Corn Laws, and burdens of every kind still pressing upon them—worse fed and if possible, worse clothed than now, and abundance of leisure time provided by the "humane" for them to turn their attention to these edifying topics? I am appalled, Sir, by the bare anticipation and possibility of such a scene of horror; but I assure you, most solemnly, I can see no other issue than *one*. It requires little imagination to fill up this grim and shadowy outline, and to call to mind the riots of Spitalfields, and the burnings of the Quartier Rousse, at Lyons.

It is commonly supposed to be the first step towards the cure of any grievance, that its Causes and Origin should be well understood, and taken into the account. It is upon this principle, Sir, that I take the liberty of pointing out to your attention the circumstances and real origin of what are termed "The evils of the Factory System." Now it boots not, in considering this question, to blink the *real causes* of the disease, unless indeed you fear that it is above your skill, and that you cannot compose any effectual prescription,—and as I have not seen the question grappled with in a bold, comprehensive, and statesmanlike way, by those who have undertaken to settle it by legislation, I will plainly state the real causes of the evils of the factory system, and what the only sound and practicable remedies. As it cannot be disguised, and ought not to be concealed, that Causes which I will enumerate are the sole adequate parents of the physical and mental condition of the working classes, so it cannot be affirmed with truth, or the slightest particle of reason, that the employers of the population have been either the CAUSES or the WILLING INSTRUMENTS of reducing all classes of industrious men to their present state. There were seeming ground for the charges of tyranny, and avarice, and oppression, so often fulminated against the manufacturers, if they were making fortunes *at the expence* of the population—if the profits of trade were so enormous, and the accumulation so rapid, as to realize wealth without risk or trouble—but all these designing charges wither away before the fact, that capital is a *drug*—profit a *shadow*—rapid riches, a tale of the last century—employment, a scarce article, often indeed a real charity, yet received with thanklessness, though bestowed at the risk, and frequently to the loss of the manufacturer.

In the first place, I point to the present *commercial policy* of this country, as one of the main causes of the evils of the factory system,—a policy, which, by restricting and coercing alternately, makes sport of the productive industry and mercantile enterprize of Great Britain—a policy which says to the working man, that he *shall* buy his loaf of the dearest grower—and to the merchant, that he *shall* be debarred from certain markets, open to all the world but himself for the sale of his goods,—a policy which renders capital a burden, and labor a drug—which turns to bitterness the ingenuity of the manufacturer and the skill of the mechanic—to whose paralysing agency, all the misery and anomalies of trade are traceable, and which, if it be suffered to exist, will, in spite of all temporizing expedients, undermine the trade, and rot " the wooden walls of Old England."

In the next place, I point to the sudden and arbitrary changes which have been made in the " *Currency*." Indeed I have done it injustice, in not giving precedence to it, for in comparison with this, all other causes of commercial distress fall back into the shade—compared with this, all the petty frauds of the vulgar are harmless pleasantries. * " Is there, " Sir, any natural want or impediment in the soil or situation " of England, which can produce all the untold misery which " exists among her population ? We have mines which

* From a Letter recently addressed to the Editor of the Morning Chronicle.

" had better have remained buried deep in the bowels of
" the earth, than afford no profit to those who work them.
" We have iron, coal, lead and tin, which had better been denied
" by nature, than continue, as at present, a bottomless abyss of
" capital, a melancholy source of ruin to their proprietors.  A
" population most industrious, but for which we cannot find
" occupation, without abandoning every idea of profit as pro-
" ducers.   We have chemical skill and mechanical power,
" such as Archimedes never dreamt of, and which, with our
" rail-roads and canals, would long enable us to hold cheap
" the rivalry of nations, if we did not presumptuously
" increase our difficulties, and so load ourselves with gratuitous
" obligations as to make equality or rivalry with communities
" of more simplicity, impossible.  By a revision of our mone-
" tary system *alone,* this fall will be averted.  Its procrastina-
" tion has made the poor poorer, and the rich less wealthy.  It
" has encumbered the opulent with the pressure of the needy
" and infected the necessitous with a deadly hatred of property
" and social institutions.  Men will bear adversity when their
" own folly has produced it—they will quietly sit down under
" privation which their own crimes or imprudence have brought
" upon them—but no number of men will or ought to submit
" to be ruined for the acquisition of a theory" which at once
increases our taxation, fetters our commerce, limits its extent,
saps its security, and indicates its decay.

I next point to " *The Debt,*"—but what is even the ever-
lasting interest of *this* immense and incomprehensible amount,
in influence, compared with the two causes I have already
named !  How vastly is " The Debt" increased in weight and
pressure by the one ;—what a hopeless scheme is its liquidation,
without the most prosperous estate, and very highest condition
of the other !

I know there are some who will ask with a self-satisfied
air, " What has debt, and taxation, and monopoly to do with

" the hours of labor, and what good can come of mixing up
" these questions with the ' Factories Bill ? ' "    To such
characters, (whether they be knavish or foolish) I will answer, that *these evils* are the *very root of the matter*, and
the adequate causes of the effects in question, and that so long
as they continue to exist, it matters not whether men work
twelve hours per day, or stand idle, for these will hang like
mill-stones round their necks, weighing them down lower and
lower ; and not only labouring men, but all the productive classes, till their employers approach nearer and more
near every year, to the condition of the unemployed.  It is
idle to pretend that national and political causes, are not the
authors of unprofitable capital, languishing manufactures, and
long hours of labour.  It is vain and silly boasting to say that
trade will be rendered prosperous or more tolerable by a bill,
which at one stroke, reduces wages and profits, and renders
the manufactured article so much the dearer to those who
wear it.   But it is presumptuous folly, to say that the modern
system of manufacturing industry, which concentrates scores
and hundreds of individuals in the same apartments, can be
divested of its inevitably contingent evils and disadvantages by
Act of Parliament, and that the dense manufacturing population of this country can be reduced to an aboriginal state of
simplicity, and primitive innocence of manners, by a Bill
which leaves them in the very midst and centre of all that is
opposite and counteracting.

I will not occupy time or space in delineating the super-
added and subordinate causes of misery in the situation of the
working classes.  Improvidence hand in hand with penury—
waste combined with want of economy, in the daily household
matters of the working classes—compassion and high-feeling,
with grovelling selfishness, and brute sensuality—these, alas !
in various ways, oft make the cup of bitterness flow over into
the bosoms of the poor.

But there is one other element of misery to England, which I cannot but allude to on this question, because it has a most serious influence upon their own condition : 1 mean—*Population*. And here, let it be remembered, I do not mean to contend that there is too great a population for the country at present, within it—nor on the other hand, that " there is too much capital"—nor again, that " population" has or has not " overtaken provision." These knotty points of disputation I leave unassailed in all their pride and prowess. But I do maintain, that so long as labor itself is subject to the unlimited competition of a yearly increasing population, and trade be systematically thwarted and obstructed—so long will length-ened hours of labor be unavoidable.

I am well satisfied with the sneer which has been thrown out against the principles laid down by the opponents of restric-tions and fetters on trade and industry. I am content take to myself and my fraternity, any epithet and opprobrium which may be bestowed on those views which have been designated " cold-hearted Scotch philosophy." A man may affect to despise the laws of material philosophy, as well as of political philosophy—he may deny the laws of animal life—he may cavil at the solar system, or dispute the theory of gravitation—but it is not therefore the less true that all these affect his exist-ence and well-being, and that every hour of his life depends upon their uniform operation, although he be as insensible to the facts and principles themselves, as the clods of the valley. So also a man may call principles, and a train of reasoning which he does not understand, or has not tried to understand—" cold-hearted" or " Scotch," but it proves less than nothing against the general principles of political economy and " non-interference" with trade and labor. But it proves this much against him, that he does not comprehend what he presumes to pass judgment upon, or he would have avoided offensive allu-sion to a *name* which is immortalized, and a *nation* which is

**F**

quite as proverbial for sagacity as himself.  It is, however, late
in the day for such puny attacks to succeed as they are intended.
Time and circumstances are bringing about changes which will
open the eyes of the politically blind and wilfully perverse, and
w   develope these principles in spite of  names and titles
of party.

I have before pointed out  the necessity of the immediate
removal of the pressure of taxation, a mitigation of  the effects
of the sudden and fraudulent changes in the currency and
the present commercial policy of Great Britain, because I cannot conceive of the most remote possibility of any change for
the better, in the character of the " manufacturing system,"
whilst these sources of  evil weigh down the energies, and
circumscribe the boundaries of this " nation of shopkeepers,"
as we have been called.   But in addition to these remedies, I
state, as of vital consequence to this country, the adoption of
two other measures, which I sum up in those emphatic words,
" *Cheap corn*" and " *Free trade.*"

When that time comes, for come it must, when all " protection" shall be denied, all patronizing and chartering
refused, all " prohibition" prohibited, all unfair one-eyed
policy discarded, when the interests of the *consumer* shall not
be sacrificed to the avarice and influence of the producer,
depend upon it, Sir, we shall hear of  no complaints of
markets glutted with goods, artisans starving by scores, and
manufacturers undersold by the foreigner.  Free trade and
unrestricted commercial intercourse with all nations is the  best
and truest interest of Great Britain ; it is a policy which every
season of distress and every cause of national fate advances,
and which every  prospect of the  times appears to indicate as
fast approaching.  Look, Sir,  at the gigantic confederation
of fifteen American States against the impositions and injustice
of their Tariff, and their plain and manly resolutions, ex-

pressly asserting their right of access as *consumers* to the *cheapest*, and as *producers*, to the *best customers* they can find to deal with. Consider the weight thrown into the scale, and the grand turn which is given to the question, by these thriving republicans, whom we have compelled to imitate our " exclusive" weaknesses, in self-defence against that policy which has excluded them from free dealing in every possible commodity. If these States see the policy, and insist upon the adoption of these principles, which secure to the consumer the best article at the cheapest rate, and to the producer the markets of all the world and the customers of all nations: how can England stand against the rivalry of such a system, by dint of dear corn, which is starvation to the manufacturers? or by such aid as short hours of labour, which render all manufactured articles dearer?

How is the British manufacturer to stand against the competition of the foreign manufacturer, who exchanges his goods for the cheapest corn he can buy, and who employs his workpeople fourteen or sixteen hours per day, and only pays them about half the price of English labor?

If this country is ever to be delivered from the " evils of the factory system," rational means must be adopted to secure this end. Hunger will not be allayed by half a meal of dear corn—employment will not be increased by bad trade—full wages will not be obtained for short hours of labor—industry cannot be rewarded if capital be unprofitable—the arts and manufactures will not be extended by prohibiting the manufacturer to sell to the best customer, and by exporting wool, the raw staple of England, at a nominal duty, for the accommodation of the foreign manufacturer. Neither will any class be benefitted by restrictions on labor, or by having goods rendered dearer, whilst the foreigner is untaxed and unrestricted, and is more benefited and encouraged, the higher that English goods rise in price—*for the higher the price of British manufactures, the better for the foreign manufacturer.*

I will not recapitulate the various arguments and opinions which I have thrown together in the preceding pages, for that might tire and disgust; but, I would, nevertheless, implore you, Sir, to consider the present state of *domestic political feeling*, the *privations*, the precarious *subsistence*, and the beggared *condition* of the mass of the *working classes*—the impaired *means*, and the straightened *circumstances* of those above them—the languishing and decaying state of the *Commercial* and *Agricultural interests*, and the prostrated powers of all the capital, talent, and honest industry of the nation. Ingenuity has strained her last effort—Genius taken her highest flight—Invention has become barren. If talent, if skill, if honourable ambition and unstained reputation, in the pursuits of industry and in the arts of peace, could have secured to England the blessings of plenty, and public happiness, her population have earned these ten times over. But still she pines away and declines!

How long will industry be fettered—will enterprise be quelled—will naval power and greatness be sacrificed—our ships rotting in our habours—our merchandise perishing by moth and worm ?

Think besides, Sir, of the present *situation* of this country ; think of her *prospects*, politically, commercially, abroad and at home ; think of an increase of machinery and a decrease of wages ; think of artificial embarrassment and wilful calamity ; think of the working man ; think of the manufacturer, and then answer, if it is not a mockery of all classes, to tell them to put their trust in a measure which will render dearer the blanket of the poor man, and the broad cloth of his employer, tie their hands upon their backs, and take the bread out of their mouths, upon the most flimsy and fanatical pretences that were ever heard of?

Let me once more point to the INJUSTICE of the bill—injustice to the father of a family, and injustice to his employer. What amount of suffering and want, in the one case, it will produce among the *hundreds* who will be thrown out of employment, and the *thousands* who will be curtailed of their wages and domestic comforts—no tongue can tell. What amount of capital it will throw down and trample under foot, in the other, my pen in vain can estimate. The engagements, leases, and contracts that will be forcibly and fraudulently violated—the thousands (may I not say millions?) which are invested in manufacturing stock, and means of production that will be locked up by the reduction made of the hours they now are in constant employment—is a question of common arithmetic which I leave to restrictionist, to reckon up his own way. When divided by a *twenty-fourth*, or a *twelfth*, or a *sixth* of the time he now employs that capital in active production, I think it would appear a monstrous sum to throw away, or to lock up and disable without good reason. But when, in addition to this sum, I add the amount of the reduction of wages, of money taken out of circulation, and out of the hands of those who are now contented, healthy, and industrious, I find myself scarce able to restrain the loud and strong expression of those feelings of indignation which rise in my breast against the injustice, incredible folly, and cruelty of this measure.

Again, Sir, let me warn you of the effects of this measure, which will not only add to the pressure now existing upon the working classes, but entailing difficulty and ruin upon the upper classes of society, will push national decay towards its catastrophe. This, Sir, is no dreamy or croaking foreboding of misanthropy. The fate which awaits England, if it be not speedily averted by sound measures, will fall upon her in her security, irresistably at last. It has been the fate of the most wealthy, the most enterprising, and the most powerful commercial states of antiquity, whose locality, whose history, and whose very names are now only " as a tale that is told." And what exemption can England claim from the common consequences of national prodigality and decay? What avail her unrivalled skill in art—what her perfection in manufactures—what the fame of her illustrious citizens and wise men— what her christian profession—if starvation, vice, and horrible distress prevail, and happiness be not secured to the " greatest number."

Thus, Sir, I have endeavoured to put together my ideas upon the main points of the question of the hours of labor in factories; and in doing this, I have stated my opinions boldly and strongly. But whatever be the feebleness, or whatever the failure of my arguments, they have the support and uncontrollable assent of my judgment and conscience. If any such bill should ever become law, *whatever* be its effects, which I believe inevitable—*whatever* its consequences, which I dread— I, at least, have this exemption from responsibility, and this satisfaction from within, that I have attempted to discharge that which I believe to be an imperative duty, by stating my conscientious and oft considered opinion without reserve.

I am, SIR,

Your obedient Servant,

A MANUFACTURER.

# POSTSCRIPT.

THE Restrictionists, it seems, have risen in their demands, and they now say that nothing less than a "ten hours' bill" will satisfy them. And accordingly, the necessities of the times have furnished them with a champion in the person of Mr. M. T. SADLER, M. P. for Aldborough, If, in the arguments I have advanced in the following pages, against *the late* factory bill, there be any cogency or force, that force is more than doubled against the proposed restrictions of Mr. M. T. SADLER. And if the worthy gentleman understands the subject at all he must know very well that his only chance of *benefiting* the working classes, and of sustaining his popularity, is in the *failure* of his own bill. Indeed, it seems odd that Mr. M. T. SADLER should have become the champion of the working classes thus late in the day, after having given such faint and feeble support to the late bill, when before the consideration of Parliament. But then, it must be remembered, by way of explaining this seeming inconsistency, that such also was his conduct on the question of " Negro Slavery ;" and that the emancipationists did not receive Mr. M. T. SADLER's active support, " till the fit and proper time" arrived for him publicly to advocate Negro Emancipation. So that Mr. SADLER's conduct is as consistent upon the Factories Bill, as upon the question of the Slave Trade.

" Perish Trade ! Sink Commerce !"—was the significant exclamation of THE AGITATOR on a late occasion,—" if they are to be supported by the present hours of labour." This ejaculation of wisdom and statesmanlike talent, is an epitome of the spirit, arguments, and notions of the party, on this subject; and as it cannot fail to carry with it its antidote into the bosom of every working man of understanding and principle, I spare all comment upon it.

If, indeed, the working classes, or any individual manufacturers are influenced by such reasoning, there is no hope of them—experience must be their school of learning—embarassment and poverty their task-masters. If combinations for temporarily raising wages, and attempts to create an artificial demand and fictitious high prices, be yet not understood by all classes of artisans—if the effects of vexatious impositions and restrictions

—delay and unnecessary obstacles to trade and manufactures, be not yet comprehended by mercantile men, more trials must be undergone, and more difficulties, beggary, and ruin, be endured by the operative and commercial classes of this country. If the real character and " working of that system" which has reduced the country to its present state, be not yet known to the working classes, in all its doubles and windings, it is high time for them to study it. Let them sit down to learn it forthwith—to trace the *effects* to the *cause*—undisturbed by the profane cajoleries and mountebank capers of the abettors of Monopolies, Abuses, and grievous Taxation. I would call upon them to remember (if they can have forgotten) that they were told these gross absurdities and injurious measures were for their benefit and advantage, by the *same friends* who now tell them to pursue as their chief good, that " ignis fatuus," a Ten hours' Factories Bill. Let the working classes reflect too, that their employers were taunted as jacobins and levellers, when they opposed those ruinous and abominable measures which have reduced them to their present condition, by the *same party*, and in the same spirit, as they are now branded as " tyrants and oppressors."

I would implore them to consider *what* the bill will do for them, and *what* it will rob them of—*whom* it is pretended that it will benefit, *and whom alone* it will serve. Let them consider the question as it respects themselves—*not* the Agitator, or Tory Candidate for Leeds;—as it concerns their *families* and *homes*,—despising and rejecting the profaned voice of abused scripture—as it affects their *employers* and their *country*, without suspicion, breach of charity, or malice.

T. WRAY, PRINTER, 18, BRIGGATE, LEEDS.

# A LETTER

TO THE

RIGHT HONOURABLE

## LORD VISCOUNT ALTHORP, M. P.,

CHANCELLOR OF THE EXCHEQUER;

IN DEFENCE OF THE

# COTTON FACTORIES

OF

## LANCASHIRE:

BY

## HOLLAND HOOLE.

---

" AUDI ALTERAM PARTEM."
" LAISSEZ NOUS FAIRE."

---

MANCHESTER:
PRINTED BY T. SOWLER, 4, ST ANN'S-SQUARE.
—
1832.

My Lord,

THE observations to which I have the honour to call the attention of your Lordship, are occasioned by a Bill now before the House of Commons, intended very greatly to reduce the hours of working in the Cotton, Woollen, Linen, and Silk Mills of this country.

I beg leave to premise that I address your Lordship in defence of the Cotton Factories only : my knowledge of the other branches of our national manufactures referred to, being limited to mere report. Moreover, the Cotton Manufacture has long exclusively enjoyed the advantage (if it be such) of Legislative interference with its hours of labour, by enactments of various dates ; and may well therefore claim another hearing, before it be subjected to further restrictions so oppressive and injurious as those contemplated by the Bill now before Parliament.

My Lord, it is a trite observation that British industry excels that of any other nation in the world ; and it is also a truism, that the artificial situation into which our political course has conducted us, requires all the exertions of all His Majesty's subjects, to preserve us from national embarrassment and decay.

The degree of labour required from, and put forth by every order of society, from the Statesman to the meanest Artizan, is often irksome, and in many cases injurious to health.

It is taken for granted, however, that the higher and middle ranks are able to protect themselves against excessive labour, and Legislative protection is thought necessary for the poorer classes only.

4

The advocate of Legislation passes by and wilfully overlooks the multitudes of mere *handicraft* labourers; not because labour both excessive and injurious to health is unknown to them, but because of the impossibility of limiting the hours of working of sempstresses, tailors, shoemakers, dyers, colliers, miners, and persons employed in a hundred other unhealthy trades,—and he fixes his attention solely upon the labour connected with MACHINERY *moved by Steam or Water power*, because there his task is easy; for such machinery being itself clockwork, is capable of being regulated with the utmost exactness of the clock. It is not because the labour connected with machinery is more excessive or more injurious to health than hand labour, but because of the facility with which it may be restricted, that the attention of the Public and of the Legislature is so frequently called to the subject.

My Lord, there are three principal classes of persons who clamourously ask for the further enactment in question.

The first is composed of the Philanthropists, so called, who generally know little or nothing of the subject, and who are anxious to shew their benevolence at the expense of other people: united to these are to be found persons who, from mistaken motives, would, if possible, entirely prohibit the use of our modern machinery.

The second are the Demagogues, who, besides their general object to promote discontent, and derange the order of society, have a special dislike to Cotton Mills, because the precision of their regulations interferes most effectually to prevent the weekly assembling of thoughtless crowds to listen to their inflammatory speeches.*

The third class comprehends descriptions of the Ope-

* It was for this reason, avowedly, that the plan of holding Seditious Meetings on the Sunday, was recently adopted here, which has been promptly suppressed by the Magistrates.

ratives themselves, who, having formerly enjoyed a sort of monopoly in their particular departments, enabling them to dictate laws to their employers, are vainly anxious for the restoration of a state of things which can never more return.

Such are the parties, my Lord, who, having long ago commenced a violent attack upon the Cotton Factory system, now seize upon the opportunity which presents itself to inflict the severest blow upon this great branch of our national industry, which it has ever yet experienced,—that of annihilating the usefulness of young persons employed therein.

It has long been the boast of our Cotton Manufacture, that thereby " the Capital of the country has been brought to the people;" but it may not be so fully known to your Lordship what is the amount of capital thus " brought" to each individual employed.

Permit me to inform your Lordship, that a Cotton Factory, upon the fire-proof principle, adapted for the employment of 1000 persons, can not be built, filled with machinery, and furnished with steam engines and gas works, for a less sum than £100,000. It follows that the capital furnished to each individual, man, woman, and child, employed therein, is (on the average) £100. In other words, each person is furnished with *tools* to the value of £100, (exclusive of the raw material) wherewith to meet the world in the market of labour.

No wonder that, with such advantages, hundreds of families have risen from the rank of mere day labourers, to opulence and independence; and that thousands more are placed in circumstances far above the fear of want, and in a state of comfort superior to that of the middle classes in any other country in the world.

It cannot escape your Lordship's attention, that the day labourers themselves derive immense advantages from this large outlay of fixed capital; both in the security which it affords them of constant employment, and the uniformity which it produces in the rate of their wages. The proprietor of a Factory which has cost £100,000, is well able to calculate the loss which he will suffer by stopping his Mill, in the total unproductiveness of his large investment of capital, and in the injury which his machinery will sustain by standing still; and he will prefer to keep working in the most unfavourable state of trade, until his loss shall actually exceed the rent of his fixed capital. This secures to his work-people a constancy of employment, which nothing else could have given them; and the same cause prevents that dreadful reduction of wages which has so long been deplored amongst mere hand labourers;—since the people in Factories being comparatively seldom thrown out of employment, are not acted upon by the same pressure which is felt in all trades where employment is fluctuating.

To obtain these advantages, submission to reasonable regulations is required from the operatives. The nature of the work will not admit of that degree of liberty which the mere hand labourer enjoys: the machinery, whilst in motion, demands little bodily exertion from the work-people, but requires constant attention. If an operative neglects his work, he must of necessity be dismissed; and in most cases no notice is required on either side for a dissolution of the compact between the employer and the employed.

These are admitted to be inconveniences connected with the system. There are others which have been grossly exaggerated, which I will next advert to for the information of your Lordship.

It has been asserted that the operatives, or, as they are technically termed, "the hands" in Cotton Mills, are crowded together in the work-rooms. How will your Lordship be surprised to learn that this crowding consists in each individual having (on an average) about twelve square yards of floor for himself and the machinery at which he is working, so that in a room containing 980 square yards, only 80 persons are employed.*

Much has been said respecting the HEAT of the rooms, and the noxious EFFLUVIA to which the operatives are supposed to be subjected.

It is true that in what are usually called "fine spinning" Mills, a somewhat high degree of heat is considered beneficial to the work, and in such Mills 80° of Fahrenheit is not unusual, and may even sometimes be exceeded, at the express request of the spinners themselves. But these Mills do not constitute above one-tenth of the whole number of Cotton Factories, and in the other nine-tenths no more heat is used than is required for the comfort of the hands. In these latter, the variation of the temperature is very similar to that of an ordinary dwelling-house, falling to 50° in winter, and rising to 70° in summer. An atmosphere above 65° is not at all required or desirable in any of the rooms.

The noxious effluvia exist only in the imagination of the declaimers against Cotton Mills. The utmost cleanliness is a real economy to the master, and where this is observed, as it is in all modern Cotton Mills, there can be nothing to create noxious effluvia. Formerly the *stock part* of the machinery was usually made of wood, which became saturated with oil, and emitted an offensive smell; now, it is almost exclusively of iron, and there is merely the smell of the fresh oil, (continually changed) Gallipoli or Sperm, as the case may be.

A large workshop in any other trade cannot be less offensive, than the large, well cleaned, and well ventilated rooms of an extensive Cotton Factory, and few will even bear the comparison.

* In five rooms of equal dimensions, 70 yards by 14, (with 46 windows in each room) replete with machinery for every operation except cleaning the raw cotton, and all in full work, 369 persons are employed.

The number of CHILDREN employed in Cotton Factories, in proportion to the total number of the hands, has
been very much overstated.

Of 768 persons employed in the establishment in
which I am a partner—

179 are above 9, and under 18 years of age,
131 are above 18, and under 21 years of age,
and 458 are above 21 years of age.

768

The number under 18 years of age is less than one-
fourth of the whole.

It is worthy of remark that of these 768 persons,
298 attend Sunday Schools, without any influence or
inducement on the part of their employers, and 41 of
them are *Teachers* in those schools; facts to which I
shall take the liberty to refer your Lordship hereafter.

The wages are paid *weekly*, not once a fortnight or
once a month, as is the case in collieries and many other
places. The youngest child in the Mill earns 3s. per
week—and the best female spinner, 21s. The total
amount paid is £356.—averaging 9s. 3d. per week to
each person employed.

Your Lordship is aware that the hours of working
in Cotton Factories, as fixed by the act of last session,
are 69 per week; that law has already gained very
general observance in Manchester. In the first five days
of the week, the working hours per diem, are twelve, and
on the Saturday, nine. The working time commences
(by the general rule) at six in the morning;—from eight
to half-past, the steam engine is stopped, and the hands
go out to breakfast. From twelve to one (or from one
to two), a full hour is allowed for dinner. At five, P. M.,
tea is brought into the Mills, and taken without stopping
the machinery, and at half-past seven, P. M., the working
day closes. On Saturday the day ends at four, P. M.

My Lord, what is there in all this requiring further Legislative interference; what is there which ought to be considered outrageous to British feelings or disgraceful to a Christian community? It is a fact, that many females who might have comfortable situations as *domestic servants*, prefer to be employed in Factories.

The advocates of further Legislation find a powerful excuse for their interference, in a practice I abhor as much as they can do, that of working all night, which exists to a very limited extent in our trade. The truth is, that no act of parliament has yet been calculated to put a full stop to this practice; because, it has been thought unnecessary or impolitic to legislate upon the labour of persons above 21 years of age. The Bill now before the House of Commons (as it stands for the second reading) is quite as inefficient for the prevention of night working, as the enactments which have preceded it. On the contrary, if passed into a law, it will encourage night working. By an undue limitation of the working by day, it will compel the masters to discharge the hands who are under age, (for it is not impossible to dispense with them,) and the law will then allow the Mills to work twenty-four hours per diem, if the better feelings and principles of the Mill owners do not hinder them from doing so.

The HEALTH of persons employed in Cotton Factories is, at least, equal to that of any other class of the labouring poor. I need not remind your Lordship that the question of *health* and *morals* is one of *comparison* only. We do not expect the lawyer and the chymist to exhibit the robust health and sturdy frame of the agriculturist, and no reasonable man can suppose that the hands in Cotton Mills ought to look as well as the sons and daughters of the farmers in Warwickshire. But their real state of health will bear comparison with that of the great majority of the inhabitants of large towns, and will be found superior to that of the labourers in the great seaports of this kingdom. My Lord, the statements made of the premature decrepitude of hands in Cotton Factories, are utterly false, as applied to our day.

Of the 768 persons already mentioned, the average of sick (absent on that account,) seldom exceeds *six*. A Sick Fund established in the Mill, (another advantage of the system, as the people are thus made to benefit by their own superior circumstances, as compared with others,) producing about £2 10s. per week, provides half wages for all who are from sickness unable to work: this allowance is continued for twelve weeks, if illness be protracted so long. In case of death, 21s. is allowed for a coffin: (in 1827 to 1831, five years, only 29 coffins were required.) This fund, established twenty-four years, has never been exhausted.

The week which follows Whit-Sunday, is an universal holiday in Manchester, and is celebrated by processions of Sunday School children, assembled to the number of 25 to 30 thousand. Your Lordship might then see the "miserable victims of the Cotton Factory system," well clad, and often even elegantly dressed, in full health and beauty, a sight to gladden a monarch—not to be paralleled perhaps in the whole of the civilized world; and your Lordship would, I firmly believe, draw this conclusion, that the hands employed in Cotton Factories, so far from being degraded below their neighbours of the same rank in society, far exceed them in comfort, in order, and even in health.

It is the fashion to take for granted that the MORALS of the inhabitants of large towns are inferior to those of the country people. It would, however, be much more difficult to prove that the *morals* of persons employed in Factories are below those of other descriptions of the labouring poor in populous districts. If the degree of knowledge and information possessed by a given number of individuals, forms a correct standard of morality, the

case would be decided at once in favour of the Factory
people against the mere hand labourers, or even the
agricultural peasantry. The regular habits created by
the uniform occupation of Factory Children, render
them some of the best attendants of Sunday Schools,
and by consequence some of the best recipients of
instruction. If, as it has been shewn, three out of
eight of all the persons employed in *a* Factory, are, at
one and the same time, regular attendants at Sunday
Schools, and 41 teachers are found amongst 300
such attendants from one spinning establishment, in a
place like Manchester, where the Sunday School system is carried to the greatest perfection, the probability of such persons acquiring moral and religious
knowledge may be fairly inferred. A more minute
observance of facts, however, by any impartial and
attentive resident on the spot, would carry complete
conviction of the superiority in morals of Cotton Factory
hands, over the labouring poor in other occupations.
In some of the villages near Manchester, where there
are no Factories, the inhabitants are notoriously more
immoral and degraded, than in those places where the
people are chiefly occupied in Factory labour. Nor are
we too far distant from the meads of Cheshire, to know
that agricultural labourers are not less vicious, to say
the least, than our much misrepresented Factory people.
If the case were otherwise, however, I am at a loss to
learn how an improvement in morals is to be the necessary consequence of a reduction of the hours of labour
from sixty-nine per week to fifty-eight. It is not
unworthy of remark, that in the numerous riots which
have occurred in this manufacturing district, during
the last twenty years, it has rarely happened that the
Factory people have been extensively implicated.

It remains for me to draw your Lordship's attention
to the probable RESULTS of the proposed measure, both as

it will affect the work-people and our Cotton Trade itself.

If Mr. Sadler's Bill becomes a law, the masters will have the choice of two evils. Either they must reduce the hours of labour to the limit proposed to be fixed for children, (fifty-eight hours per week,) or they must place their establishments without the pale of this enactment, by discharging all persons under eighteen years of age from their Factories.

In the former case a reduction of the *wages* of all persons employed, whether children or adults, corresponding with the reduction of the time of labour, must inevitably take place. The state of the trade, the present comparatively high rate of wages paid in cotton spinning, and the plentiful supply of labourers, preclude the possibility of any advance whatever in the *rates* by which the wages are calculated: the earnings of the hands must, therefore, experience a reduction in the proportion of 11 in 69, or nearly one-sixth. This certain effect of the Bill is carefully kept out of sight by most of its public advocates, or if hinted at by some of them, it is in the hearing of that class of operatives only, whose high wages and frequent disputes with their masters make them reckless of consequences. The great mass of the hands—the women and the children—know full well that *they* are destined to be the great sufferers, by a reduction of the working hours which they have never solicited, but which, knowing the consequences, they earnestly deprecate.

I beg to assure your Lordship, that not a few of the master cotton spinners have determined to adopt the other course above mentioned, namely, to *discharge* from their employment all the hands under 18 years of age, as soon as the proposed law comes into operation.

The deplorable effects of a general, or even partial discharge of the young persons now employed in Factories, are sufficiently obvious to every reflecting mind.

Many families would be utterly deprived of support, and driven upon the parish. Great numbers of young persons, able and willing to earn their own livelihood, would become beggars and vagabonds: the gaols would be filled to overflowing with juvenile offenders against the laws, already too numerous; and the habits of industry, which can only be acquired in youth, would be wanting for life.

It is not an empty threat that the masters now referred to have uttered. Some of them are of opinion, (I am not) that the work might be better, and even cheaper done, without the young hands than with them, if once their arrangements were made. At all events, in many establishments this mode of proceeding will be adopted, in preference to shortening the time to 58 hours per week; on account of the otherwise enormous extra charges, in rent and expenses which cannot be reduced.

Is it better that the mother of a large family should herself go to the Factory, to earn bread for her children, who are idle in the streets, or that the children should be employed, (even in a Factory), and the mother be found attending to her domestic duties at home?

My Lord, genuine benevolence will not look with a short-sighted policy to some isolated advantage, real or supposed, which it is desirable to confer on the community, but will take into its range of vision all the circumstances connected with the case before it, and will be cautious not to aggravate the evil which it attempts to relieve.

It is not easy to calculate the effects of the proposed measure upon our Foreign Trade. This part of the subject is often very cautiously avoided by the advocates of this Bill. One eloquent speaker, at a public meeting in this town, held last week, was bold enough to face this difficulty; and he informed us, that if it were true that we could not meet our Foreign Competitors with a reduction in the hours of labour, the Government could immédiately remedy this trifling inconvenience, by a *repeal of the Duty upon raw Cotton*. That a repeal of this duty would be in itself very desirable, is of course the general opinion of the trade, but upon very different grounds than those assumed by this gentleman. If your Lordship and the House of Commons will entirely abolish a *few* of the duties on the great articles of our Consumption, the impolicy of a reduction in the hours of labour will·not appear so glaring, nor the consequences so much to be dreaded, as far as the Cotton Trade is concerned! Absurd and impracticable as such propositions must appear to your Lordship, they pass current with the unthinking part of the community, and are adduced by those who seek the popularity of a seeming benevolence, as matters of easy accomplishment.

If WE are unmindful of the advantages this country has derived from the Cotton Manufacture, other nations are fully alive to its importance, and their anxiety to encourage its introduction and to promote its extension, is shewn by their prohibitions of, or exorbitant duties upon, our British yarns.

From FRANCE and SPAIN, our Cotton Twist is entirely excluded, except it be introduced indirectly by the smuggler.

AUSTRIA prohibits the importation of our yarn under certain numbers of fineness, composing the great bulk required for her manufactures; and exacts upon such qualities as she permits her subjects to purchase from us, a duty of very nearly 6d. per ℔., being from 30 to 40 per cent. upon the prime cost of the article.

In SWITZERLAND, in the canton of Zurich, Cotton Spinning is rapidly extending, the spinners obtaining a plentiful supply of the raw material from the free port of Genoa.

RUSSIA has long and zealously promoted and supported the establishment of Cotton Mills. The duty on our exports of Cotton Twist to that Empire, has recently been advanced 12½ per cent., being now (at the present exchange) upwards of 6d. per ℔., or 45 per cent. on the prime cost of the descriptions of yarn required by her subjects. It is not merely for the increase of her Revenue, that Russia exacts this enormous duty, but at the suggestion, as I am well informed, of those who are at the head of her infant Cotton Spinning Establishments, in whose prosperity her government appears to take the deepest interest.

The Ruler of Egypt has engaged most extensively in this branch of business, and the produce of his Mills meets us in the markets of the East Indies.

In the neighbourhood of Calcutta, Cotton Factories upon a large scale have been erected, and from the favourable circumstances in which the spinners are placed, in reference to the raw material, and the cheapness of labour, the undertaking appears likely to succeed.

As an extensive Exporter, as well as Spinner, of Cotton Yarn, I feel considerable alarm at the rapid advances which our rivals are thus making on every side; but when, in addition to Foreign Competition, I am threatened with a Law to cripple still further our exertions *at home*, my alarm partakes of the character of despair.

My Lord, the Cotton Manufacture is not indigenous to Great Britain. It has been invited here by the industry of her inhabitants, and fostered by their capital. It will one day (I hope at a very distant period) find its most congenial and lasting soil in the United States of America. Let not its removal be hastened by rash and injudicious legislation. Whilst it contributes so large a share to the support of our national burthens, it claims, at least, to be exempted from unreasonable and oppressive restrictions.

If the Act of last session requires a more general enforcement of its provisions, the Legislature can secure its universal observance, by fixing the time upon the moving power. An extension of that Act to the Linen, Silk, and Woollen Mills of the Kingdom, would remove that just ground of complaint which the occupiers of Cotton Mills now possess, that hitherto their branch of Factory labour has been unfairly singled out as the only subject for legislation.

Before further restrictions are imposed, let a COMMISSION OF ENQUIRY be issued by the Government, to competent and impartial individuals, who may, by personal investigation, ascertain the real condition of persons employed in Cotton Factories.

The Question is one of sufficient importance to warrant such a measure, involving as it does, in Cotton spinning alone, a fixed capital of at least Fifteen Millions Sterling, giving employment to 150,000 persons.

Allow me to conlude, by apologizing to your Lordship, for having stated many facts with which your Lordship must previously have been perfectly familiar,—arising from my anxiety to place before your Lordship, a full view of this important question.

I have the honour to be,

MY LORD,

Your Lordship's very faithful and most obedient humble Servant,

**HOLLAND HOOLE.**

*Manchester, 12th March, 1832.*

---

T. SOWLER, PRINTER, ST. ANN'S-SQUARE.

# SADLER'S BILL.

---

## Cotton Branch.

---

MANCHESTER:

PRINTED BY T. SOWLER, ST. ANN'S-SQUARE.

---

1832.

It has been a primary object, in these pages, to introduce as few words as possible, and such remarks only as
may interest Members of Parliament, in considering the
subject to which they relate.

I AM interested in a Cotton Manufactory, which, in spinning and in weaving one-third of the weight which it spun, paid last year in weekly wages, to about 1,580 persons, £41,300.—This sum, at 50 working weeks, allows 10s. 6d. weekly to each; at 52 weeks of the year, 10s. 1d. to each.

This Manufactory uses much coarse Cotton for low priced goods, and therefore furnishes less than the average rate of wages per pound weight; but I will suppose it to give a full average. In 1831, Great Britain spun 259,837,350lbs.; this concern spun 2,000,000lbs. If two millions paid £41,300, then 260 millions paid £5,369,000., which, at £26. each, employed 206,500 persons, at as high a rate of wages as the father of a family obtains in most of the Agricultural districts. What was the entire amount of weekly wages obtained from the 259,837,350lbs. of Cotton, through its various processes, and changes of character and place, I do not presume to say; but it will assist conjecture to assume, that the average value of the Cotton was about 7d. per lb., and that the goods produced from it enhanced its cost to about 1s. 7d., the difference in value chiefly arising from labour, interest on sunk capital, and manufacturers' profits.

Suppose manufactured value 1s. 7d. per lb., interest and profit.... 1$^d$.9 first cost.................... 7, } deduct 8$^d$.9

there remains for various labour 10$^d$.1 per lb.; or for labour, on 260 millions, at 10d., £10,833,333.*

This sum, at £26 for each, shews 416,666 persons employed, and each may reasonably be presumed to support at least one and a half person besides himself: thus 1,041,665 persons were supported,—all, more or less, paying

* The data are throughout taken from Burns' "Glance;" and detailed calculations are avoided, except that a profit is here assumed, for the purpose of shewing the amount left for the wages of labour. The "Glance" gives £11,153,469 as the balance in favour of spinning and manufacturing Cotton in England only—excluding Scotland and Ireland. The exported value of manufactured Cotton last year, was £7,707,020.— the weight, 70,760,783lbs. at 2s. 2d. : thus we were enabled to sell to Foreigners, £4,713,333. 6s. 8d. of labour, on 70,700,000 lbs., at 16d.

Taxes, and contributing to the welfare of the
Agricultural and Colonial interests, instead of
being burthensome.

It is a most important fact, that the Cotton
trade of Great Britain has encreased, as the cost
of the commodities made from it has been reduced,* and such of necessity must be its course.

The Cotton trade in Foreign States has
encreased of late years, at least as rapidly as
in Great Britain.—The weight spun during
the two last years, as ascertained from circulated documents, was—
In the United States 101,860,000 ⎫ Or in one
In France ... ............ 148,000,000 ⎪ year,
—————— ⎬ 124,920,000
249,860,000 ⎭ lbs.

If these countries spin to disadvantage, it
has not been such as to prevent them from
spinning to the extent stated.—Machinery is
now removed from this to any other country
almost as easily as ships; and if with previous
difficulties this extent of spinning has been
attained, it will encrease much more as those

* In 1819, the quantity of cotton spun, was 110,000,000lbs.,
worth 15d. per lb.
In 1831, ——————————————— 259,800,000lbs.,
worth 7d.

impediments are abated, and facilities are acquired by experience, and as bounties are offered by the self-inflicted impositions upon the trade of Great Britain.

Every station of life has, more or less, its abuses—and workers in Cotton Factories are not exempt. Isolated cases, some true, some coloured, some entirely false, some of old date,* are no proof of general suffering. It neither is the practice nor can be the interest of the owners of Factories to enervate or otherwise injure the persons whom they employ—on the contrary, it is necessary that they be alert and attentive; for attention, and not hard labour, is their constant duty. Let a commission prove the truth or falsehood of this assertion, if the common sense of the thing does not sufficiently guarantee its truth. Tales of sorrow, got up for a Parliamentary Committee, cannot establish the justness of a sweeping accusation.

Capital sunk in Factories, of whatever sort, tends to insure to labourers unceasing employment at remunerating wages; for every

* The wider the field the greater the probability that such cases may be found: and it must be obvious, that over whatever number of years the enquiry may extend, the aggregate number of persons employed, during each of those years, must be taken into account to form a correct judgment.

well-managed concern will, if possible, be kept going even in bad times to avoid the loss on stagnant capital.

If the Manufacturers of this country be fairly treated, they will go on encreasing this assured employment and diminishing the cost of the articles they make, to the benefit of all persons of every rank, but more especially the poorer members of the state. If they be vilified and fettered as ignorant meddling enthusiasts and philanthropists, are now attempting, but not at their own expense, establishments for spinning and weaving will still flourish,—but not in Great Britain. The advantages which England has derived from them are well understood and rightly appreciated elsewhere.

The benevolent innovators who are attempting the very course which our Foreign rivals desire, ought to be prepared with a remedy for the evils which must ensue on the accomplishment of their project. Its effect must be greatly to enhance the cost of the manufactured articles, to reduce the earnings of the persons employed, and consequently to diminish the amount which they are enabled weekly to circulate, and which continues afterwards in restless activity.

Men of private fortune do, or should for the most part, confine their annual expenditure to their income. Manufacturers circulate annually, some nearly all, some all, and some much more than all the money they are possessed of, yet with perfect prudence.

They who contribute largely (no matter their motive) to the steady employment and support of the labouring classes, should not, on imaginary charges, or on light grounds, have their spirit of enterprise crippled—and if it be crippled as proposed, it will ere long be destroyed or be carried out of this kingdom.

This is a subject which Statesmen should well consider; they need not in so doing dwell upon the interests of the owners of Factories, on their particular success or ruin, but on the benefit or injury of their establishments to the labouring population, commercial and agricultural, and to the national prosperity.

JOSEPH BIRLEY.

*Chorlton Mills,*
*April 6th,* 1832.

PRINTED BY T. SOWLER, COURIER AND HERALD OFFICE.

MR. SADLER, M. P.,

HIS

# FACTORY TIME BILL,

AND

## HIS PARTY,

*EXAMINED.*

---

LONDON:

JAMES RIDGWAY, PICCADILLY.

MDCCCXXXII.

CHARLES WOOD AND SON, PRINTERS,
Poppin's Court, Fleet Street.

# MR. SADLER'S

# FACTORY TIME BILL,

&c. &c. &c.

---

So much has been said about an intended act of
parliament now before a committee of the House
of Commons, called by many Mr. Sadler's Bill to
ameliorate Slavery in Cotton and other Mills and
Factories, and so much has been written and
spoken by the promoters of the Bill before mentioned against the mill-owners or master manufacturers, that it is considered high time to endeavour at all events to disabuse the public generally, and legislators who may be called upon
to decide as to the merits or necessity of Mr. Sadler's Bill. It is intended therefore, in as brief a
manner as possible, to show what is the actual
condition of the operatives employed in the cotton, woollen, silk, and flax mills of the kingdom;
how it is that their numbers have increased and
are increasing so rapidly, and what effect the
Bill will produce upon that condition, should it

become a part of the law of the land. An attempt will then be made to show how fit or unfit Mr. Sadler is for the work he has undertaken, *viz.* to make a law to affect most seriously the daily bread of more than two millions of his fellow creatures, and the intrinsic value of all the cotton, the woollen, the silk, and the flax mills in the United Kingdom. And we declare here once for all, that our intention is only to show that Mr. Sadler's Bill is unnecessary ; that if it pass into a law it will be a curse and not a blessing upon those for whose benefit (we are willing to admit) it is intended. We have a right to do this, and if we succeed, Mr. Sadler himself will give us his thanks. It is to Mr. Sadler as a member of the legislature merely, and to his act and its consequences, that we address ourselves. But in the first place we must say a few words as to the way in which Mr. Sadler's bill has thus far been promoted or advocated.

We have had speeches and preachments made for it, from the Right Reverend Father in God our holiest Bishop by Divine permission, to the man of unknown tongues, and thence to the lowest Maw-worm in Yorkshire, who preaches and sells butter and brickdust. We have had petitions to the legislature from the rick burners round Maidstone, the web-footed oyster dredgers of Colchester, and the pitchy boat builders of Rochester; none of whom in all probability ever saw a cotton or other mill in their lives. The Quakers too are on the alert, and have shown as much anxiety for the success of the Bill as they did to save the neck of Friend Joseph Hunton. The gentlemen of the Press have perhaps been paid for telling the country that factories are Bastiles, in which are done all sorts of crimes and cruelties; that the master manufacturers or factory owners, with the fear of the Gazette and the workhouse before their eyes, destroy other men's children to have the means of feeding their own. To these assertions of the Public Press it may be sufficient to say, that they are false: and it may be said too of the Public Press, that there is no reptile of quackery, sedition, and obscenity, who cannot for a trifle buy himself commendation in the newspapers: there is no deformed monster of malice, rebellion, and impiety, who cannot for a few pence enlist on his side the Public Press. Talk of the Gazette! why the Gazette *can* have no terrors for a penny-a-line-man: the poor-house he should speak of with reverence, for in some such asylum the penny-a-line-man generally pays his debt to nature, and receives at last the decencies of Christian burial.

We now proceed to show what is the condition of the people employed in cotton and other mills, and our observations will have reference more particularly to the mills and factories in the town and neighbourhood of Manchester. The poor's rate for the township of Manchester, as shown by an official document signed by the comptroller (Lings), a copy of which is subjoined*,

| * RATE OF | DATE. | £. s. d. |
|---|---|---|
| 5s. | Poor's Rates collected from 25th March 1826 to 25th March 1827 | 59,216 16 8 |
| 5s. | Ditto from 25th March 1827 to 25th March 1828 ............... | 70,159 0 5¾ |
| 4s. | Ditto from 25th March 1828 to 25th March 1829 ............... | 55,704 6 6 |
| 4s. | Ditto from 25th March 1829 to 25th March 1830 ............... | 52,247 16 4½ |
| — | Arrears of 1829-30, collected in 1830-31 ..... .................... | 9,760 15 4½ |
| 3s. | Ditto from 25th March 1831 to 1st March 1832 ................. | 44,080 0 4 |

Population of the Township of Manchester...... 142,026
Ditto of the Parish of Manchester............... 270,963
Ditto of the Hundred of Salford.................. 612,414
Ditto of the County of Lancaster ..............1,335,600

GEO. LINGS,
Comptroller.

*Manchester, Town Office,*
*March* 10, 1832.

is on an average of six years, ending March,
1832, exactly three shillings and sixpence in the
pound, upon an assessment professing to be upon
the full rent; and in this sum of three shillings
and sixpence is included all county rates and
constables' accounts. This fact, as the saints of
the Bible club would say, speaks for itself without note or comment; and whether three shillings
and sixpence in the pound is a higher or a lower
rate than has been paid in six years in agricultural counties, where factory slavery does not
prevail, it is not necessary to inquire. However,
in those six years no gangs of parish-paid stone
breakers have been seen; no roundsmen; no
soup charities; no separation of man and wife;
nor has money been given to emigrate with. The
statement signed by Mr. Lings is a document deserving of attention, for it refers to a population
of 142,026 souls.

It is very true that many thousands of industrious individuals are obliged to labour during the
night, because they cannot by any possibility obtain employment by day: and it will be necessary to say a few words here, with a view to show
how it is that night working has arisen among us,
as well as to show that the obloquy and the
abuse which is so unsparingly heaped by factory
time bill makers upon those mill owners who
work by night is not merited; it will on the con-

trary, it is hoped, be shown that those gentle-men are deserving of the thanks, not only of the operatives who are so employed, but of the country generally.

The panic in 1825-26 is in the recollection of many, who will also recollect what was said in the House of Commons at that time against a class of men called country bankers. It will be recollected, that the great Bank herself in Thread-needle Street was obliged, in that moment of dis-tress, to pay as gold a very considerable sum of old worn out paper money notes, and she was relieved by that means; and indeed saved herself; but her children, the country bankers, were many of them left to shift for themselves, or to perish. The great Bank herself (Sycorax, as she has been called) was taught a lesson at that time, which was of use to her. She has made fewer paper pro-mises, and has been more careful how she has used them. She has not allowed the country bankers to make hardly any at all. The thinking people would not any longer lend the country bankers their savings, and they (the country bankers), who until now had lent their paper promises to build mills or factories with, had nothing to lend. The mother bank would lend nothing : and it is a fact, that scarcely one (if one) cotton mill has been built in the town of Manchester since 1826. At length came the glorious days of July, 1830. Since then it has been evident that the Bank of England, like Noah's dove, has found no resting place: the exchanges have been generally and often unfavourable; she has one day discounted commercial bills, the next day she is selling Exchequer bills, and often at one shilling and at two shillings premium. It is clear, then, if these statements be true, that the great Bank has been in no condition to lend paper promises to her children, the country bankers, and so through them to people who would use them to build mills with.

The Club Banks, or, to speak more genteelly, Joint Stock Banks, can lend nothing: they are themselves borrowers, and have (it is firmly believed) not paid up into the club box the money which they would have the world believe is there: and in proof of this it is notorious, that the great club bank in this place, or, as it is called, *The* Bank of Manchester, is working on no more than three shillings in the pound: that is, if a man subscribed for a share, and promised to pay one hundred pounds into the stock, he has as yet only paid fifteen pounds. It is not meant to say that this bank has not kept faith with the public, although their Prospectus is not at hand to prove whether it has or not — it is only intended to show that these Joint Stock Banks are not, and are not likely to be, free lenders of money, or paper promises, to build mills with.

Old George Rose's banks, the Savings' Banks, can lend nothing. The savings, as they are called, are not available for building mills with ; the money being gone Heaven knows where ! It went from the poor folks to whom it belonged into the national debt. So that there are no banks to lend paper promises to build mills with ; and it is notorious, that nine-tenths of the mills which were built before 1826, were built with country bankers' paper promises, and nothing else.

It has been stated, that since that glorious year of prosperity (1825) so well pictured by the Chancellor of the Exchequer of that day, Mr. (Aislabie) Robinson, there has scarcely one (if one) mill been built in the town or parish of Man-chester. No man, being in his right mind, looking at his own age, if he be past the middle of life, will lay out ten or more thousand pounds in a mill, even if he had by industry and frugality acquired that sum : the low rate of profits itself would prevent him. But all this while the population has been and is increasing, and thousands upon thousands of operatives are pressing daily and nightly and hourly for employment and for bread.

The mill-owner himself, from competition, can hardly obtain interest even for his perishable capital, and is compelled as it were to work dou-ble tides. He desires to relieve himself from a mortgage — he desires to recover what he may

have lost by bad debts or fall in stock, when the
Bank of England is selling Exchequer bills; seeing
his days passing away, and seeing too how little
a cotton mill sells for when the man who had
raised it sleeps with his fathers — desirous to
make a better provision for perhaps his helpless
family, whilst he has some health and strength
left. Thus, urged often by necessity, or considerations such as have been mentioned, and having
operatives of all ages continually applying for
employment, he begins to work in the night, and
to make one mill do the work of two. Hence
comes night working. It is to be lamented that
our fellow-creatures should, urged by their numerous wants and necessities, be as it were compelled to work by night: but that is not all; we
declare that there are thousands who cannot even
obtain work by night. Will any man say then
what should be done with all who work by night?
There are perhaps forty thousand who work by
night, or are depending upon those who do: will
any man say that, situated as they are, they had
not better be fed by their earnings than out of the
earnings of others, taken by law in the shape of
poor's rate? Ask a man who has a night place,
what would become of him if he were to lose his
employment? he will tell you that he must starve
or go to the Poor-house. Wherefore it is con-

tended, that those gentlemen who do work their mills by night, are not only not deserving of the reprobation which is so unsparingly laid upon them, but they are entitled to the best thanks of their neighbours and the country in general, for they save those who are ready to perish: they save them from being a burthen to their neighbours, a burthen to themselves, and from the degradation of being led into the parish poorhouse.

We have said so much about night working, because it seems to be the grand pretext for Sadler's Bill: and it is also very true, that the operatives in mills and factories do work eleven or twelve hours per day or by night, to obtain a supply of food and decent clothing; but they are paid almost universally by the piece, or, which is the same thing, by " good hand, good hire." Those who are paid by the day are paid for extra or over hours; that is, for all above eleven or twelve, as the case may be. If in some instances (and there may be a very few such) longer hours are exacted, it is because the labour of those who submit to such hours is too abundant in the market. Sadler's Bill would make such people's condition worse than it is; for if the employment were spread over a greater number, the wages of the whole would be reduced, even if the manufacturer were to increase his machinery one-sixth part. The operatives in all the mills are at liberty to leave their employers' service at the end of any one week; so that the operative employed in a cotton or silk or other mill has more than fifty opportunities in a year of finding himself a better or more beneficial place, if he can. We will give a short account of a cotton mill, for which we are indebted to Mr. Hoole*, who is himself a cotton spinner: we are indebted to him the more, because if what he asserts is untrue it may be contradicted by not fewer than four hundred of his work-people, and no such contradiction has been made as yet.

Number of operatives............ ...... 768.  Of these —

179 are above 9 years of age and under 18.
131 ......... 18 .............................. 21.
458 above 21 years of age.

Earnings, one with another, on an average of several years, 9s. 3d. per week.

Number absent from sickness, seldom more than 6.

The temperature of the mill about 50° of Fahrenheit in winter and about 70° in summer.

Wages range from 3s. to 21s. per week: mean, 9s. 3d.

Hours of labour, 69 hours per week by Hobhouse's act; and every operative, with the machinery, occupies 12 square yards; that is, one operative and the machinery at which he or she may be employed, occupy a space of 12 yards square.

---

* See Hoole's Pamphlet, published by Sowler of Manchester.

Cotton mills are much the same in all respects, only the wages of the mill alluded to are perhaps less than in many others. An account of a silk mill will be given as a Postscript. These statements as to the health and earnings are correct, and deserve attention.

The mill-owners are charged with cruelty, slave-dealing, with living by slave labour, and so forth. When the proper time arrives they will show, that the operatives employed in the cotton and silk mills in Lancashire are better fed, better clothed, and far better instructed in their duty to God and in their duty to their neighbour, than any other description of operatives whatever, taking in even those in the metropolis itself. They will prove, that young persons are not destroyed by excessive labour in their mills.

It may be remarked here, that Hobhouse's Bill came into effect in November last; in March following we have a Bill of the same breed from Mr. Sadler. If acts of parliament against the mill-owners and their operatives are to be multiplied at this rate, can any one think that our ablest capitalists will not leave the country, will be compelled to leave the country, and turn their energies and their means against their native land?

Let Sadler's Bill pass into a law, as he and his party would have it, and Lancashire would soon become what Bedfordshire is said to be, a mass of bankrupt farmers and pauper workmen. Sadler's Bill should be entitled, a Bill to decrease Wages, and to increase Poor's Rate. Let any man only look at the population of Lancashire, and say what would be the condition of England if night fires were raging there, as they were raging but lately elsewhere, and for the same causes.

It is hoped that his Grace the Archbishop of Canterbury will attend to the statement with respect to the earnings, &c., just mentioned.; for his Grace is reported to have said, that all young people under fourteen or fifteen years of age, should play about and go to school, and that the master manufacturers should no longer be suffered to *enrich themselves* by the labour of such young persons; which is all mighty fine, and becoming the benevolence of his Grace; but let us ask his Grace, whether the young cottagers and children of the rick burners in his Grace's diocese play about and go to school until they are fourteen or fifteen? Does his Grace not think, that if the wages of seven hundred and sixty-eight labourers and their families, all above nine years of age, who live in any part of the garden of England, called Kent—"where are valleys filled with waving corn"—were earning on an average of years 9s. 3d. a week, that this 9s. 3d. a week would not be a sovereign remedy for rick burning, stone breaking, rounding, and emigrating? What a glorious addition would be made to his Grace's tithe, if the cottagers and their children above nine years of age were earning 9s. 3d. a week!

But if his Grace will have it, that young persons under fourteen or fifteen should play about or go to school—if his Grace will have it so, would it not be better to send for Mr. Owen, commonly called Old Bob Owen, obtain an act of parliament, and convert the hundred of Salford, in which Manchester is situated, into a city of mutual co-operation? The number of souls is only six hundred and twelve thousand four hundred and fourteen. His Grace would of course reign over all in the said city supreme. Mr. Sadler might, if politely requested, take charge of the children under nine years of age, be professor of humanity and justice. The Rev. W. B. Collyer would take care of the men; for his love for mankind is undoubted and unbounded: he could occasionally give lectures on lending money to princes and nobles. Mr. Owen could take care of the women and girls; he could also teach the newest rules of Harmony, and conduct the music. Under such regulations as would be named in the act of incorporation, and under such professors, it is possible that the young people in the hundred of Salford might be reared until they are fourteen or fifteen without work.

It is not intended to approach his Grace but

with all the respect which his rank requires ; but
the manufacturers of Lancashire, masters and men,
beg to remind his Grace, that as far as their spiri-
tual affairs are concerned they are under his especial care ; and they ask of his Grace, that when he
speaks of their worldly affairs he will do so with
candour and with consideration, and after having
heard both sides. Another holy Bishop is reported
to have said, that it was high time for the legislature
to interfere on account of the children employed in
cotton and other mills, for their masters were giving
them gin to enable them to endure the great fatigue
they were obliged to undergo in their employment.
His Lordship should have said where such a practice
prevailed. To say the least of this declaration of
his Lordship's, such a course is highly improbable.
Is the cotton trade, the silk trade, the woollen
or the flax trade, so prosperous at this moment,
and is human labour so scarce in the market, that
the masters are obliged to give wages in gin and
in money also? Does his Lordship think that such
prosperity prevails in the silk trade? If his Lordship ever reads these pages, he would see what is
said about working by night, and then say if it is
likely that gin is given as well as money in the
cotton trade. All cotton and other mills are full
of complicated machinery, which require great
attention, or else the work which is going on will

B

be valueless : does his Lordship think that gin is calculated to produce increased attention, increased care and accuracy ? His Lordship has all his life been employed in teaching men to be careful how they believe, and more careful how they speak : surely his Lordship has not on this occasion taken his own advice. Suppose we were to give his Lordship the dimensions of a cotton mill and the number of operatives, and then ask how much gin the mill and the people would absorb, at the temperature of his Lordship's palace, and under the pressure of the wages of a Bedfordshire labourer. His Lordship remembers his great master Socrates is said to have been asked, when a gnat hummed, whether the sound issued from mouth or tail—the answer we have no occasion to give. His Lordship however is an excellent bishop ; we would have said admirable, only that Pascal used that word in speaking of the Jesuits. The Jesuits are admirable men, said our Author of the Pastoral Letters.

We have next to show how it is that the people increase so rapidly in the manufacturing towns and districts, although they do endure there such a load of factory slavery. The increase of course is partly from within, and considerably from without ; but it will only be necessary to say a few words as to the increase from without. Young people, fathers and mothers with large families, industrious shopkeepers, artizans, such as joiners, bricklayers, shoemakers, &c., all with factory slavery before their eyes, all flock to the manufacturing towns and districts; out of Ireland there is a constant stream; out of Wales, from adjoining and distant counties, they come, as they say, to mend themselves, to do better for themselves and for their children; and that they do so in almost every case is perhaps proved by the amount of poor's rate already stated.

But there are some minor causes to show why people come into these towns and districts, which may be mentioned here. If any member of a family is sick, there are infirmaries, where medical assistance is to be had free of charge; schools there are for the children free of charge: if any of the family go to church, they are not driven into a corner in which is a board with the humane inscription "Sittings for the Poor:" if the whole or any of the family go to a dissenting chapel on a Sunday, they are shown into a pew, spoken to by the clergyman, and treated like gentlefolks. If any of the family wish to keep a dog, they can do so, although it should be a lurcher: there are no 'squires to Hector it, nor Lord to treat them as if they were slaves and beings not having the same origin, although so much *has* been said to the contrary. And these are a few of the reasons why people flock to the manufacturing towns and districts, full as they are of factory slavery.

We have now to show what effect this celebrated Bill will have, if it ever becomes a law. The Bill, in effect, shortens the time of labour from six days per week to five—and the staunchest advocates for the Bill do not deny that its first operation will be to lower wages generally *, fully or more than one-sixth part. This point admitted, it is easy to perceive that the comforts of the operatives will be diminished. Three shillings out of eighteen is a fearful sum: in numberless cases it cannot be spared, and the falling off must be made good out of the Poor's Rate, which, be it remembered, is wrung from many who are often sadly distressed to raise it. If the Bill, then, *can* decrease the hours of labour, it will increase the hunger: it will derange or destroy numerous contracts between mill-owners and their tenants; derange or destroy numerous indentures between masters and ap-

* It seems that about one half (or more in many instances) of the operatives employed in mills are under twenty-one years of age; these discharged by Sadler's Bill at the hour appointed, leaves less than one half above twenty, and for these it will not be worth while to work the steam engine or moving power.

prentices. The land-owner, who is the law-maker, will be heard bawling for remunerating prices; the Temperance Clubs will have no occupation, for gin-drinkers will nowhere be seen; Mr. Chancellor Althorpe will make more mistakes; the revenue will fall off. Let only one day a week be struck off, let only one-sixth part of productive industry be destroyed, and the national creditor will not get his paper-money notes from the Threadneedle Street Bank; the Lord Harry will be called upon to sign a fiat against the *Grey*-headed taxers of raw cotton, if in the mean time no other settlement takes place by a shorter and ruder method.

Again, this Act says, that it shall be highly penal to give employment for more than ten hours per day to any young person under eighteen years of age, or by night under twenty-one years of age. Why, there are thousands married, and are fathers and mothers before they are twenty-one; but they must not work by night whatever may be their necessities, or by day more than the law allows. No judge will punish a man for stealing a loaf of bread, after sufficient proof, that but for that very loaf the poor creature would have perished from hunger. This is the consideration on which poor laws are founded; yet by this Bill a judge is called upon in effect to punish a man under twenty-one for working in the night, although it should be to save the life of his father or mother, his wife or his child. At all events, the Bill will punish any one who shall employ a young person, although he should be circumstanced as has been stated; and so then by this *humane* Bill the nursing wife and nestling infant of a young cotton-spinner under twenty-one years of age may want the comforts which their trying situation require, and which might be honestly obtained for them but for this precious piece of legislation.

Another effect of the Bill will be, constant instances of perjury: this may be shown by the working of a similar bill, which came into operation only in November last, and was the handy-work of Worsley, of Stockport—Brotherton, high-priest of the Salford Pythagoreans, bean-haters, and egg and spinach eaters — and the Right Honourable Sir John Cam Hobhouse, the King's Secretary at War. We will give a short statement of a case which was decided in the Salford Court House but a very few weeks since under this delectable morsel of legislation. A poor woman, urged by hard necessity, had obtained a night place for her daughter in the mill of a most respectable man (Mr. Thos. Harbottle), having first given a certificate that the girl was of the proper age required by law: it turned out, however, that the girl was not of the proper age, and against Mr. Harbottle and his manager an information was laid by a common informer. The mother, in order to preserve the place and bread for her child, offered to swear in open Court that the girl was of the full age required ; but the justice refused to receive her oath. Mr. Harbottle pleaded the certificate, explained how he had understood the clause in the act which refers to certificates, and declared upon his honour, that he had acted, as he thought, correctly ; that if he had offended, it was from not knowing the law. Mr. Harbottle's character is out of the reach of the slightest suspicion even ; yet, after all, he was condemned in a penalty of ten pounds, and five pounds costs in addition to all his own costs. The poor woman was rebuked, and then with her daughter left the Court, no doubt to obtain that relief from her parish, to which this act had in effect entitled her ! Here is law and justice,—law with a vengeance ! It seems to be true, then, that the belly has no ears, nor has necessity any law.

We will state one other case, which was decided in the same Court, and under the same act, within the last ten days. It seems that two poor boys, living at some distance from the mill in which they were employed, had brought their dinners with them, and when the hands, or operatives, which is usual, were turned out for dinner, the two poor boys, in order to eat their scanty meal in warmth, in quiet and comparative comfort, secreted themselves amongst the machinery rather than be turned into the street in one of the coldest days in the month of February; and for the supposed offence, namely, for working the poor lads too many hours, or during the dinner hour, Mr. Patrick, one of the principals of the establishment, was informed against, and an attempt was made to take from him forty pounds for two penalties, besides costs. However, after a hearing which occupied a very considerable time, it was decided that no offence had been committed, and Mr. Patrick was allowed to depart after a suitable admonition.

These informations were laid at the instance of a club of mill-owners, an account of which was given the other day at a public meeting by a Mr. Hindley. He is reported to have said, " I would refer you to the history of the association formed in this town (Manchester) for the very purpose of enforcing Sir John Cam Hobhouse's Bill, which has expended nearly one hundred pounds and *obtained* only five convictions." Now the club have the valuable services of Byers, Worsley, and Mr. Foulkes the attorney. Surely it is not too much to say, that Hobhouse's Bill has been a failure—and it would seem that few offences are committed, or convictions would

be cheaper—that it gives a pretext for perjury
has been shown in the case against Mr. Harbottle.
It is a means by which the master is harassed
and annoyed, and, to say the least of it, has been
alike injurious to the operatives and their employers. Sadler's Bill is the same as Hobhouse's,
only the time allowed for labour is shortened in
Sadler's; and Sadler's Bill includes the silk, the
woollen, and the flax mills, whereas Hobhouse's
Bill only refer to cotton mills. Hobhouse's Bill
came into effect in November last, and although
it has been aided by a club of informing mill-
owners, all they have done is to *obtain*, according
to Mr. Hindley, only five convictions. It may,
perhaps, be now asked, can Sadler's Bill then be
otherwise than injurious to the operatives and their
employers? But a new idea seems to have
sprung up among the factory time bill makers,
and Sadler is in danger of being thrown over-
board; for at a public meeting held in the Town
Hall of Manchester on the 10th instant—for the
avowed purpose of promoting Mr. Sadler's Bill
— there is in the report of the proceedings
a resolution concluding with these words:—
"Resolution IV, That no legislative enactment can
be effective without placing the restrictions upon
the moving power." The meeting approved of
Sadler's Bill, and seemed to regret that he had not
fixed a limit to the working of the steam-engine

or water-wheel. We must leave our erudite Mr. Sadler to ask a few questions of these *new* factory time bill makers, for they leave Sadler far out of sight : Sadler's is only a half measure ; this is Cæsar or nothing. They would fix a limit to the working of the steam engines and water wheels employed in all the cotton, woollen, silk, and flax mills in the kingdom ; they would have one of the King's men to watch the mill-owners by day and by night, and with the King's lock, the King's key, and the King's seal, open and lock up our furnace doors by act of parliament. Can they not see that thousands upon thousands of industrious and well-disposed work-people are daily and hourly pressing upon the mill-owners for employment and for bread, and yet do they propose to restrict the moving powers of our mills ? Can they not perceive the imminent danger of not keeping the mighty masses of population which are crowded together in the manufacturing districts in employment, and in tolerable comfort even ? Can they not perceive, that if these masses before mentioned are meddled with rudely, if they are interfered with in their pursuits, and hindred by unjust and unreasonable enactments— such as Mr. Sadler's or other Factory Time Bills —that they will, like the whirlwind, in an instant lay temples and palaces and laws and order prostrate ! Will they say that the steam engine has not become essential to the very existence of millions of their fellow creatures, and it may be said, to the peace, to the order, to the government, and to whatever makes life desirable in this country? And yet, to use their own words, they would place "restrictions upon the moving power" of our mills.

Again; according to the wisdom of these men, we have then been mistaken all these years in speaking of the philosophic Dr. Black with the purest veneration, and the sincerest affection and gratitude; we have been wrong in our estimate of the services of the ingenious and able Watt. These philosophers left us the steam engine nearly forty years ago, as it is unaltered at this moment: but it would seem they did too much for their fellow men. Will they say, that in cultivating the arts of peace, we are multiplying by means of the steam engine the necessaries, the comforts, and the elegancies of life, at too low a cost of human labour, and that we have arrived at a point from which we are to retrograde, to turn back, for that onward there is nothing but "rocks and brawling waves, and mists and fogs and murky darkness." It was a holy Christian Bishop in his blind zeal who destroyed the valuable library at Alexandria (called the new library). Christian Baptist saints have lately preached one of our oldest colonies into rebellion; and in England in the nineteenth century, Christian *philosophers* and saints would lay their rude hands upon our proudest triumph of philosophy (the steam engine), and place a limit to its usefulness.

We had better have no laws whatever than laws made up or even tainted with the prejudices and the passions of the party who propose and promote factory time bills, and would limit the employment of man's most powerful auxiliary, the steam engine.

> " *Seeming* saints they are,
> Famous sophists, fortune tellers,
> Quacks, med'cine mongers, bards bombastical,
> Chorus projectors, and star interpreters,
> And wonder-making cheats.
> Cloud-inspired worthies, children of fog,
> And dew, and dusky vapour."

If the man of unknown tongues were made a native god by act of parliament, what a glorious host of bishops, priests, deacons, groaners, and gapers, experienced in sighs and tears and ejaculations, might he not enlist among factory time bill makers and promoters!

We must now return to Mr. Sadler, of whom we had almost lost sight, having already shown (imperfectly), that if his bill should become a part of the law of the land, it will be, as Hobhouse's bill now is, injurious alike to master and man. We proceed now to inquire, as we promised, who

Mr. Sadler is, and to account, if we can, for his introducing a law so tremendous in its consequences.

Mr. Sadler is a member of parliament for the town of Aldborough; and we have great pleasure in stating, that he is out of all comparison the best educated linendraper in the House of Commons. He stands up and says what he has to say like a gentleman, he never doffs his shoes, his gloves, or his stockings, and holds them up as helps to his argument. Mr. Sadler has published a book, and John Chidley in the City Road said it was a book of some value. Mr. Sadler has made an outline of an act of parliament for destroying infant slavery in cotton and woollen and silk and flax mills; but it is firmly believed that he has never been in a cotton mill these many years, certainly he has never been in a silk mill in Lancashire; and therefore, as far as the silk mills are concerned, and in all probability the cotton mills also, he knows nothing whatever, that is of his own knowledge he knows nothing whatever; and then it follows, that all the facts (as he calls them), with which he has made his proof of the necessity for his Bill are merely ex parte, and the sayings, the ravings, and the cant of others. He is reported to have said, in moving the second reading of his Bill, that down in Lancashire men and women entered into the con-

tract of matrimony with no other consideration
on earth than to beget children for the purpose of selling their labour, or in other words,
for the purpose of selling their children as slaves
to the master manufacturers. If Mr. Sadler's
followers and promoters of factory time bills were
made of common stuff, the declaration given
above would have the same effect upon them as
a blade of grass has upon a sick dog. If after
such a declaration as this his followers continue
to yelp and yell, the flail or the flogger must and
will be used unsparingly; and if they should still
go on, it will be absolutely necessary to separate them from their leader: tie them "fast,
and treat them as of old, with phlebotomy, and
whips and chains, and dark chambers and straw."

As we do not "hate Mr. Sadler with a cordial
hatred," and as we have as yet no "private injury
to revenge," we may try to find out (if we can)
some good or reasonable motive from which his
Factory Time Bill is derived. Mr. Sadler is an
anti-reformer, and may believe in his heart that
the Reform Bill is a fallacy, that it will neither
make men wiser nor better, that it will not make
two blades of grass grow where only one grew
before; and therefore he hopes by this Bill of his
to set the master manufacturers and their men together by the ears, and so get quit of the Reform
Bill: in this we can tell he will be mistaken, the

manufacturers of Lancashire will have a change; they *will* have their own representatives in the national council; they think they ought to sell the labour of their hands for untaxed bread-corn; the tax-gatherers are never from their doors, and they ask why they are not governed as cheaply as the Americans are in the United States. The manufacturers know their numbers, and thanks to the schoolmaster they know their strength too. In the county of Lancaster alone there are one million three hundred and thirty-five thousand souls.

Does Mr. Sadler think that by his Bill he can raise a sort of antagonist irritation, after the fashion of that distinguished philosopher St. John Long? Why the Reform Bill has already, like the mist at the heels of the countryman, enveloped one thing after another; and although Mr. Sadler's Bill holds out the temptation of working only five days a week instead of six, the manufacturers are not to be caught by such a bait, they will not be diverted from their purpose for one instant. Mr. Sadler may think that the moment the Reform Bill becomes a law, that the nobility and the church (objects of his dearest affection and regard) may be reformed also. If Mr. Sadler has such forebodings, the manufacturers have none. They know little of the nobility, except by the pensions which many of them have out of the taxes: they have never in their distress received

relief from the nobility, and they have had precious little consolation in their afflictions from the
Church. They know the Church chiefly by its
grinding exactions, often by its prejudices and
ignorance, and always by its ungovernable pride.
It cannot be believed, that at Mr. Sadler's advanced age, when in a very few years, in the order of nature, he must be numbered with his
fathers, that he will be found popularity-hunting,
that he would be pleased at seeing his name in
capitals in the nastiest corners of the streets, close
to the name of Dr. Sibley, and the great ox, and
the learned horse, and the great boa. Mr. Sadler surely cannot be alarmed lest he should not
obtain a place in the new parliament, meaning
the next after the Reform Bill becomes law ;
where only one member is allowed, he would be
sure of success : it is true that he has not shown
much liking for the puzzling intricacies of trade,
foreign exchanges, the Bank, bank notes, Exchequer bills, loans domestic and foreign, and their
effects upon the profits and losses of *shopkeepers* in
general ;—only except these, and Mr. Sadler may
be likened to Gibbon the historian, who, as an
able critic said, could write inimitably fine, and
had as much to say on a *Ribbon* as on a *Raphael*.

Looking at the way in which Mr. Sadler's Factory Time Bill has been advocated, looking at all
its clauses, particularly the Time Book clause

(indeed they are all alike), it must be clear to every one that it is intended to deliver over the mill-owner, or the master manufacturer, bound hand and foot to the common informer and the law-making justice. Well may the master manufac-turers lament, bitterly lament, that there is now no Canning in the senate, to hold up in that sacred place the mirror to the seeming saints, the mockers of the poor and the needy, who in-trude themselves there, and make use of their office of legislator to introduce their schemes, their bills, and their fallacies, to gratify their own low-bred vanities, and to raise expectations in the country which never can be realized ; and it may well be regretted too, that as yet no able scholar is recognized in the cloister, to point at such men and their measures the finger of scorn and derision, and to direct against them the of-fended spirit of criticism with "viper hair and sounding lash."

In conclusion, it is submitted to the Factory Time Bill makers, not forgetting the philosophers and saints, the steam engine restriction act makers of Manchester, whether, if they really wish to im-prove the condition of the operatives employed in the cotton, woollen, silk, and flax mills of the king-dom, it might not be worth their while to set about delivering the country from those unreasonable laws

c

called the corn laws; to relieve their country from
the whole or a part of that unsightly feculent
heap the national debt, and to do away with all
trading and banking corporations. If they really
intend to serve the operatives in the manufacturing districts, had they not better set about devis-
ing some plan, either to increase the quantity of
employment, or to decrease the price of food?
If they succeed in increasing the quantity of employment, better wages and fewer hours of labour will be the consequence, and the operatives
will owe them a debt of gratitude. If they succeed in making a law to restrain but one operative from working as long as he has a mind,
being paid "good hand, good hire," or by
the day or week, they will deserve the bitterest and deepest reprobation of every operative
in the King's dominions; for it should be remembered, that Sadler's Bill is only to run against
the operatives in cotton, woollen, silk, and flax
mills; all other operatives whatever may work
as long as ever they please, as heretofore.

V. R.

Manchester, March 26, 1832.

# POSTSCRIPT.

THE Certificate here annexed refers to about eight hundred individuals, and is not a bad description of Factory Slavery. Dr. Carbutt is and has been Physician for fourteen or fifteen years to the Manchester Royal Infirmary.

" I have this day made a general examination of the Silk Mill of Messrs. Royle and Crompton, in Great Bridgewater Street, Manchester, and found the work-people, whether adults or children, to have a very healthy appearance; indeed, quite as much so as could be expected in persons whose employment is not entirely in the country. Many of the children whom I questioned have been in the business three or four years, and have a healthy, cheerful aspect, with sufficient alertness of manner.

" The temperature I found to range from 60° to 70° of Fahrenheit, which I do not consider too high for health.

"The labour appears very light and easy; and the hours I found from inquiry are, for the women and girls 63½ hours per week, and for the men and boys 68½ hours; which period is certainly not too long.

"EDWARD CARBUTT, M.D.

"Physician to the Manchester and
Dispensary Fever Wards, &c. &c. &c.

"Manchester, April 5th, 1831."

CHARLES WOOD AND SON, PRINTERS,
Poppin's Court, Fleet Street.

# PETER THE PEARKER'S LETTER

TO

## MICHAEL THOMAS SADLER, ESQ. M.P.

Sir,

Your sworn friends,—the Ultra Tory Castlereagh faction in Leeds, are, at this early period, stirring up the strife; and have commenced a most insidious and hypocritical canvass in your name.

A few of the Operatives have been persuaded to join them in this untimely project; the native generosity of their character having led them to give ear for a moment to the voice of the *blue serpent:* but, "*charm he never so wisely,*" depend upon it, they will soon return to join their old comrades, the great body of the Operatives, in the front rank of the Orange Volunteers.

I do not ask if you, Sir, are connected with these proceedings; for I have learnt, from experience, the folly of attempting to draw from *you* a straight forward and satisfactory reply to *any* question: so, leaving your cross-examination to be effected by the Electors, when you appear on the hustings, (if, unhappily for you, that period should ever arrive) I shall proceed to tell you a little plain, unadorned truth.

Permit me, by reminding you of the *past*, to show your true Political character; that the persons your Castlereagh canvassers wish to mislead, may have truth to assist them in forming a correct estimate of what they may expect from you for the *future.*

You *have been* the "thick and thin" supporter of the Boroughmongers!—You *have been* the bitterest enemy of Parliamentary Reform!!—You *have been* the decided opponent of the grant of the Elective Franchise to large towns!!!—You *have been* the bigotted opposer of Religious Liberty!!!!—You *have been* the persevering eulogizer of the System which contracted the Eight Hundred Millions of Debt, crippled the Manufactures, undermined the Commerce, and nearly ruined the Agriculture of your country!!!!!—You *have been* the strenuous advocate of the Corn Laws, which compel the Operatives to eat dearer

Remember Macaulay is also your opponent—the eloquent Macaulay.—He has already entitled himself to the gratitude of his countrymen in all future ages, by his strenuous, powerful, and successful support of the Reform Bill. He claims our suffrages as a tried Reformer; who has met, and fought, and defeated you and your corrupt coadjutors—the Rotten-borough members. Macaulay is emphatically one of *the People;* who has risen to his present elevation by his industry, his genius, and his eloquence. If such men, receiving their character from the People, are employed in the service of the King, and particularly as the controlling minds at the India Board, Leeds may confidently anticipate the extensive consumption of her manufactures by the populous nations of the East.

From the hands of such men as Marshall and Macaulay, we may reasonably expect to receive the legitimate and constitutional fruits of Parliamentary Reform; but who could be so absurd as to expect such fruits from your hands? We call "*legitimate and constitutional*" what you call "*revolutionary.*" The People have secured the interminable hatred of the Castlereagh faction, by the triumphs they have enabled the Grey and Brougham Administration to achieve in the passing of the great Charter of Reform. Depend upon it they will uphold that Administration; with whom they have shared the calumnies and abuse of you and your party; with whom they have fought the great battle of Reform, and won a triumphant conquest.

The *People* regard the Reform Bill as a means whereby the country is to be renovated; and, if possible, delivered from all the evils which have resulted from the long continued misrule of your friends and supporters—the Boroughmongers.

The *People* look for Retrenchment in every department of the State, at home, and in the colonies. Can they expect this from you and your friends and supporters—the Boroughmongers? The *People* look for the total Abolition of Negro Slavery. . . . After fifty years of hypocritical pretence, combined thus secured every [famous colonial corruption, and] West India Proprietor in Parliament to strengthen their selfish policy!!!!!!—You *have been* the extoller of the Irish Clergy; though the abuses, and jobbing, and bigotry of that branch of the establishment have degraded Protestantism, endangered true Religion, and alienated the hearts of the millions of Ireland!!!!!!!—*You have been* the flatterer of the Party which suspended the Habeas Corpus Act,—passed Gagging Bills,—and sent Spies to entrap the advocates of Liberty and Reform amongst the Operatives, to treason and the gallows!!!!!!!!!

*In all* these mischievous proceedings *your* party have gloried, until you were driven out of your beloved Rotten-boroughs, and compelled to *ask the People* for their votes. I do not affirm that you, *personally* maintain every one of their opinions; but as your *past* political life has been exclusively devoted to the maintenance of the borough faction, your future votes—if you were sent to Parliament—would, no doubt, be directed to the same object; and thus your success would be identified with danger to all the important national interests which I have enumerated. Are these *your claims* on the Electors of Leeds!—What a contrast!—the deformity of your *past* political life, and your *present* professions of patriotic, liberal, and benevolent sentiment. Under what spell were your patriotism, your liberality, and your benevolence reposing, when Castlereagh and the Boroughmongers, with their friends Oliver and Castles, rode rough-shod over the field of Peterloo, and the liberties of your country?

I have no right to accuse you *personally* of being a selfish and unprincipled politician; but I have a right to accuse you, before the Electors of Leeds, of aiding, abetting, and conspiring with, the most selfish, the most unprincipled faction—the Boroughmongering faction—that ever disgraced the annals of a free country. The misguided Operative, the time-serving Tradesman, the apostate Reformer, who should give you *one* of his two votes, would be doing his utmost to re-organize that defeated faction; to neutralize the Reform Bill; to perpetuate every unearned pension, and every unnecessary place at home and in the colonies; to continue every abuse in the united churches of England and of Ireland; and to effect the ruin of the empire.

But when I remember who are your opponents, I have no fear.

Marshall, the son of our staunch old Reformer, appears before the Electors of Leeds, not to mystify his father's principles, but to claim and support them. He is, and always has been, consistent as a Parliamentary Reformer; an economical Reformer; a church Reformer; and an advocate of every enlightened measure, calculated to extend the happiness and welfare of his native land.

heads and supporters—the Boroughmongers—whose great rule of finance was, to relieve themselves by taxing the poor,—or, as they used to call them, the "swinish multitude?" The *People* look for the Revision of the Corn Laws; which at once limit the quantity of food, and diminish the quantity of labour. Can they expect this from your friends and supporters—the Boroughmongers who passed the Corn Laws; or from you, who maintain they ought to be rendered more severe? The *People* look for the opening of the Markets of the East to the products of their skill, and industry, and energy. Can they expect this from your friends and supporters—the Boroughmongers—who for half a century, to extend their patronage and their power, have uniformly opposed all the efforts of the manufacturing and commercial classes to abolish the East India Monopoly? The *People* look for the modification of Tithes, the removal of Church Abuses, and the application of the Surplus Wealth of the Establishment for the real advantage of the Nation. Can they expect these ameliorations from your friends and supporters—the Boroughmongers—who have degraded religion by making the churches of England and Ireland markets for Parliamentary corruption; have mingled with the sincere ministers of Christ, a large proportion of men who entered the Church solely under the influence of avarice and ambition: and thus have again verified, to an alarming extent, the declaration of the great Founder of christianity, "My house shall be called the house of prayer; but ye have made it a den of thieves?"

No, Sir, the People will not be deceived any longer by the Boroughmongers and their adherents. They will give their confidence to men like Marshall and Macaulay; who have adopted such political principles as will advance the prosperity, not only of this country, but of the whole civilized world.

I have the honour to be,

Sir,

Your's in much faithfulness,

PETER THE PEARKER.

———

P.S. Peter is particularly anxious that the merits of Mr. Sadler should be fully discussed; and, therefore, he requests that his letter may not only be read by those who have received a copy, but afterwards widely circulated among their friends and neighbours.

JOHN HEATON, PRINTER, 7, BRIGGATE, LEEDS.

# British Labour Struggles:
# Contemporary Pamphlets 1727-1850

### An Arno Press/New York Times Collection

The Factory Act of 1833. 1833-1834.

Richard Oastler: King of Factory Children. 1835-1861.

The Battle for the Ten Hours Day Continues. 1837-1843.

The Factory Education Bill of 1843. 1843.

Prelude to Victory of the Ten Hours Movement. 1844.

Sunday Work. 1794-1856.

Demands for Early Closing Hours. 1843.

Conditions of Work and Living: The Reawakening of the English Conscience. 1838-1844.

Improving the Lot of the Chimney Sweeps. 1785-1840.

The Rising of the Agricultural Labourers. 1830-1831.

The Aftermath of the "Lost Labourers' Revolt". 1830-1831.